The Hampsh...

THE LION
&
THE EAGLE

THE LION
&
THE EAGLE

IAIN MANSON

SPORTS
BOOKS

Published in Great Britain by
SportsBooks Limited
1 Evelyn Court
Malvern Road
Cheltenham
GL50 2JR

Front cover designed by Alan Hunns.

A catalogue record for this book is available from the British Library.

ISBN 9781899807 67 3

Printed and bound in England by
Cromwell Press

CONTENTS

ACKNOWLEDGEMENTS

I OWE a debt to a number of people, without whose assistance this book would be a lesser work.

Alan Collinson, a direct descendant of Tom Sayers, helped me greatly by lending me his copy of Tom Langley's brief biography of his ancestor – not an easy work to get hold of. He was also able to give me some family memories of Tom Sayers which contributed usefully to my understanding of my subject.

Boxing writer Tris Dixon was most generous in sharing his knowledge of the big fight, and in pointing me in the direction of some very useful sources.

Also of great assistance was *Bare Fists* author Bob Mee, whose knowledge of the bare-knuckle prize ring is matchless. He was able to help with queries which might otherwise have gone unanswered.

On the other side of the Atlantic, I could not be more grateful to Elliott Gorn, author of *The Manly Art* – probably the most scholarly work yet written on the bare-knuckle era. My Chapter 6 simply could not have been written without him, and this book would unquestionably have been the poorer.

Further American assistance was offered by martial arts expert Frank Allen, co-author of *Classical Northern Wu Style Tai Ji Quan* and *The Whirling Circles of Ba Gua Zhang*. In *Kung Fu Magazine*, Frank has himself contributed usefully to the literature of the bare-knuckle prize ring.

No individual helped me more than Brighton historian Roy Grant, without whom my account of the early years of Tom Sayers would be thin and colourless. The assistance which Roy gave me went beyond anything I might reasonably have expected.

Another vital source of information on Tom Sayers was the Camden Local Studies & Archives Centre, the staff of which were singularly helpful. My account of the domestic life of Tom Sayers in London depended crucially on their input.

The association of Tom Sayers with neighbouring Islington was much slighter, but still required some research. In this context, a small but significant contribution was made by Martin Banham of Islington Local History Centre.

Honourable mention has also been earned by Gad's Hill School's Press and PR Manager Sarah Garratt. In going out of her way to answer just one query, she saved me from making a fool of myself in the very first paragraph.

I made one invaluable visit to Brighton Museum to check up on one or two facts about the early life of Tom Sayers, and the staff there could not have been more helpful.

The same may be said of the staff of the National Archives at Kew, where the collection of materials relating to the Sayers–Heenan fight is a must for anyone interested in the subject.

Finally, and most importantly – though they would all say that they are only doing their job – the staffs of the British Library at St Pancras and its Newspaper division at Colindale were my most vital helpers, whether they knew it or not. My most valuable research was done at these two places. We should never forget what a wonderful resource the British Library is.

Iain Manson 2008

NAMES

The true name of a prize fighter is not always easy to establish. Some boxers, like Yankee Sullivan, used a number of aliases in order to stay ahead of the authorities, while others simply preferred to fight under a *nom de guerre*: Bill Bainge fought as Bill Benjamin, Tom Winter chose the more upbeat Tom Spring, and so on. I have drawn attention to the pseudonym in some instances, but not in all.

One case worthy of mention is that of the first formal opponent of Tom Sayers. Whether his surname was Couch or Crouch is impossible now to determine; both names were used.

Even where we know what to call a man, we may still be unsure of how to write his name. Many prize fighters, like Tom Sayers himself, were illiterate, and would therefore have been unable to offer any assistance on the matter. Where one name can be spelled a number of different ways, there is seldom any unanimity over which is correct. Thus we have Stevenson or Stephenson, Humphries or Humphreys, and a number of others. You can take your pick of how to spell Macdonald or Molineaux.

I have for the most part been content to abide by majority opinion, but there are two exceptions. Harry Paulson's name is usually given as Poulson, but I prefer to use the version that he himself favoured. Most importantly of all, there is the name of one of my two principal characters: John Camel Heenan insisted that 'Carmel' was an erroneous spelling of his middle name, and as in the case of Paulson, I think it perverse to ignore the wishes of the name's owner.

CHAPTER 1

A SHORT
JOURNEY...

WEDNESDAY, NOVEMBER 15th, 1865. The final monthly instalment of *Our Mutual Friend* is now on sale, and its author is at Gad's Hill Place, the house which he had coveted as a boy and which the success of his writing has finally enabled him to buy. To the north lies the Thames and to the south the Medway, presently home to a vessel that Alice might have seen in the Wonderland which she entered through a rabbit-hole four months ago: Brunel's *Great Eastern* is five times the size of any other ship afloat. As he works on his weekly, *All the Year Round*, Dickens no doubt reflects sadly on the death three days previously of Mrs Gaskell, one of its finest contributors. It was for this publication that he once commissioned a report on the prize fight between Tom Sayers of England and America's John Camel Heenan.

At work that same day in the office of the South-Eastern Railway Company is Samuel Smiles, author of *Self-Help*, one of the defining documents of Victorian sensibility. Mr Smiles is company secretary, and his mind surely strays from time to time back to the dreadful accident which befell one of South-Eastern's trains at Staplehurst in June. Charles Dickens was among the survivors.

Dickens had not, however, in spite of his original intention, been on either of the trains which Mr Smiles had arranged for Sayers, Heenan and their supporters in April 1860. William Makepeace Thackeray, on the other hand, quite possibly had. We cannot be sure, for he could never subsequently make up his own mind: the event, for all its éclat, had after all been neither legal nor, still more serious, respectable. But he may well have been present, and he was almost certainly responsible for the mock epic, *The Combat of Sayerius and Heenanus*, which appeared in the next issue of *Punch*. On November 15th, 1865, however, Thackeray is responsible for nothing at all, for the very good reason that he has, for almost two years, been lying under the neatly trimmed grass of Kensal Green Cemetery.

Equally dead is Lord Palmerston, who has only recently taken up permanent residence in Westminster Abbey. At the time of the fight he was prime minister, and his evident sympathy with the disreputable pugilists and their still more disreputable followers was, like so much of Palmerston's life, something of a scandal in polite society. It was even rumoured that he had been one of the passengers conveyed to Farnborough that day by Smiles's railway, but that is certainly false. So, sadly, is the oft-repeated tale that his death, less than a month before the day in question and just two days before his eighty-first birthday, occurred on a billiard table in the arms of a parlourmaid. Palmerston was, however, beyond doubt a tremendous rake, one of whose amorous exploits caused him to be cited in a divorce case when he was seventy-nine.

With prostitution rife, and twelve the age of consent, it was a good time for rich dirty old men. Palmerston would have loved, had he only known her and had she only given him the chance, Adah Isaacs Menken. Actress (of sorts), poet (ditto), virtuoso seducer of the famous, Miss Menken has attributes of Jackie Kennedy, Madonna and even Maria Callas. On November 15th, 1865 she is appearing in London in Henry Brougham's play *The Child of the Sun* at Astley's Amphitheatre, the scene of her extraordinary 1864 triumph in the title role of *Mazeppa*, the part which had earned her the soubriquet of the Naked Lady.

Six years earlier, in her native America, she had married (bigamously) one of the men who was to fight at Farnborough, the redoubtable John Camel Heenan, commonly known as The Benicia Boy. Now retired from the ring, Heenan has chosen to sit out the Civil War in England. The old South is no more, slavery has ended, Abraham Lincoln has died in his hour of triumph, and Jack Heenan has missed it all. On November 15th, 1865 he is at Shrewsbury races in furtherance of his trade as a bookie. Many people think he should be in London, for Tom Sayers is in London. And this is Tom's day.

A short journey...

――――――――

London was dirty. London stank. It stank mostly of horses, of which there were tens of thousands, but also of sewage – though matters had improved somewhat since the Great Stink of 1858 when the stench from the city's biggest sewer, the Thames, made people sick and disrupted the business of Parliament. And London smoked. According to the *Oxford English Dictionary*, by 1864 country people going there would talk of going to the Smoke, for the city could be detected from a great distance by the dirty yellow pall which overhung it.

With great frequency, the pall would descend onto the streets, seeming to transform the city into its own ghost. Nathaniel Hawthorne described the scene one day in December 1857:

> I went home by way of Holborn, and the fog was denser than ever, – very black, indeed more like a distillation of mud than anything else; the ghost of mud, – the spiritualized medium of departed mud, through which the dead citizens of London probably tread in the Hades whither they are translated. So heavy was the gloom, that gas was lighted in all the shop-windows; and the little charcoal-furnaces of the women and boys, roasting chestnuts, threw a ruddy, misty glow around them.

London was also phenomenally noisy. Horseshoes made quite a clatter on stone roads, but nothing to the constant rasping of iron-shod wheels. So tremendous was the din in any busy street that you could not make yourself heard in a shop unless the door was closed. And if you took a stroll in one of London's parks, you were hemmed in by a great ring of noise. In an attempt to keep the volume down, some roads were even paved with blocks of wood. Streets were frequently jammed by horse-drawn traffic: two-wheeled hansom cabs, with the driver perched birdlike up behind; four-wheeled broughams and clarences; horse-drawn omnibuses, wretched in wet weather if you had to climb the ladder at the back and take one of the seats on the roof.

And this was England's capital. 'That great foul city of London,' John Ruskin cried in exasperation in that year of 1865, 'rattling, growling, smoking, stinking – a ghastly heap of fermenting brickwork, pouring out poison at every pore.'

But Victorian England was on the move. There was the electric telegraph and Morse code, city streets were lit by gas. Railways linked the great centres of population, and London's first underground line had recently opened. There was Big Ben and there was Nelson's Column (though no lions as yet). Whitbread's brewed beer, and a refreshment contract for the Great Exhibition of 1851 went to Schweppes. Fagin was the archetypal evil Jew, the Marquess of Queensberry was a twenty-one-year-old tearaway.

People worried about the cattle plague which had driven up the price of beef and which many expected to worsen. They were horrified by the stories of black insurrection in Jamaica, where a white clergyman was said to have had his tongue torn out before being butchered. They swapped grisly urban myths: quite recently it had been said that a cat, handily skinned alive to preserve the lustre of its fur, had lived long enough to mew pathetically outside its mistress's door and leap into her lap when admitted.

Tom Sayers, however, was at peace with the world that Victorian autumn day. He had begun it at number 257 Camden Town High Street, and ended it some three miles further north. Alone in a gleaming carriage drawn by four black horses, he had followed a brass band and preceded an endless procession of friends and admirers along a route lined by people in their thousands and their tens of thousands. He had then attended a brief church service before being carried shoulder high to his grave in Highgate Cemetery.

Death was never far from people's thoughts in Victorian England, for the Industrial Revolution had brought an enormous increase in population, and more living people meant more dead people. It had also created a new wealthy middle class who were always determined to go out in style. And the poor, whose wretched living and working conditions ensured a high mortality rate, would put money aside throughout their working lives for fear of the shame of a pauper's grave. Professional mourners could be hired – Oliver Twist, for instance, in his days with Mr Sowerberry – and real ones might keep an onion handy just in case the absence of genuine tears should cause them to appear stony-hearted. No one ever did funerals quite like the Victorians. They certainly did one for Tom Sayers.

The arrangements were made by John Mensley, who had always made Tom's fighting boots, and at whose London and North Western Strong Boot and Shoe Manufactory at 257–261 Camden Town High Street Tom had died. He was from Brighton originally, but it was fitting that he should end his life in Camden Town where he had spent so much of it.

His doctor, Mr Adams of Harrington Square, stated that, while Tom was suffering from diabetes – itself a death sentence in the days before insulin – the sole cause of death was consumption, which had virtually destroyed one of his lungs. Even so, his intemperate lifestyle, said Mr Adams, had speeded his end: 'It is with sorrow I record my conviction that to the errors of his life may be ascribed the beginning and the end of his disease, and that England's Champion has fallen a victim to England's curse.'

———————

He died on November 8th, and now, a week later, two grim-faced mutes, clad from head to foot in black, stood guard outside Mr Mensley's door. Behind it, and behind the Venetian blinds which protected them from the gaze of the crowds, the principal mourners waited in the first-floor drawing room for the arrival of the vehicles which would take them on their sombre journey. It was three o'clock in the afternoon.

Sitting with his silver head bent over his chest and his hands clenched on his knees, Tom's father stared at the floor. His daughter and Tom's elder sister, Mrs King, peered out through the blinds and observed that she would have preferred not to see so large a crowd. 'I hoped never to have seen it,' replied Mr Sayers flatly. The same sentiment might have been echoed by Tom's brothers Charles and Richard – the latter resembled the dead man closely – but they were silent.

The most visibly affected of all, in fact, was not even related to the dead man. Harry Brunton, who had seconded Tom in some of his greatest battles, sat alone in a corner, weeping silently and wiping his eyes from time to time with a white handkerchief which he had not even thought to unfold. Also present, though less demonstrative in his grief, was Jemmy Welsh, the other man in Tom's corner on the day he had faced Jack Heenan at Farnborough.

Then there was Tom's daughter Sarah, fifteen years old, her face partly obscured by her mourning hood. She controlled her emotions well enough until her brother Tom, two years her junior, entered weeping. Seeing him so affected, Sarah too broke down, and brother and sister cried bitterly in each other's arms. For the boy it was all too much, and he was to remain visibly distraught for the rest of the day. But at least his immediate future was decided, for he was to go back to boarding school in Harlow after the funeral. Sarah's fate was less certain: all that had thus far been determined was that she would remain for the time being with John Mensley.

Mr Mensley, it was said, had wanted to keep the time of the funeral secret, but the elaborate arrangements strongly suggest otherwise. What he and others organised amounted to an unofficial state funeral for a working-class hero. The show that they staged was designed to be seen. And seen it was, by tens of thousands, for November 15th, 1865 was a very fine day, and the crowds had been gathering since early morning. From all over London and beyond they had come, and they had waited, more or less patiently, for a performance which would not begin for many hours.

By the middle of the afternoon, the crowds were reminiscent of those which had turned out for the Duke of Wellington thirteen years previously almost to the day. The great majority were men. Shapeless caps, dusty white flannel jackets and corduroy waistcoats defined them as representatives of the urban working class created by the Industrial Revolution; their great boots, even when new, could never have adorned the feet of a gentleman. Brightly coloured neckties suggested that some of them were costermongers, as indeed they were.[1] They formed a crowd to terrify respectable people, but within two years a number of them would have the vote, when Parliament would seek to ease dangerous social tension by widening the franchise dramatically.

There would, of course, be no question of enfranchising any of the women who were present in the High Street that day. In their worn shawls and faded bonnets, few had any pretensions to respectability. But no woman, however prosperous, would benefit from the efforts of the recently formed Committee for Women's Suffrage. For one thing, you needed property before you could vote, and married women had none: their property, and even their earnings if they had any, belonged to their husbands. And anyway, why should men take seriously the butts of so many *Punch* cartoons? Tightly corseted above the waist, voluminously crinolined below it, fashionable women had long borne something of the appearance of handbells. The poor could afford no such extravagance: sharp outlines, in all ages, are the prerogative of the rich; the poor are always blurred.

And this, of course, goes for men as much as for women. Tall silk top hats, sombre frock coats and heavy gold watch-chains were tokens of prosperity. And such tokens, it should be said, were not entirely absent from Camden Town that day, for less than six years had passed since Tom Sayers had been the toast of all the nation, not only of the lower orders.

The closure of almost all the High Street shops was generally interpreted as a mark of respect for the departed, but the more cynical suggested that the real reason was that shopkeepers feared for their property when the followers of the prize ring, the Fancy, were around.

The Fancy had a reputation not unlike that of English soccer fans more than a century later. Peaceable people quailed in their presence, the trains on which they travelled to fights were shunned by others, and their depredations in the locality where a fight took place were legendary. *Bell's Life in London*, the weekly which defined sporting journalism, reported that, from early morning on the day of the funeral, Camden Town was

> ... crowded with roughs and riff-raff, who were anything but grave in their deportment, who had evidently assembled as they would on any occasion which attracts a mob, and whose conduct presented a marked contrast to that of the respectable portion of the community...

But business would have to go on sooner or later, and shops would not be closed all day. The passing of Tom Sayers even presented opportunities for the astute trader. The photographic saloon opposite number 257, for example, exhibited a sombre-edged placard bearing

Tom's image and the inscription 'Peace to his ashes. His portrait in his favourite attitude, sixpence plain, ninepence coloured.' A black border also surrounded the announcements in the window of the cookshop round the corner: 'Superior brisket one and three' [one shilling and three pence] and 'Accommodation for refreshments on the first floor'. Even the Fancy would have to eat at some time.

Their traditional enemies – crushers, they usually called them, or sometimes blues – were also present. The Metropolitan Police Force had been in existence for a generation and more, and its officers were still often referred to as bobbies and peelers in memory of their founder, Sir Robert Peel. With the replacement in 1864 of the old top hat by a rounded helmet, and the simultaneous shortening of the tunic, the officers on duty at the funeral of Tom Sayers did not look so very different from those of much later days.

The sheer number of onlookers gave them a busy time of it, and they had to telegraph to Scotland Yard for reinforcements. People watched from the windows of shops and houses, they watched even from the roofs, they overflowed from the pavements onto the road. By mid-afternoon it was as much as the police could do to keep open a narrow channel in the middle of the High Street.

Most of London's pugilists were there, including Tom King – who had fought Heenan in '63 – Jem Ward, Bos Tyler, Jerry Noon... Their attendance was doubly appropriate, for the dramatic decline in the fortunes of the prize ring since the retirement of Tom Sayers persuaded many that his funeral was also that of the ring itself. But why was Jack Heenan not there? He of all people should have been, and such was the expectation that several impressive figures were mistaken for his. Tom King, discomfited by the attention he was attracting, managed to get a hansom to take him further up the road where the crowds were thinner.

The Pall Mall Gazette, no friend of the prize ring or its followers, thought that the people behaved

> ... exactly like the mob at a Newgate hanging... Within
> 40 yards of the door where the mutes were stationed was
> a public house, at the open upper windows of which was
> seated a convivial party of ladies and gentlemen, the former

with glasses of gin-and-water on their laps, cheerfully carolling Whitechapel ditties, while the latter joined in chorus, cracking walnuts at intervals.

The same newspaper also reported the presence in a nearby side-street of a group of Ethiopian serenaders, singing lustily to the twanging of banjos.

The most interesting thing about the *Gazette*'s report, however, is that it should have appeared at all, for such a respectable organ normally ignored anything pertaining to the disreputable prize ring. Harry Broome, who had been champion not long since, had died less than a week before Tom Sayers, and his early demise had gone almost completely unnoticed outside the ranks of the Fancy.

That of Tom Sayers, however, was impossible to ignore, for the fame he had earned in his great battle with Jack Heenan had immortalised him. *The Daily Telegraph* had opened its obituary with the simple statement 'Tom Sayers is dead', an implicit acknowledgment of the resonance of his name. The fastidious distaste expressed by *The Pall Mall Gazette* probably had a good deal to do with sheer annoyance at finding it necessary to cover such a defiantly proletarian event.

For the fact is that, whatever the *Gazette* might have thought of the mourners, there was almost no real trouble in the High Street that day, the number of reported thefts being surprisingly low. The sort of decorum expected of the middle classes might have been absent, but most of the people behaved decently enough.

Their patience was finally rewarded shortly after half past three when the door of Mr Mensley's at last opened, and a plain black coffin was carried out. Such was the press that the police had to work hard to force a path through to undertaker Samuel Freshwater's hearse – a glass showcase on wheels, drawn by four black horses with black plumes nodding on their heads. It was preceded by a brass band, but most eyes were on neither band nor hearse, but on the vehicle behind.

In the years following his retirement from the ring, Tom Sayers had often been seen driving about town in his phaeton, an open-air four-wheeled carriage with two back-to-back bench seats separated by a rail. At his funeral it was drawn as ever by his little dun cob, a black velvet pall over his back, and led by one of Mr Freshwater's men. Resting in his usual place on the imitation leopard skin covering the rear seat was Tom's frequent companion, the mastiff Lion, his collar wrapped in black crape. Tom's place in front was empty.

When the coffin was safely aboard Mr Freshwater's hearse, the principal mourners filed out of Mr Mensley's and went to the large closed mourning carriages drawn up behind the phaeton. Into the first climbed Tom's father, his brother Charles and the two children. Five more followed for the rest of the party who had endured the painful wait at John Mensley's. Among them, conspicuous in a red Garibaldi shirt, was a pale and sick looking Nat Langham, the only man ever to have beaten Tom Sayers in the ring.

Behind the mourning coaches was an extraordinary succession of coaches – the drivers' whips wrapped in black crape as they had been for Palmerston three weeks before – and workmen's carts of all descriptions. To the rear a few horsemen mingled with thousands on foot, including a number of non-commissioned officers and men of the Life Guards and Blues.

It was quarter to four when, after one false start, Mr Freshwater was finally able to get the vast procession moving. The musicians played the Dead March from *Saul*, but not, we are told, very competently. Mr Mensley had tried hard to engage a military band, but without success, and had had to be content instead with a group of players from the music halls. Handel was not a regular part of their repertoire, and it showed. Other pieces received similar treatment, and *Bell's Life* observed that their performance 'would have gone much better and accorded more with the solemnity of the scene had they tried over their pieces together once or twice beforehand.'

They had plenty of scope for demonstrating their incompetence, for Highgate Cemetery is some three miles from the top of Camden Town High Street, and there were crowds of people all the way. At the Britannia tavern, where five roads converged and where Tom had been a familiar figure, carriages of all sorts were drawn up wheel to wheel as if at a racecourse. All the length of Kentish Town Road they marched before bearing left to begin the long slow climb up Highgate Road. People still crowded at the windows and lined the sides of the way, but the houses were sparser here, almost all of them recently constructed, for Highgate Cemetery was well to the north of the built-up area.

This in fact was the whole point, for the safe disposal of London's dead had become an urgent issue. Arrangements had been haphazard until well into the century, with bodies usually being interred in shallow graves within the city. And these could pose a serious risk to health if, as often happened, a coffin was accidentally disinterred, for the ungrateful dead could and sometimes did poison the living. By the 1830s, a fast-increasing population was making things still worse, and space was at a premium. An 1832 Act of Parliament established Kensal Green Cemetery, Thackeray's resting place, and Highgate soon followed.

Flags flew at half mast, black banners were draped across the road and in front of buildings: 'FAREWELL TOM OF THE LION HEART' said one, while Mr Cockin's Bull and Last, the northernmost tavern in Highgate Road, displayed one which read, in white letters on a black background, 'PEACE TO ENGLAND'S CHAMPION'.

By the time they passed it, the cortège had already covered two uphill miles, and the hardest part of the journey, the great upward curve of Swain's Lane, was yet to come. It was a long and weary climb, but shortly after half past five they came at last to the gates of Highgate Cemetery.

Thus far, even if the Fancy had been somewhat disorderly, even if the band had been less than brilliant, things had gone smoothly enough. But that was now to change. A hundred or so of the men crowded outside the entrance to the cemetery had managed to force their way in much earlier, and many more were now waiting for the gates, presently closed against them, to be opened. And in spite of the efforts of the crushers, sheer weight of numbers carried them through when, after the carriages with the principal mourners had been admitted, the gates were unwisely reopened to admit the band.

Respectable onlookers watched with horror, and some of their comments reveal, as much as anything, a very Victorian fear of the lower orders. The *Daily News*, for instance, informed its readers that:

Hundreds of the foulest scum of the back courts and alleys of London, the creatures who only come to light in the aggregate at an execution, or race-course, or an illegal betting ground, rushed in to hold saturnalia at the graveside.

Bell's Life said that, while the service was in progress in the chapel, 'the mob climbed weeping willows... or clambered up or on broken columns and funeral urns... and made the usual stillness of the cemetery horrible with their howlings.'

Still, proceedings in the chapel were not disrupted, and neither was the short interment service. The Fancy may have been rowdy, but they were genuine enough in the desire to bid farewell to their hero. The grave was very deep, with yellow sandy soil heaped beside it, and red berries just beginning to appear on the spreading holly tree at its head. It was now too dark for the photographers who had hoped to record the scene, but Dan Collins, George Sims and Jack Grant, all early victims of Tom's, were there to salute their conqueror for the last time. The black fighter Bob Travers seemed especially moved, 'his face having', in the words of *The Sporting Life*, 'an intensity of sorrow and awe in it we have never seen exceeded.' His eyes remained fixed on the coffin as he let fall grains of gravel on the lid.

It was almost dark by the time that Tom's friends and family trudged from the graveside back down the hill and out into the world again. And then the mass of unruly extras came forward, tactfully enough avoiding the main cast, to gaze into the open grave. The coffin bore a brass plaque which read simply 'Tom Sayers, born May 15, 1826; died November 8, 1865.'

William Jeffery Prowse of *The Daily Telegraph*, less troubled than some by the behaviour of the intruders, was moved by the melancholy of the occasion:

The shadows and the chill of evening had crept over the scene... Now purple mists were rising among the bare trees, down in the valley which this pleasant burial-ground overlooks, and met the fading orange sky with the sadness of a cold November twilight.

But the *Daily News* struck a less elegiac tone altogether. Remembering the subscription which had been got up for Tom Sayers after the great battle at Farnborough, the *News* noted with distaste that 'the respectable classes... subscribed to keep him in idleness for life; who had become the idol of pothouses, and died of drinking, and whose funeral was a riot.'

You paid your money and you took your choice.

―――――――

The shades of Victorian England haunt Highgate to this day. Mary Ann Cross, better known as Mary Ann (or even Marian) Evans, still better known as George Eliot, was laid there on the cold and slushy Boxing Day of 1880. And within three years she had been joined by Karl Marx, who lies now beneath his famous bust, truncated in accordance with planning permission so that he seems to rest on his beard.

There is also Mrs Henry Wood, author of the fabulously successful *East Lynne*, published in 1861, the year of *Silas Marner* and *Great Expectations*. Across the way is Dante Gabriel Rossetti's wife, Lizzie Siddal, who took her own life in 1862, and with whom the distraught aesthete saw romantically fit to inter the only complete manuscript of his poems. (Seven years later she was to suffer the indignity of disinterment when Rossetti, his ardour having cooled, decided to retrieve his work in order to make some money from it.)

And then there is George Wombwell, who died in 1850, the year that Rossetti and Siddal first met. Wombwell owned a menagerie, and on his tomb rests an effigy of the lion Nero, whose peaceable disposition had once ruined a projected fight with six bull-mastiffs.

But there is another sculpted Lion in Highgate. If you take the right-hand path which winds uphill from the chapel just inside the gates of the west cemetery, you will find it very near the highest point in the burial ground. The stone image of Tom Sayers's dog rests, head on paws, beneath the bas-relief medallion of his master's profile on the front gable of a tomb shaped like a classical temple with low-pitched roof. Lion is the epitome of canine devotion, and the somewhat faded medallion shows not a man but a hero in the classical mould, a Hector or

Achilles. It is less the face of Tom Sayers than an icon, a personification of manly virtue.

The bones which lie beneath were once covered with living flesh, nerves, sinews. And muscles of steel. The heart within once pumped blood to a brain which thought of wife and children, food and drink, gaslight and London fog. This was once a man. And one glorious spring day in 1860, all England held its breath to know his fate.

CHAPTER 2

... AND A LONG ONE

SUNDAY, NOVEMBER 2nd, 1873. Charles Dickens is in Westminster Abbey, where he has been at peace for the past three years. His last novel, *The Mystery of Edwin Drood*, has been left incomplete, and the world is not quite the same without him.

Brunel's mighty *Great Eastern*, by contrast, is doing well. Having failed as a passenger ship – smaller vessels were well capable of handling the demands of the time – she has found her vocation as a cable-laying vessel for the telegraph system which, along with steam power, is shrinking the world as never before. Jules Verne's *Around the World in Eighty Days*, published in 1872, was making a serious point. Thanks to the *Great Eastern*, Europe and America are now linked by Morse code: a few minutes now suffice to send messages which previously took ten days or more to arrive.

Dickens had lived to see it, but not to see his own sixtieth year. Some say that he never fully recovered from the crash of South-Eastern's train at Staplehurst in June 1865.

As for Samuel Smiles, he quit his job as South-Eastern's secretary in 1866 – the year in which the *Great Eastern* laid the Atlantic cable – to become president of the National Provident Institute. Five years later, he suffered a severe stroke, but has made a remarkable recovery, relearning the skills of literacy sufficiently to enable him to return to authorship.

Smiles seems to have been one of the few literary celebrities who did not fall under the spell of Adah Isaacs Menken, the Naked Lady, who collected literary friends and lovers as others of the age collected rare insects. Charles Dickens was among her specimens. On Sunday, November 2nd, 1873, however, Menken's collecting days are over, for, still in her early thirties, she has preceded Dickens in death by a couple of years.

Dying in Paris, she was first laid to rest at Père Lachaise, but her remains have since been moved to the cemetery of Montparnasse. Her bigamous husband, John Camel Heenan, the Benicia Boy, the toast of all America when he fought Tom Sayers to a standstill at Farnborough thirteen years before, is more than three thousand miles away in his native New York. Again he is the centre of attention, for Sunday, November 2nd, 1873 is the day of his funeral.

———————

It was eight years and more since Robert E. Lee had surrendered to Ulysses S. Grant at Appomattox Courthouse, and the victorious Union commander was now into his second term in the White House. Another Federal general, the flamboyant George Armstrong Custer, had led the Seventh Cavalry into their first clash with the Sioux, near the Tongue River in Dakota Territory, less than three months previously. Custer's brief had been to protect a railroad survey party.

Since the War, the protection of railroad workers had occupied much of the army's energy. Between 1865 and 1873, thirty-five thousand miles of new track had been laid, much of it in Indian country, with the transcontinental railroad itself reaching completion in 1869. And just to confirm that the Frontier really was becoming civilised, Jesse James had recently pulled off the American West's first successful train robbery, at Adair, Iowa.

But not everyone was having fun. Only a month had passed since the share-price crash which had forced the New York Stock Exchange to close its doors for ten days, and the nation was now in the depths of a severe economic depression, of which unwise speculation in the burgeoning railroads had been the major cause. The extraordinary construction boom couldn't last, and when the Philadelphia banking firm of Jay Cooke had to declare bankruptcy after overextending themselves to finance the projected Northern Pacific Railway, the effects were catastrophic. The official completion of Central Park that year was not of much comfort to the many New Yorkers who had been ruined.

And nothing could be of comfort any more to John Camel Heenan, who had died eight days previously and two thousand miles away, at Green River Station, Wyoming Territory, on the Union Pacific Railroad. It was a place dominated by the sort of arid, towering butte, topped by a stark platform of rock (Castle Rock), that instantly evokes wagon trains and horse-rustling, outlaws and Indians, gunsmoke and the US cavalry.

The transcontinental railroad, its last link sealed by the golden spike at Promontory Summit, was only four years old, and it was now five years since Union Pacific's railhead had reached Green River. Like so many other places along the line, Green River had had its brief moment of dubious glory as a Hell on Wheels town, when the railroad workers set up camp there.

Some tales of their wildness may have grown taller with the telling, but these truly were hell-raisers. At Green River as elsewhere, they threw up flimsy constructions of wood and canvas which did duty for dance halls, saloons, gambling dens and brothels, often all rolled into one. Places of worship were conspicuously absent, and gunfights were so common as to pass almost unremarked.

At Green River, as at countless other locations, they left a ghost town when they moved on, the population swiftly declining from two thousand to fewer than two hundred. What remained was a forlorn scattering of adobe walls and a few dwellings which, according to one contemporary observer, might with equal justice have been defined as houses with canvas roofs, or as tents with board sides.

And this was where John Camel Heenan, the Benicia Boy of legend, died. He had been injured in a train crash just a year before Charles Dickens suffered a similar experience, and, as with Dickens, there were those who said he had not been the same since. It happened in England in June 1864 when he was on his way home from Ascot races, where he had been plying his trade as a bookie. His train was stationary at Egham in Surrey when it was rammed from behind by another.

When the first alarm was given, he had craned his neck out of the window to see what was happening, and, realising that a crash was inevitable, had leapt out onto the platform. He had fallen, sustaining injuries so serious that two doctors remained with him for the next twenty-four hours, during which he suffered constant fits. His recovery thereafter was halting. Five people died in the crash, and Jack Heenan was one of twenty-five hospitalised. The South-Western Railway Company paid him damages without going to court.

Something more than a year later, within a month of the funeral of Tom Sayers and still suffering from the effects of the accident, he had left England. By the end of 1865, he was back in the United States.

Whatever the ultimate cause of his ill-health, his condition was giving grounds for serious concern by the autumn of 1873, when he was living in New York. He was attended by Doctors Carnochan and Willard Parker, who agreed – wrongly, it was later established – that his lung haemorrhages were the result of pneumonia rather than of tuberculosis (or consumption, as they termed it). In response to their recommendation that he seek drier and purer air, Jack left home on September 3rd and headed west, for Denver in Colorado Territory. It was a formidable journey for a sick man, but nothing to what it had been before the coming of the railroad – nothing to what such a journey had been twenty years before, when Jack Heenan had quit New York State to seek his fortune in California.

Before the rails were laid, it had taken anything from eight weeks to eight months to get from New York to San Francisco. The forty-niner gold prospectors and others had to choose between the ocean trip – either round Cape Horn or via Panama – and the overland trek by wagon train. Whichever route they took, they faced a perilous journey of months. Now it took little more than a week to get from coast to coast. When the golden spike joined the Union Pacific and Central Pacific railroads at Promontory Summit, the fate of a continent was sealed.

Now the iron horse plied the plains, and there was nothing that the Cheyenne, the Sioux or anybody else could do about it. Trains thundered across the lands of the native Americans, their plough-shaped cow-catchers making short work of animals which strayed onto the line, their huge cone-shaped funnels – essential as spark traps for the many wood-burning locomotives – framing the great headlamps which blazed the trail by night.

The sick man travelled first to Omaha, Nebraska, where the Frontier began – where Union Pacific had laid its first rails eight years before. From there, it was Wild West all the way – through Nebraska and into Wyoming Territory at Pine Bluffs, then on to Cheyenne, where the local newspaper, the *Leader*, ran a daily column entitled 'Last Night's Shootings'. From Cheyenne, the Denver Pacific Railway covered the hundred miles south to the new city of Denver.

For the pale-skinned colonists flooding in with the railroad, everything between Omaha and California was new and wild and woolly. The aspiring middle classes of the new settlements were keen to share the sophistication of New York and San Francisco, where fashionable women now wore bustles which suggested elephantiasis of the bottom, and where top hats were no longer so elevated as to merit the designation stovepipe.

But the men who kicked open the doors to the West wore the clothes that suited their way of life. Stetson hats covered heads, neckerchiefs offered some protection against the ubiquitous dust, stout leather chaps protected trousers tucked into high boots and held up by braces. It was in 1873 that Levi Strauss, who had begun selling his denim Levis to the gold diggers of California in the 1850s when Jack Heenan was there, patented the riveting of stress points. Trousers – some called them jeans – had never been tougher.

Everyone carried a gun. Eighteen seventy-three was the year of Colt's most famous revolver, the Peacemaker, and also of Winchester's most successful rifle, known to some as the gun that won the West. Life was tough and life was cheap. It was seldom long.

Certainly Jack Heenan's condition held out little hope of longevity. In Denver, he felt better for a time, but in the middle of October, news reached New York that he had taken a turn for the worse. And no one was more upset than his old friend and mentor Jim Cusick, the man who had launched his prize-fighting career.

Cusick, English by birth, never boxed professionally but had achieved great success as trainer and manager. Seldom seen without a bow tie, he was a small bustling man of terrific energy, some of which found an outlet in incessant talk. He was also a brilliant manager, without whom the easy-going Jack would never have made it as a prize fighter. Their relationship even survived Cusick's intense dislike – returned in full measure – of Adah Menken.

Jim Cusick was the most faithful friend Jack Heenan would ever know, and, busy though he was, he did not hesitate when he heard the news from Colorado. He left New York on October 18th, and reached Denver four days later. His former protégé was so moved to see him that he wept.

Well aware that the sick man might not have long to live, Cusick had hoped to take him back to New York, that he might at least have the comfort of dying at home. The Benicia Boy, however, preferred to go to California, where he and Cusick had first met, and where he had made the name that was to serve him so well in his prize-fighting days.

Accordingly, they left Denver on the twenty-fourth, rejoined the Union Pacific at Cheyenne, and pushed on to Laramie, the epitome of Hell on Wheels in 1868 when the railroad arrived. With twenty-three saloons, one hotel and no churches, it took five hundred vigilantes to bring the town under control on one night of mayhem in October that year. After a bloody gun battle in which most of the town participated, a number of public enemies were hanged from telegraph poles. It was little more than par for the Frontier course.

Anyway, by 1873 it was history, and of no concern to Cusick and Heenan. On they went to the ghost town that was Green River, and there Jack Heenan spoke his last words: 'I'm gone, Jim.'

'The innumerable caravan' was, in the words of the *New York Clipper*, 'longer by a soul.'

It was no surprise. Cusick telegraphed ahead to Salt Lake City, to ask for a metal coffin to be sent to the nearest station at Ogden. The coffin was waiting when they arrived, but, failing to find an embalmer as he had hoped, Cusick left Ogden the next morning, to accompany his friend's remains on the long journey back to New York. From Utah they retraced their route back into Wyoming at Evanston, back to Green River, back through Rock Springs, along Bitter Creek, through Rawlins and Medicine Bow and Laramie and Cheyenne, back through Pine Bluffs and into Nebraska, all the way to Omaha. And then back to New York.

———

The body of John Camel Heenan arrived in the metropolis late on the last night of October, and was taken from the station to his late residence at 16 Clinton Place, where it was finally embalmed.

The following afternoon, some three thousand people came to pay their respects. Nearly all of them, according to *The New York Herald*, 'belonged to the sporting or gambling fraternity.' The black-draped catafalque on which the coffin lay was that on which, five months previously, had rested the remains of James Gordon Bennett, founder, editor and publisher of the *Herald*, the only American daily to have given extensive and ungrudging coverage to Jack Heenan's career.

The body, dressed in a dark suit, was visible through a glass plate in the coffin lid – a sight distressing to some, the dead man's face being, in the words of the *New York Clipper*, 'much puffed up and of a ghastly hue'. And just in case anyone wondered why, the *Clipper* was ready with an explanation which many might have done without:

> ... when placed in the coffin the body bled profusely from the nose, and in order to stop the effusion of blood Mr Cusick was obliged to put cotton in the nostrils, as also to remove the support from the head. The blood being forced back, combined with the gases used in embalming, caused the features to swell...

One candelabrum stood at the head of the coffin and one at the foot, seven wax candles burning in each. Accompanied by her two young daughters, the dead man's only sister, described by the *Herald*'s reporter as 'a very comely woman of perhaps thirty-six years of age and bearing a strong personal resemblance to her brother', remained in the room all afternoon, overcome with grief.

The next day, Sunday, November 2nd, crowds lined both sides of Clinton Place to see the cortège move off at nine o'clock. A squad of police preceded the hearse, which was drawn by four grey horses, and closely attended by the eighteen principal male mourners, including Jim Cusick and former police superintendent James J. Kelso – four in front, four behind, and five to each side. Then came four carriages carrying the dead man's sister, aunt and nieces, and a number of female friends of the family. Behind them, a long line of friends and admirers walked two abreast, their numbers supplemented here and there from the sidewalks.

The procession made its way to the Church of the Holy Innocents on Thirty-Seventh Street near Broadway, where the crowds made it hard for police to clear a way for the principal mourners to take their places. The presence of such numbers, however, gave a slightly misleading impression. The *Herald* observed that almost all of them had been attending early mass, and had stayed on largely out of curiosity. Still, they would not have remained for just anybody.

The coffin was placed on a catafalque at the foot of the chancel, with lighted tapers at either end, and the altar was decked out for a full requiem mass, a crown of gas jets surmounting the apex of the shrine. The Reverend Father Larkin officiated.

One unexpected absence was the cause of some comment. In 1858, Jack Heenan had fought John Morrissey for the American championship. Morrissey, a somewhat lucky winner, had then retired from the ring to make his fortune in gambling and extortion rackets. He had also found time to set up Saratoga Racetrack and to serve two terms in Congress. He and Jack Heenan were old foes, their enmity going back to childhood, but most had thought he would at least turn up at the funeral. Morrissey, however, played the part at Heenan's funeral that Heenan had played at that of Tom Sayers.

When the service was over, the coffin was taken to the Grand Central depot, where a large and curious crowd was waiting. At ten past eleven, the special train made up of two drawing-room cars pulled out of the depot to begin its journey north to Albany. Crowds had gathered at all the stations along the way, but none as large as that which waited at Albany itself, where the train arrived in mid-afternoon.

There twenty carriages stood ready to carry the mourners the four remaining miles to St Agnes Cemetery, where Jack had bought a plot and where a crowd of several hundred was waiting for them. The dead man's sister and nieces had not come to Albany, but his uncle John, a blacksmith in the arsenal, was there to witness the interment. The remains of Jack Heenan went to join those of his parents and two brothers, just a mile and a half from Watervliet Arsenal where he had been born.

The life of the Benicia Boy had come full circle.

CHAPTER 3

BRIGHTON TO LONDON

DESTINED TO die in the high noon of Victorian England, Tom Sayers had been born into the Georgian twilight of the 1820s. To be more specific, he was born in Brighton (which many still called by its old name of Brighthelmston) in May 1826.

It was an age of elegance. The King's favourite architect, John Nash, had recently laid out Regent's Park, Regent Street and Trafalgar Square, and was now transforming Buckingham House into a new palace. Beau Brummell had long since fled to the Continent to escape his gambling debts, but his exacting sartorial standards had left an indelible mark on the upper classes. The King himself was something of a dandy, determined to be known above all as a man of taste and style.

It was an age of misery. The new industrial working class lived brief lives of relentless toil in burgeoning cities which would soon be blackened by the smoke billowing from petrified forests of factory chimneys. Small children worked amidst dirt and danger in mines and mills and factories for twelve hours a day and more. Others choked on soot inside the chimneys they had to climb.

The Industrial Revolution ground on, crushing the lives of its children beneath its steam-driven wheels. The world's first railway, from Stockton to Darlington, had just been completed, and the Liverpool & Manchester line was now under construction. On the high seas, the world's first iron steamship had made its maiden voyage in 1822.

Unsurprisingly, the victims of Progress felt they had a right to better lives – to something, at least, of the enormous wealth enjoyed by the upper classes and the new capitalists who controlled the means of production. Lord Liverpool's Tory government, however, had other ideas, and resisted with determination the aspirations of the dispossessed. At St Peter's Fields in Manchester in 1819, cavalry had, at a conservative estimate, killed eleven and injured four hundred at an orderly demonstration in favour of political reform. Just four years after Napoleon's defeat, no one missed the ironic allusion in the name swiftly given to this tragedy: the Peterloo Massacre. Trade unions were largely impotent, their legalisation in 1824 having been followed within a year by an effective ban on strike action.

The mushrooming industrial cities already covered much of the landscape, yet the bulk of the population was still to be found in the countryside. John Constable painted deceptively idyllic scenes of the lives they lived in the south of England, while William Cobbett, in *Rural Rides*, revealed the wretchedness to which many had in reality been reduced. Meanwhile at Haworth on the Yorkshire moors, it was in 1826 that the curate, Irishman Patrick Brontë, brought home the box of toy soldiers which was to inspire his remarkable children to create the imaginary world of Angria, and later of Gondal.

In London at the same time, Charles Dickens, now fourteen years old, was attending school in Camden Town. While his father had been in debtor's prison just two years previously, he had endured, in Warren's Blacking Factory on the Thames near where Charing Cross Station now stands, the most miserable months he would ever know. The memory would for ever darken his life.

All this was Georgian England. But only just. After a lifetime of debauchery which had made of his person a bloated ruin, George IV did not have long to go. Respected by none, openly ridiculed by many – Leigh Hunt, author of 'Abou Ben Adhem (may his tribe increase!)', had been imprisoned for daring to commit his low opinion to print – George was now in the habit of regaling listeners with the fanciful story of his exploits on the field of Waterloo. The Duke of Wellington, now prominent in the political world, found it most tiresome.

It had all been so different once. The young George had been handsome as well as clever and charming, worshipped by men and women alike. But he had never learned to control his appetites. George simply couldn't get enough food or drink or sex or drugs, and a lifetime's indulgence had wrecked him. He was still in his early thirties when James Gillray memorably caricatured him as a bloated sybarite, and by the time of his coronation in 1821, he was an old man before he was sixty.

That coronation, however, had been truly splendid, with all the pomp and pageantry which George so much loved. It had almost been ruined by the attempt of his estranged and hated wife, Queen Caroline, to gatecrash, but George had taken precautions against such an eventuality. With the soldiers on duty being there in a ceremonial capacity, he had arranged a more functional guard in the shape of nineteen bare-knuckle prize fighters, all dressed as pages. Chief among them was John 'Gentleman' Jackson, who, it was said, had taught a third of England's peerage to box at his gymnasium in London's Bond Street. Queen Caroline – who died within three weeks of her humiliation – was never going to make it into Westminster Abbey.

In an unparalleled age of invention, George might himself be said to have invented one thing: the seaside holiday. And Brighton was his resort of choice. The most determined and the most illustrious holidaymaker the town would ever see, George was to make his final visit just three years before his death. But he had discovered Brighton as Prince of Wales in his early twenties, when he was as much admired as he was despised in later years. He was a true leader of fashion. Where George went, the fashionable – and still more, those who wished to be fashionable – followed.

But Brighton, as it happened, was up and coming even before George made his first appearance. The town's fame as a health resort began in the 1750s, and is generally attributed to Dr Richard Russell of Lewes, who claimed (in a paper published in Latin in 1750) that drinking and bathing in seawater could cure many diseases. Russell was not in fact the first to make such an assertion, but his was the one that stuck. By the 1820s, Brighton beach was home to scores of bathing machines, individual wheeled changing rooms, usually drawn into the water by horses.

From 1750 to 1820 Brighton underwent a transformation. The old town was rebuilt, the surrounding farmland was swallowed up, and the population rose from two thousand to twenty-four thousand. And as it became more fashionable – the destination of choice for wealthy Londoners who fancied a holiday by the seaside – so a tourist industry developed, often employing on a seasonal basis people who would have to find other work outside the summer months. In 1825, Dr Struve of Dresden boosted tourism still further when he constructed an artificial spring in Queen's Park. More and more fashionable visitors poured in.

Then there was the growth in cross-Channel traffic after the Napoleonic Wars. The popularity of the Brighton–Dieppe crossing soon necessitated a better means of embarkation than the small boats launched from the beach to meet larger vessels, and in 1823 the chain pier (now replaced by Brighton Pier, formerly Palace Pier) was constructed for the mooring of ships.

But much of the Brighton into which Tom Sayers was born three years later was dreadful. The Industrial Revolution was in full swing, but the legislation which would gradually improve the lot of the poor – regulating work in mines and factories and mills, establishing decent sanitation, ensuring at least elementary education for all – lay very largely in the future.

Where London smelt of horses and sewage, Brighton smelt of horses and sewage and fish. There was virtually no subsurface drainage, with the result that domestic and industrial waste ran past house fronts in open gutters which also contained fish intestines and blood and flies from slaughterhouses. Effluent from cesspits would sometimes ooze through the walls into the basements of houses, its ingress eased by inferior bricks, and mortar made of unsuitable sea sand.

It was an age of cruel contrasts, but the rich and fashionable lived lives largely insulated from the poor, and the social conscience of the nation was as yet little developed. Certainly, there is scant evidence of a social conscience in King George, who, while taking no noticeable interest in the poor, marked the Brighton of wealth and fashion with his own unique personality, tangibly expressed by John Nash in the form of Brighton Pavilion.

A dazzling example of the frivolity which only serious money can buy, the Pavilion, completed in the early twenties, has never quite found a secure place in the public estimation. England's Gothic cathedrals are universally loved, her mid-twentieth-century skyscrapers universally loathed, but we have never quite made up our minds whether to admire or to despise George's Pavilion. Reminiscent at first glance of the Taj Mahal, the popular oversimplification is that the Pavilion is Mogul on the outside, Chinese on the inside. In a later age, it might have been called postmodern. But whatever anyone might think of it, Brighton Pavilion is a creation which is determined, like the monarch who conceived it, to be unique. And to be noticed for it.

An early detractor was William Cobbett, who likened it to a square box with turnips on top. This was not altogether fair, but Cobbett was one of the most perceptive commentators of the age, and it would have been interesting to have had his views on another Brighton location entirely. Pimlico, only five minutes' walk away, was the birthplace of Tom Sayers, who came into this world just three years after the completion of George's pleasure dome. And it could scarcely have presented a starker contrast.

———————

Long since lost under Tichborne Street, Pimlico was no more than an alley with a gutter running down the middle. The two-roomed houses had no water supply, the toilets were stinking holes in the ground, and effluent from the communal cesspool, very deep and seldom emptied, leaked into the wells from which the people drew their drinking water. There were several unregulated slaughterhouses close by, and the fishermen's wives, when they cleaned fish, would simply leave the intestines in the gutter. An 1849 report on the health of Brighton cited Pimlico as an area where disease was especially prevalent, and it is highly unlikely that it had been any better in the 1820s.

It was at number seventy-four that Tom Sayers was born, the youngest in a family of five. His father, William, a shoemaker, was thirty-three years old, and came from the little Sussex village of Storrington at the foot of the South Downs. His mother, Maria, was some ten years older than her husband. On the last day of 1826, Henry Waghorn, who had once been tutor to the two sons of the Duke of Wellington, baptised the infant.

The Sayers family, like so many others, lived on the breadline, and Tom was obliged to work from an early age. He was only six years old when he went into the tourist industry as a Jack in the Water, helping to push pleasure boats out from the sand, to beach them when they were not being used, to clean them, and generally to serve the needs of Brighton's well-to-do holidaymakers.

But, the holiday trade being seasonal and dependent on the weather, Tom was obliged also to make himself useful to the fishing industry. He would, for example, help to push out the hog-boats, dumpy little fishing vessels peculiar to the Brighton area. Boys like Tom worked freelance, patrolling the beach in the hope of a few coins from anyone – holidaymakers or fishermen – who just needed a little unskilled assistance of the sort that a young boy might be able to offer.[2]

Although he certainly never learned to read or write, it has been claimed that Tom did once attend school. The records of the Union Charity School of Brighthelmston (now Middle Street Primary School) near Pimlico show the enrolment of a Thomas Sayers in June 1836. His father's name, however, is given as Richard, and his address as 45 Bread Street, so it seems that this cannot have been the future pugilist.

It was at the age of thirteen that Tom Sayers staked a claim to his own place in the world, asserting his independence by striking out alone for London. There would have been no question of coach travel – which, although the railway was under construction, was still the only means of passenger transport – so, aged thirteen, he must have walked, hitching lifts when he could get them.

At least he had a place to stay when he arrived in the capital, for his sister Eliza, sixteen years his senior, was already living in north London, on Marylebone High Street not far from the new Euston Station. He was also assured of a job, since Eliza's husband, Robert, was a builder. In this his first taste of regular employment, Tom seems to have done well enough, but his combative personality was a little too much in evidence. According to his brother-in-law, who otherwise thought well of him, 'he was always fighting with some boy or other. I used to talk to him and so did his sister, but all to no avail, for it appeared fighting was his delight.'

In the circumstances, it is hardly surprising to learn that he fell out so seriously with a sea captain on whose house he was working that man and boy nearly came to blows. The real Tom Sayers had arrived.

But he had had enough of London, at least for the time being, and went back to Brighton. There he remained in the building trade, becoming an apprentice bricklayer on the new houses being built for the town's growing number of wealthy visitors. And it was now that he began to take a serious interest in the activity which was to become his life.

Brighton was not – like Nottingham or Bristol – one of the great centres of pugilism, but at the Druid's Head tavern, Joe and Harry Phelps offered coaching to those interested in learning to box. It was in the Phelps blood, for their elder brother, known as Brighton Bill, had attained immortality of a sort when he was killed in a bout with Owen Swift at Royston in Hertfordshire in 1837.

Properly directed, Tom's great natural ability shone through, and was first seen in public in 1842. It was really a matter of luck, for he had gone to Newmarket Hill near Brighton Racecourse as a spectator, not a participant. The contest he witnessed was between Jack Grady, a boxer of no great distinction, and a novice whose name has not even come down to us. When the battle was over, a man by the name of Haines entered the ring and threw out a challenge to all comers. Tom stepped forward.

There is no detailed record of the fight, but he seems to have held his own against a bigger, older and more experienced opponent. How the fight might have ended had it run its course can only be a matter of speculation, for local magistrate Colonel Paine arrived to put a stop to proceedings after seventeen inconclusive rounds. He was doing no more than his duty, for prize fighting, however common and however popular, was illegal.

From now on, it seems that Tom was happy to exercise his talent whenever the occasion arose. But apocryphal tales have always been told of heroes, and one story of this time which must surely be filed under too-good-to-be-true tells of a fight he got into on one building site. Young Tom, so the story goes, dealt in true knightly fashion with two labourers whom he caught molesting the foreman's daughter. But the villains had powerful friends, and the biggest navvy on the site – six feet two inches tall to Tom's five feet eight – decided to teach the whippersnapper a lesson. They fought for five shillings a side, and Tom (naturally) won.

However that may be, it was not long before his restless feet took him back to London. There he resumed employment with his brother-in-law Robert King, who tells a more reliable story – one which sounds rather like the germ of truth behind the tale of the foreman's daughter – relating to this period. While Tom was working on the Hippodrome Racecourse at Notting Hill, he stood up for a Russian immigrant worker who was the butt of cruel jokes by some navvies. Tom, not yet seventeen years old, thrashed two of them, one after the other.

But this was a small matter compared with his next fight. Again we are indebted to Robert King for the story. Some months later, while working for his brother-in-law at Wandsworth in south London, Tom had an argument with an unnamed Irish labourer, said to have stood over six feet tall. King would not allow them to fight at work, so they adjourned to Wandsworth Common. Such arrangements were not unusual at the time.

During the first hour, unable to keep his footing on the slippery ground, Tom was 'thrown tremendously'. His solution was to remove his boots and fight barefoot. It worked. After a battle lasting close on three hours, Tom, who was left only with a few bruises, won by a knockout. His vanquished opponent did not get off so lightly. He was carried to his lodgings, where, according to King, three doctors attended him all night, unsure whether he would live or die.

The blues were informed, and, in the midst of a hue and cry, Tom's friends took him to some stables in Tooting, where they hid him in a corn bin. Then at three in the morning, they smuggled him back to north London under a cartload of hay. There he hid out three days with Robert and Eliza, till the search was called off. After such an experience, Tom Sayers could hardly help but take pugilism seriously.

'Many more rough fights he had', according to Robert King, before his formal entry into the prize ring. It was not to be wondered at. Navvies were notoriously combative, and a young man with a big fighting reputation but without the physique to match, was always likely to face challenges from those who sought to enhance their own reputations as hard men. It suited Tom well enough. 'I have often heard him say,' said Robert King, 'that he would rather go out and have a fight than go to work.'

It was a time of economic depression and industrial unrest. Chartism, considered by some to be history's first mass working-class movement, thrived, and the Chartist struggle for democracy would be one of the defining features of the 1840s.

But for most poor people, keeping food on the table left little energy for other activities, and Tom Sayers was not an exception. In 1845 he entered into the biggest construction project the world had yet seen, the building of Britain's railways. This time, there was nothing random about his return to Brighton, for he was now a fully-fledged bricklayer, and bricklayers were in great demand in his home town. Tom worked with his elder brother Jack on the London Road Viaduct, a massive undertaking which employed three and a half thousand men and nearly six hundred horses between May 29th, 1845 and March 28th, 1846. The result was a structure four hundred yards long and sixty-seven feet high, its twenty-seven arches towering over the tree-lined slopes of the Preston Valley.

There cannot have been much free time for the workforce, but Tom found a profitable way of using what little there was. Through Jack he got to know a man well qualified to supplement the training which he had already received from the Phelps brothers. Bob Wade, one of their workmates, was the Dover champion, and was happy to pass on to the young bricklayer the benefits of his own experience in the ring.

When the viaduct was complete, Tom returned once more to London. It was the fifth time he had walked the London to Brighton road since 1839, but this time he would settle in the capital. It seems likely that he travelled in company with Jack, because he now moved into Jack's house in Agar Town, an area which included St Pancras Workhouse and St Giles Cemetery, and which lay just to the north of today's St Pancras Station. They were not far from their sister Eliza.

In the mid-eighteenth century the whole area had been rural, but was now densely populated. In 1862, speaking in terms which would have been valid sixteen years earlier, *The St Pancras Directory* expressed pride in the achievement:

The once desolate district has become densely populated;
the fields, farms, and nurseries, are converted into squares,
crescents, and streets. The old watchmen are superseded
by the metropolitan police,– the dim old oil lamps,
which on winter nights made darkness visible, and thick
darkness sensibly felt to be terrible, are things of the past;
and people can now walk alone at any hour of the night,
which duties may require of them, lighted by cheerful gas
lamps, and consciously free from lurking dangers. Nor is
this all that has happened in the way of change; for the old
coaches through St Pancras, from the City to Paddington,
Highgate and Hampstead, have now given way to much
more numerous and economical Omnibuses...

But this was not quite the whole story. Much of St Pancras was indeed
desirable, and the middle classes had claimed it for their own, but Agar
Town was different. It was to gain notoriety in 1851 when it was the subject
of a piece contributed by W.M. Thomas to Charles Dickens's weekly
Household Words.

Thomas describes a squalid shanty town, full of Irish – so often at the
bottom of the social heap in Victorian London – and costermongers, a
breed considered almost feral by respectable society. The houses, he said,
were ramshackle constructions unfit for human habitation. What appeared
on the map as streets were in reality little more than sluggish rivers of mud,
into which refuse of all kinds was indiscriminately tossed. The area was
unlit at night.

In fact Thomas, who may have had little idea of how the urban poor
normally lived, was not being altogether fair. One commentator said of
the habitations of London's poor generally, that they were frequently
built near open sewers, cesspools, and cemeteries whose shallow graves
allowed the dead to infect the living, and were unfit for human habitation
by reason of location alone.

But parts of Agar Town were bad even by these standards, and there
was a reason. As a housing development, it was built piecemeal from
1840 on small plots of land offered with twenty-one-year leases by the
widow of William Agar, a lawyer in the Court of Chancery. Some of the

first houses were built by working men in their free time, and the short leases gave them no incentive to build to last. Nor was an area with such an uncertain future likely to be a priority for improvements by the local authority.

Still, for the most part Agar Town was no worse than other areas where the poor lived. And Tom Sayers, having been brought up in Brighton's Pimlico, is unlikely to have been at all shocked by the conditions. Life at the bottom was tough in Victorian cities.

The very worst slums of London were the so-called rookeries, of which St Giles, standing roughly where Tottenham Court Road now meets New Oxford Street, was the most notorious. According to *Knight's Cyclopaedia of London* (1851):

> It was one great maze of narrow crooked paths crossing and intersecting in labyrinthine convolutions, as if the houses had been originally one great block of stone eaten by slugs into innumerable small chambers and connecting passages... Hence whoever ventured there found the streets (by courtesy so called) thronged with loiterers, and saw through the half-glazed windows the rooms crowded to suffocation. The stagnant gutters in the middle of the lanes, the accumulated piles of garbage, the pools accumulated in the hollows of the disjointed pavement, the filth choking up the dark passages which opened like rat-holes upon the highway – all these, with their indescribable sights and smells, left scarcely so dispiriting an impression on the passenger as the condition of the houses. Walls the colour of bleached soot – doors falling from their hinges – door-posts worm-eaten and greasily polished from being long the supports of the shoulders of ragged loungers – windows where shivered panes of dirty glass alternated with wisps of straw, old hats, and lumps of bed-ticken or brown paper...

It is unlikely that W.M. Thomas had ever ventured into the rookery of St Giles.

Such places were so vulnerable to disease that it seems remarkable that people could survive in them at all. In 1847, the driving of New Oxford Street through the rookery made things a little better, but even in 1849, fifty-four of the inhabitants of St Giles expressed in a letter to *The Times* their justified dread of Victorian London's deadliest killer:

> Sur, May we beg and beseach your proteckshion and power...
> We live in muck and filthe. We aint got no privez, no dust
> bins, no drains, no water splies, and no drain or suer in the
> whole place... if the Colera comes Lord help us...

Sadly, cholera did come to St Giles in 1848–49, but other areas were worse hit in an epidemic which killed some fifteen thousand Londoners.

As it happened, Dr John Snow was already working on the theory which he would prove a few years later – that cholera was caused by polluted water – and the end was in sight for a fearsome killer. Thus far, however, London's slum dwellers lived in constant dread of the next outbreak.

Recreations for the London poor included brothels, cockfights and ratting – in which a fighting dog was required to kill as many rats as possible in a given period. Then there were the music halls – sometimes made by the simple expedient of knocking down a dividing wall so that two rooms could be turned into one just large enough to accommodate a stage of sorts and a bit of standing room for the audience. Lewd dances and crassly suggestive songs always went down well in such places. And if escape wasn't enough, there was always oblivion, to be found in many thousands of gin shops and alehouses.[3] Alcohol consumption was enormous.

This was the London of Tom Sayers. Bricklayers were far from being the lowest of the low, but, like all of the poor before the coming of the welfare state, they lived precarious lives. If illness or injury interrupted their work for any length of time, the consequences were devastating. The possibility of a more lucrative career would have been enormously tempting.

And such a possibility was open to Tom Sayers. He had not yet begun to box seriously, but he must surely by now have had it in mind. His next noteworthy informal fight would have dispelled any doubts that might have remained.

John Garrett, proprietor of the Copenhagen Running Grounds in Islington, employed him part-time as a sort of caretaker, one of his tasks being to stop people evading payment by climbing in over the fence. In this capacity, he fell out with Islington grave-digger Con Parker, and a fight was arranged that evening. The battle, still undecided when darkness fell, was resumed at seven the next morning. It should have been an unequal struggle, since Parker was also a professional prize fighter who stood six feet tall and weighed around one hundred and seventy pounds, but the outcome seems to have been inconclusive. Tom could already hold his own against just about anyone.

And at around this time – the sequence of events is not quite clear – he met the woman who was to become his wife. He had not chosen the most convenient of partners, for Sarah Henderson's paper-hanger father, Charles, would not give her permission to marry the combative young bricklayer.

But Sarah, who was only about fifteen at the time, had a mind of her own, and she and Tom set up home together. The story goes that, by 1847, he had saved enough money to buy the tenancy of the Laurel Tree, a downmarket alehouse in Bayham Street. In fact, though Tom was for a time closely associated with this establishment, there is no evidence that he ever ran it – and it seems inherently unlikely that a twenty-one-year-old bricklayer would have been able to afford the tenancy.

But whatever the nature of his association with the Laurel Tree, he and Sarah did go to Bayham Street, setting up home at number forty-five, which they shared with gardener William Bale, his wife Mary, and their two children. They were to remain there for several years. Charles Dickens, who had lived in Bayham Street for a time as a boy, would later call it 'as shabby, dingy, damp and mean a neighbourhood as one would desire not to see.' But for Tom Sayers it was a step up in the world.

Even so, a shared house in Bayham Street did not, it seems, satisfy the aspirations of his young partner. What Tom thought of it is hard to say, but the chances are that natural inclination would have persuaded him to try his luck in pugilism even if it had not held out the prospect of a more comfortable life. It was in 1849 that he made his formal entry into the prize ring.

Although mills, as the Fancy preferred to call them, were common, the prize ring was illegal, an awkward circumstance for which there was a well-tried solution. In order to give the authorities the least possible chance to intervene, the organisers would keep the venue secret from all but those who absolutely had to know, and those wishing to see the fight would have to buy a ticket the night before from a sporting tavern. Ticket sales would be advertised in *Bell's Life in London* on a Sunday, with the fight scheduled for the Tuesday. The ticket would name a railway station and a time of departure, but specify no destination.

Thus it was that, on the late morning of Tuesday, March 19th, 1849, a small crowd of men poured out of a train at North Woolwich Station, and into a flotilla of small boats. These took them to a deserted stretch of the Kent marshes at Greenhithe, where everyone disembarked and followed old Tom Oliver, who, in his capacity as commissary general, was the man in charge of setting up the ring. When he and his assistants had hammered the stakes into the ground and arranged the ropes, all was ready.

Tom's opponent was Abe Couch, a Camden Town dustman, who, having already fought and won twice in the prize ring, had scoffed openly at the young bricklayer's pugilistic pretensions. The taller by three inches and the heavier by nearly thirty pounds, Couch seemed to have all the advantages. Full of confidence, and intent on winning a quick victory, he went off like an express train.

But fire and fury was all he had to offer. Tom, seconded by Jack Grady (whom he had seen fight at Brighton seven years before) and Dan Collins, stopped Couch's initial rush easily, and outclassed him thereafter. In the words of *Bell's Life*, 'a merry contest which lasted 12 min 28 sec, was decided in favour of Sayers, who proved himself too quick and severe in his deliveries to afford a chance to his adversary.' Tom Sayers had made his mark.

His friends, having helped him raise the £5 stake required of each man, were happy to let him keep all of the £10 which his victory was worth. Working ten hours a day, six days a week as a bricklayer, it would have taken him five or six weeks to earn as much, but still the prize ring could be very much more lucrative.

With this in mind, he wasted little time. On April 1st, less than a fortnight later, the following advertisement appeared in *Bell's Life*:

Tom Sears, alias Brighton Tom, is prepared to make a match with Collyer of Wandsworth for from £15 to £25 a side, and will meet him to-morrow (Monday night) at George Robinson's, the Laurel Tree, Bayham Street, Camden Town.

CHAPTER 4

WEST TROY TO BENICIA

EVERYONE AGREES that John Camel Heenan was born in West Troy, New York; everyone agrees that he was born in the month of May. Doubt exists only as to the year. Many suggest 1835, but, if the *New York Clipper* is to be trusted, the plate on his coffin gave it as 1834.

Either way, he was born into the America of Andrew Jackson, a president who represented both the past and the future of his country: the last to have taken part in the War of Independence, and, in his determination to base federal appointments on merit rather than on social standing, the first to show a genuinely democratic spirit.

With huge distances to travel and a less developed infrastructure, the United States still more than England was the land of the horse and the stagecoach, but the Industrial Revolution had crossed the Atlantic, and the railroad had already arrived. Eighteen thirty-four was the year in which America's first railroad tunnel was opened, and the far-sighted could already see where it might lead.

The Capitol's Rotunda had been completed just a decade previously, and the north portico of the White House, finished in 1830, had replaced the south portico as its main entrance. The cool neoclassical architecture of the president's residence and of the heart of government showed a nation that took itself seriously, a nation determined to play a major part on the world stage.

Sadly, it was a nation which did not take all of its own people very seriously. In the South, some two million slaves worked the plantations, while the American Indians, having already been displaced in the East, were now being rooted out of their lands further west also.

And even the country's own citizens might live lives of abject misery in the land of opportunity. Pre-teenage girls sold themselves on the streets of American cities, and the old and infirm, unless they had money, could choose between miserable almshouses and starvation. Within fifteen years of Jack Heenan's birth, there were an estimated forty thousand homeless children in New York alone. Many of these were to be found around the city's most notorious slum district, lower Manhattan's Five Points.

Charles Dickens, after visiting New York in 1842, wrote of

> ... narrow ways diverging to the right and left, and reeking everywhere with dirt and filth... See how the rotten beams are tumbling down and how the patched and broken windows seem to scowl dimly, like eyes that have been hurt in drunken frays.

And the people impressed him no more favourably than their homes. Having noted the extraordinary number of pigs in the streets, he asked, 'Do they ever wonder why their masters walk upright instead of going on all-fours, and why they talk instead of grunting?'

Former congressman Davy Crockett, who had served under Jackson in the Creek War of 1812, was of the same mind. Of the denizens of the Five Points, he said in his 1834 autobiography, 'I thought I would rather risque myself in an Indian fight than venture among these creatures after night... these are worse than savages; they are too mean to swab hell's kitchen.'

The Old World had no monopoly on poverty.

But still the huddled masses of Europe poured in, for America was, despite everything, the land of opportunity, and everybody knew it. It could hardly be otherwise. For those who arrived in New York and stayed there, things were not necessarily so different from what they had been back home. But only a little further west, there were vast empty spaces just waiting to be settled – for the primitive people who already lived there were few and insignificant.

As yet, nothing much was colonised between the Mississippi and the Pacific coast. But, for the American Indians, all the warning signs were there. By the Louisiana Purchase of 1803, France had ceded to the United States all claim to a vast tract of land from Montana to Louisiana. As yet, the United States had not really taken up the interest which it – or they, as it was more often expressed at the time – had acquired, but it took no great genius to see that it was only a matter of time.

Anyone who doubted it had only to consider the implications of the Monroe Doctrine of 1823. A recently-established New World nation which was prepared to warn all European powers against extending their existing interests in any part of two entire continents was hardly going to be content forever to control only a small part of one of those huge land masses.

For now, however, the new Americans were chiefly concerned to secure their grip on lands east of the Mississippi. The Indian Removal Act of 1830 allowed President Jackson to conclude treaties clearing the aboriginal inhabitants from this desirable area. Although in theory voluntary, it felt like compulsion to the Indians, and in 1832 the Black Hawk War had ensured that the Sauk and Fox peoples would leave Illinois and Michigan Territory (which included today's Wisconsin) entirely to the colonists.

And the year following Jack Heenan's birth saw the beginning of the Second Seminole War. The future President Jackson had played a prominent part in the first war in 1817–18, but it was the prolonged and bitter second conflict which effectively ended Seminole resistance, and ensured that the new Americans could do as they pleased with Florida. Although the war would drag on until 1842, the decisive moment had come five years earlier, when the Seminole leader, Osceola (known to some as Billy Powell), paid with his freedom for the naïve belief that his enemies would honour a flag of truce.

For the most part, the new Americans had as yet made little impact west of the Mississippi, but they were beginning to make their presence felt on the other side of the continent. Alta California, comprising the present-day states of California, Nevada and Utah, as well as parts of Arizona and Wyoming, was governed by Mexico, but trappers and settlers from the United States and from Canada were already moving in, and there was trouble ahead.

Then there was Texas, which was also part of Mexico. Anglo-American settlers, known as Texians, now far outnumbered the Hispanic Tejanos, and both groups had issues with the increasingly centralised Mexican rule. One bone of contention was slavery, which, in defiance of Mexican law, was practised by some of the Texians. By the time Jack Heenan was born, matters were coming to a head. Davy Crockett would go there the following year, and would never leave.

Further north, twenty-five-year-old Abraham Lincoln, named after a grandfather killed by Indians in 1786, was a member of the Illinois state legislature. He was doing well already for one who had been born in a genuine log cabin. Three years earlier he had been elected captain of a militia company during the Black Hawk War, though he never saw action.

Washington Irving was one of many Americans who were disgusted by what was happening to the Indians in such conflicts. Writing of his experiences on the prairies in the early 1830s, he said:

> It has been the lot of the unfortunate aborigines of America, in the early periods of colonization, to be doubly wronged by the white men. They have been dispossessed of their hereditary possessions by mercenary and frequently wanton warfare, and their characters have been traduced by bigoted and interested writers.

And the Indians were not alone in their suffering. Britain had abolished the slave trade in 1807, and 1834 was the year in which the British Empire outlawed slavery itself; but it was nearly sixty years since the United States had been part of that empire, and slavery was crucial to the economy of the southern states.

Even among white people, some were more equal than others. Most strikingly, men were more equal than women. It was in 1835 that Edgar Allan Poe, highly successful assistant editor of the *Southern Literary Messenger* in Richmond, married his cousin, Virginia Clemm. The strange aspect of the marriage was not that she was his cousin, but that she was thirteen years old. Still, it was all perfectly legal. In most states of the Union, the age of consent was ten or twelve. Only Delaware was seriously out of line: in Delaware, the age of consent was seven.

Virginia Clemm was the same age as Hiram Ulysses Grant (who would later become Ulysses S. Grant rather than risk being known as

HUG to his classmates at West Point). The future general and president lived in Ohio with his tanner father, and was already developing the equestrian skills which would distinguish him throughout his life.

Grant was of Scottish ancestry, as was Poe. James Gordon Bennett, on the other hand, was the real thing, having been born near Keith in Banffshire in 1795. It was in 1835, the year after Jack Heenan's birth, that he finally achieved his ambition of founding a newspaper. And *The New York Herald* was to be a groundbreaking publication which, turning its back on funding from political interest groups and a core of regular subscribers, would rely instead on wide circulation and consequently high advertising revenue. The inevitable result was a populist style, the reporting of lurid and sensational stories, and the distaste of polite society.

All this and more was the United States of Andrew Jackson. The President himself had played a major part in the dispossession of the Indians, and was himself an unapologetic slave-owner. But there was much more to him than that.

Jackson was as hard as George IV had been soft. Awed by his toughness in the War of 1812 against Great Britain, his soldiers called him Old Hickory, a name which would stick with him throughout life. His great victory at New Orleans had given him immense satisfaction, for Jackson had issues with England.

Aged thirteen, he had been a courier for a Carolina regiment during the War of Independence. Along with his brother, he had been taken prisoner by the British, and had been lucky to survive. In addition to almost starving to death, he had been wounded by a British officer who, angered by Jackson's refusal to clean his boots, had slashed at him with his sword. Then he and his brother both contracted smallpox. Only Andrew survived. Small wonder that he remained an Anglophobe for the rest of his days.

He was denied the presidency in 1824, when the House of Representatives, effectively choosing to ignore the will of the voters, appointed John Quincy Adams to the office. But four years later, Jackson proved unstoppable, swept into the White House on the crest of a wave of popular enthusiasm.

There was something oddly appropriate about his riotous inaugural reception in March 1829, when thousands got into the White House. The mob broke windows, tore down curtains, stood on furniture with muddy boots, and smashed several thousand dollars' worth of china and glassware. In a final desperate attempt to get them out, staff pulled tubs of punch and other refreshments onto the lawn. The President escaped almost unnoticed through a window.

An interesting testimony to his popularity was occasionally to be heard on the Erie Canal. Completed in 1825, the year before Tom Sayers was born, the canal was notorious for its low bridges, which frequently caused damage to goods and injuries to passengers. The warning 'Low bridge!' sometimes drew a jocular 'All Jackson men bow down!' A Jackson man was defined by his support for the president's disregard for social standing.

Jackson, as it happened, had witnessed the celebration of the canal's opening, as had two former presidents: James Monroe, author of the Monroe Doctrine, which told Europeans to keep their hands off the Americas, and Thomas Jefferson, who, in 1809, had considered the idea of the canal 'little short of madness.'

Many people thought he had a point, for it was a gigantic undertaking. Nearly four hundred miles long, and with its western extremity almost six hundred feet higher than its eastern, the projected route lay through virgin forests of huge trees, malarial swamps, deep valleys and lofty escarpments. But the potential rewards were enormous. If Buffalo on Lake Erie really could be linked by waterway to Albany on the Hudson, then the Great Lakes would have their outlet to the Atlantic Ocean at New York. The benefits both for the city and for upstate New York were incalculable.

Work finally began in the summer of 1817, when Andrew Jackson was engaged in the First Seminole War down in Florida. Despite horrendous difficulties, it was triumphantly concluded eight years later. And despite the massive expense, it was turning a profit by the time Jack Heenan was born less than a decade on from that. The population of upstate New York rocketed, with Buffalo, Rochester and other places on the route becoming boom towns. As for the metropolis itself, before the canal it had been only the nation's fifth largest seaport, behind Boston,

Baltimore, Philadelphia and New Orleans; within fifteen years of the canal's opening, it had outstripped them all, handling more freight than Boston, Baltimore and New Orleans combined.

No longer did the Alleghenies represent the effective western frontier, no longer did it take weeks of arduous travel to reach the Northwestern Territories that would later become Illinois, Indiana, Michigan and Ohio. The canal was responsible for the first great westward surge of white settlers.

And a remarkable number of these settlers were Irish, one reason for which was that so many of the canal builders were Irish – fully a third of the workforce by the time the project was completed. Nor was this to be wondered at, for, during the years of construction, Ireland never furnished fewer than one third of all immigrants to the United States. Irish Catholics had been migrating across the Atlantic even before the Revolution, but it was in the 1820s that their numbers really surged, and civil construction works such as the Erie Canal were in large part responsible.

The Europeans already settled in the New World watched the influx with growing alarm. The young nation was emphatically Protestant in religion and in ethos, and there was real prejudice against Roman Catholics. In the year of John Camel Heenan's birth this prejudice found ugly expression in Charlestown near Boston, where the large Irish Catholic population was most resented among poorer people, who saw the incomers pricing them out of the job market.

When a rumour spread that Charlestown's Ursuline convent was holding a young Protestant woman against her will, the city fathers failed to appreciate the strength of feeling among the less privileged. As a result, the convent was attacked and burned down, though mercifully without loss of life. The account of one witness – that the mother superior had exacerbated the situation by informing the rioters that 'The Bishop has twenty thousand of the vilest Irishmen at his command' – may tell us more about Protestant prejudice than about Catholic arrogance.

Whatever the truth of the matter, with the Irish still pouring across the Atlantic in huge numbers, there was every reason to expect more trouble in the future.

———

If so, it was likely enough to affect John Camel Heenan. The future pugilist was of Irish parentage, his mother and father both coming from Templemore in County Tipperary. His home town of West Troy (now Watervliet), on the west bank of the Hudson, was one of many New York towns with a strong Irish heritage. The town's biggest employer was the Federal arsenal, and it was there that his father Tim worked. John had the education that Tom Sayers lacked, for it was not until he had completed elementary school that he joined his father in the arsenal. By the time he did so, he had developed a powerful physique and a fearless character, in which respects only one local boy could match him.

It was a curious business altogether. Tim Morrissey and Tim Heenan, whose sons were both called John, were both from Templemore. In the thirties, both had decided (independently) to emigrate to America, and both had found their way to upstate New York – Morrissey to Troy, and Heenan to West Troy on the other side of the river. They were old friends, but it was not to last. The story is that Morrissey's gloating over his bird's victory in a cockfight infuriated Heenan, leading to a fist fight which ended their long friendship.

Their enmity was inherited by their children, and the two Johns would be at loggerheads throughout their lives. John Morrissey was born in Templemore in 1831, but was already in Troy by the time John Heenan entered the world on the other side of the river three years later. It seems likely that the two clashed even in childhood, but nothing is known for certain.

What we do know is that Morrissey showed early in life the combative spirit which was to be the making of him. Troy, like West Troy, stood on the Hudson a hundred and fifty miles north of New York, and the vast increase in river traffic which came with the Erie Canal gave both towns a huge boost.

But it also created problems. The Watervliet Cut, a lateral section of the canal giving access to Troy, was lined with saloons where many of the drinkers made ready use of fists and also of more dangerous weapons. There were alarmingly frequent tales of bodies being found floating in the Cut. It was useful to have a reputation for toughness, and none more justly earned such a reputation than John Morrissey.

By 1850, he had been indicted for burglary, assault, and assault with intent to kill. Under the circumstances, he was fortunate to have spent no more than sixty days in the county jail. He was not yet nineteen years old.

Three years his junior, Jack Heenan was less lawless, but equally adventurous. Aged seventeen – around the time that Harriet Beecher Stowe stirred the conscience of a nation and a world with *Uncle Tom's Cabin* – he set out on the long and perilous journey to gold-rush California. By another strange coincidence, John Morrissey was there before him, though there is no record of their paths having crossed.

The California that both young men experienced was very different from the Alta California of the time of their birth. In the late 1840s, under President James K. Polk (such an avid supporter of Andrew Jackson, whose old congressional seat he was to win eight times, that some called him Young Hickory), the doctrine of Manifest Destiny had taken a firm grip on the imagination of the American people. This was the quasi-religious belief that it was the destiny of the United States to rule from the Atlantic to the Pacific. The application of this doctrine, the significance of which for the Indians was unmistakable, was also extremely threatening to Mexico.

Back in 1836, when Jack Heenan was a toddler, Davy Crockett, Jim Bowie and the rest had died at the Alamo for the independence which Texas was shortly to win from Mexico at the Battle of San Jacinto. This was bad enough, but still worse was to come. In 1845, the year of Andrew Jackson's death, Texas became the twenty-eighth state of the Union, destroying Mexico's hopes of reclaiming what she still saw as Mexican territory.

President Polk's continuing expansionist policies made war virtually inevitable, and that war came in 1846. An uneven conflict ended inside two years with total victory for the United States. By the time Jack Heenan got there, California had gone the way of Texas, and was now formally part of the Union. It was also, thanks to the gold rush, in turmoil. By 1852 the population had increased more than tenfold from the twenty thousand who had called it home in 1849.

There is no reliable and detailed account of what Jack Heenan did there. It has been said that he tried gold prospecting, it has been said that he spent time just travelling around, but what is certain is that

Benicia was his home for most of the five years which he spent in the far west.

And it was during his time there that the town reached its zenith. California spent some time deciding where its capital should be, and in February 1853 Benicia got its chance. But the legislators were not happy with it, and, after just a year, returned to Sacramento whence they had come. Benicia would never rise so high again.

It had been conceived in 1846 by Lieutenant Robert Semple, a dentist from Kentucky, who had talked the owner of the site, Mexican general Vallejo, into the idea. Semple had advertised the new town extensively in his newspaper the *Californian*, but when the first settler arrived in June 1847, he found only surveyors' stakes in the midst of undulating fields of grass. Such things were not uncommon, as Dickens's Martin Chuzzlewit had discovered when he found that the settlement of Eden, in which he had acquired land, was in fact a malarial swamp.

But the town of Benicia was duly built, and with its wooden frame buildings flanking unpaved streets bordered by plank sidewalks, it looked no different from most Californian pioneer towns.

Semple's hopes had soared when the news broke – in Benicia, according to local legend – that gold had been found at Sutter's Mill in January 1848. Semple was sure that the gold rush would be the making of Benicia, but he was wrong: it was the making of San Francisco. Which rather added injury to insult, since he had already had to abandon his plan to name his town Francesca when Yerba Buena decided to change its name to San Francisco.

It was around the time Jack Heenan arrived that the army moved into town, and established in Benicia the arsenal which was to be the dominant fact of life there for a century. With his experience at West Troy, young Jack might have been expected to look for work there, but he did not. He found employment instead in the workshop of the Pacific Mail Steamship Company, the other justification for Benicia's place in the world. Having come into being in 1848, the company was perfectly positioned to benefit from the gold rush, and returns on investment reached thirty per cent in some early years.

Far from investing in the company, Jack Heenan merely worked in it, but he still made a considerable impact. Six feet two inches tall, and weighing not far short of two hundred pounds, he was enormously strong. According to legend, he once wielded a thirty-two-pound sledgehammer for twelve consecutive hours. And his size and strength were to serve him in other ways, too.

He was generally known to be easy-going and affable, but he had a temper which got him into fights. In much the same way as with Tom Sayers six thousand miles away and several years earlier, casual brawls developed into more formal contests as he began to make a name for himself. And the name he made was the Benicia Boy.

No detailed record of these early fights survives, but according to *The New York Herald* he recorded impressive victories over a well-known New York boxer called Sam Banta, and over a 'powerful desperado' by the name of Gallagher. He was noticed by itinerant English trainer Jim Cusick, who thought him a real prospect, and it was probably under Cusick's guidance that he took part in a sparring exhibition arranged by Yankee Sullivan, one of the most extraordinary characters ever to disgrace the prize ring.

CHAPTER 5

ENGLISH FISTS

IT WAS L.P. Hartley who told us, in *The Go-Between*, that 'The past is a foreign country; they do things differently there.'

Take, for example, an incident which occurred near Windsor at four o' clock on the afternoon of Monday, February 28th, 1825. Stripped to the waist, and watched by an eager crowd, two young men named Cooper and Wood squared up to each other to resolve in the old-fashioned way a difference which had arisen between them the previous day.

As the battle went on, Cooper, the smaller man, was kept going only by the quantities of brandy poured down his throat between rounds by his seconds. And even this could only prolong his ordeal. After some sixty rounds occupying nearly two hours, by the end of which Wood too was in need of liquid sustenance, size and strength finally told.

The affair would have been quite unremarkable but for two facts. First, Anthony Francis Ashley Cooper died that night. And second, he was the son of the Earl of Shaftesbury. George Alexander Wood, fourteen years old like his opponent, was the nephew of the Marquis of Londonderry. Such battles, fought in accordance with the rules of the prize ring, were not uncommon at Eton College, but they did not normally end in death. The victor and his opponent's second were charged with manslaughter – it was said that Wood had no formal second – but walked free when no one was prepared to testify against them.

A foreign country. But what sort of country can it be in which the boy children of the aristocracy fight formal battles in the most prestigious school in the land? In which they are plied with brandy to keep them going when otherwise they would collapse? In this perplexing and distressing place, only one thing seems clear: in such a country, boxing must be much more than just a sport.

Pugilism had existed in antiquity. As far back as 4000 BC, a millennium and a half before the Great Pyramid, representations from Egypt show something like fisticuffs, but it hardly resembles anything which might today be called boxing. On Crete some two and a half thousand years later, a Minoan vase depicts boxers in a rather more recognisable way. Best known to us through the legend of the ferocious, bull-headed Minotaur which lived in the Labyrinth, the Minoans had by trade earned wealth sufficient to enable them to enjoy organised leisure pursuits, and the only sport which rivalled boxing in popularity was bull-jumping.

Around the same time, a mural from Thera to the north of Crete clearly shows two youths boxing. It is a poignant image, dating as it does to a time very shortly before the volcanic eruption which, dwarfing that of Vesuvius which was to entomb Pompeii a millennium and a half later, effectively destroyed the island and may have contributed to the demise of the whole Minoan civilisation.

In all probability, it was Minoan influence which took boxing to the mainland of Greece, where it would attain great popularity. Sometime in the eighth century BC, Homer included an account of a bout in the *Iliad*. At the funeral games for Patroclus, Epeius and Euryalus fought for the prize of a mule. Epeius was bullish: 'The mule is mine... I'm going to tear the guy's flesh to ribbons and smash his bones. I'd advise him to have all his mourners on standby.' His confidence was justified, for the fight ended with Euryalus being dragged senseless back to his corner, spitting blood.

By this time, it is clear that boxing was well established in Greece: we know of one variety in which opponents sat face to face on flat stones, and simply walloped each other until one was knocked out. But it was not until 688 BC that inclusion in the Olympic Games gave boxing its ultimate seal of approval. Pindar himself celebrated in verse the triumph of Diagoras – a giant of a man, he tells us, who fought fair and despised arrogance – at the Games of 464 BC. Boxing had arrived.

The thongs which Olympic boxers wound round their wrists and forearms may originally have been for protection, but as time went on, harder leather was used, turning the thong into a weapon. As so often, however, it was not until the Romans took over a Greek institution that its full potential for brutality was realised.

The Romans weighted the leather with lead and studded it with brass, turning it into a deadly weapon known as a cestus. They even added a bronze spike called a myrmex, or limb-piercer. The Greeks would have been horrified, but Roman boxers who used the cestus were gladiators, prisoners of war or slaves required to fight in the arena for their lives.

What Homer had done in the *Iliad* to mythologise Greek boxing, Virgil was to do seven hundred years later in the *Aeneid* for the Roman version. At the funeral games for Anchises, in token of acceptance of the arrogant challenge thrown out by the mighty Dares, old pro Entellus throws into the ring a blood-stained and brain-spattered cestus so terrible that Dares refuses to fight. In the end, they face each other on equal terms, and Entellus is victorious. His prize is a bullock, whose skull he shatters with one blow.

Boxing became so popular in Rome that even patricians took it up. This was too much for the emperor Augustus, who passed a law against their participation in AD 30. It was not until AD 500, however, decades after the collapse of the Western empire, that Theodoric the Great outlawed pugilism altogether.

His ban seems to have been totally effective, for boxing as a sport disappeared in the Western world for well over a thousand years, not being seen again until the late seventeenth century. It was in England that it resurfaced, and it would seem a safe bet that the pugilism of antiquity is in no sense the lineal ancestor of today's boxing. With the exception of the Oriental tradition exemplified by kickboxing, all present-day pugilism is directly descended from the early English prize ring.

———————

Common sense alone tells us that unarmed combat is always with us, but for many centuries, it seems that the Western world practised only wrestling as a sport. In 1520, for example, at the Field of the Cloth of Gold, England's Henry VIII was disappointed when supper interrupted his bout with Francis I of France.

John Milton, not a man known for levity, took the exercise rather more seriously. In his treatise *Of Education*, he said that young men 'must be also practiz'd in all the Locks and Gripes of Wrastling, wherein English men were wont to excell, as need may often be in fight to tugg or grapple, and to close.' And need often was, for he was writing in 1644, at the height of England's bloody Civil War.

Still no boxing, though, and no sense that the exercise is recommended for any purpose other than educational. In a sense (but only in a sense) Samuel Pepys takes us a little further in the account he gives of a fight which he witnessed on June 1st, 1663. It is worth quoting at some length:

> And here I came and saw the first prize I ever saw in my life: and it was between one Mathews, who did beat at all weapons, and one Westwicke, who was soundly cut several times both in the head and legs, that he was all over blood: and other deadly blows they did give and take in very good earnest, till Westwicke was in a sad pickle. They fought at eight weapons, three boutes at each weapon. This being upon a private quarrel, they did it in good earnest; and I felt one of the swords, and found it to be very little, if at all blunter on the edge, than the common swords are. Strange to see what a deal of money is flung to them both upon the stage between every boute.

Whatever this is, it is not boxing. It is, however, a formal and organised fight, taken very seriously on both sides, and for money. It would never have been permitted in Cromwell's puritanical Republic, but this was three years after the restoration of the monarchy, and public entertainment was back. Take the weapons out of the men's hands, and you have something very like prize fighting as England was soon to know it.

Since England was unquestionably to become the home of boxing, it is curious that the first known illustration of a European boxer beyond classical times is Dutch. An illustration accompanying Nicholaes Petter's

Clear Education in the Magnificent Art of Wrestling (published in 1674, the year of Milton's death) shows a pugilist in southpaw stance, right fist forward. The text makes clear that one-on-one unarmed combat, blending boxing and wrestling, was common in Holland's golden age, when the Dutch East India Company was the world's first multinational corporation, and the Netherlands was the world's leading slave-trading nation.

But for the first account of a genuine and indisputable boxing contest, we must return to England, and *The True Protestant Mercury* of January 1681:

> Yeſterday a match of boxing was performed before His Grace, the Duke of Albemarle, between the Duke's footman and a butcher. The latter won the prize, as he hath done many times before, being accounted, though a little man, the beſt at that exerciſe in England.

Boxing at last, though the sport so called was – as it would remain for two centuries and more – a blend of boxing and wrestling.

And within forty years, the country had her first heavyweight champion. It was the England of George I, of Dean Swift, Daniel Defoe and Alexander Pope, when no gentleman was seen in public without a wig, when sedan chairs disputed the cobbled streets with carriages. And James Figg was the outstanding exponent of the martial arts. Six feet tall, Figg was as much at home with sword and quarterstaff as he was with his fists, and by 1719, the year that Defoe published *Robinson Crusoe*, he had staked a secure claim to be England's heavyweight boxing champion.

Backed by the Earl of Peterborough, Figg opened an academy of martial arts to the north of London where Tottenham Court Road now meets Oxford Street – a stone's throw from where the city's expansion would later create the dreadful rookery of St Giles. He was well connected, though the business card depicting the 'master of the noble science of defence' at his premises was not the work of the young William Hogarth but a later forgery.

In addition to teaching, Figg acted as promoter, and a little later he opened nearby an amphitheatre where paying spectators could witness the increasingly popular sport of prize fighting. Amongst them, at one time or another, were prime minister Robert Walpole, literary lions Swift and Pope, and even the king. Bouts would take place on a raised platform, the fighting area being enclosed within wooden rails. In effect, Figg invented the boxing ring.

The sport was now so well established that just about anyone was ready to take part. On June 23rd, 1722, *The London Journal* reported that:

> Boxing in publick at the Bear Garden is what has lately obtained very much amongſt the Men, but till laſt Week we never heard of Women being engaged that Way, when two of the Faeminine Gender appeared for the firſt Time on the Theater of War at Hockley in the Hole, and maintained the Battle with great Valour for a long Time, to the no ſmall ſatiſſaction of the ſpectators.

The winner was Elizabeth Wilkinson, who had challenged her opponent in the press:

> I, Elizabeth Wilkinſon of Clerkenwell, having had Words with Hannah Hyfield, and requiring ſatiſſaction, do invite her to meet me on the ſtage, and Box me for Three Guineas; each Woman holding Half-a-Crown in each Hand, and the firſt Woman that drops her Money to loſe the Battle.

Elizabeth Wilkinson was to fight (and win) at least three more times, after which she styled herself 'European Championess'. It is clear nonetheless that women's boxing was regarded as a curiosity, and the few bouts which took place were never the subject of detailed press reports.

That they were even permitted, however, suggests that there was little controversy about pugilism at the time. The King himself was happy to approve in 1723 the establishment of a ring in Hyde Park, where men could settle their differences with their fists. Boxing was now well established as both a spectator and a participant sport.

Swiss traveller César de Saussure observed this clearly in 1728, the year after the death of George I. When two Englishmen quarrelled, he reported in *A Foreign View of England*, they would

> ...retire into some quiet place and strip from the waist upward. All who see them preparing... surround them, not in order to separate them, but on the contrary, to enjoy the fight... The spectators sometimes get so interested they lay bets.

The scene was set for the arrival of the man who would be called the Father of Boxing.

Jack Broughton, a Figg protégé, was an all-round sportsman. He first rose to prominence in 1730, when, in his mid-twenties, he won the Doggett's Coat and Badge race. This event, claimed to be the oldest sporting contest in continuous existence, is a rowing race from London Bridge to Chelsea, and Broughton's victory reflects the fact that he was a waterman at the time.

But pugilism was his main interest, and, having earned a considerable reputation from semi-professional contests in the 1730s, he finally became a full-time prize fighter. It was in this capacity in 1741, when he was in his late thirties, that he fought his most famous bout. His opponent at the Great Booth in Tottenham Court Road was the one-eyed fighting coachman George Stevenson. Three years later, in *The Gymnasiad*, Paul Whitehead described Stevenson's condition at the end of the fight: 'Down dropp'd the Hero, welt'ring in his Gore, / And his stretch'd limbs lay quiv'ring on the Floor.' Broughton was invincible.[4]

By 1743, he was prosperous enough to open his own amphitheatre, which soon eclipsed all others, and it was there that he made the contribution to boxing which ensured his immortality. To replace the no-holds-barred brawling which many found unseemly, he formulated a set of seven rules which might diminish danger and enhance decorum.

Henceforth, a man who had fallen could not be hit, and no wrestling holds were permitted below the waist; the round ended when a man went down, and if, after a thirty-second break, he was unable to take his place on one side of a square chalked in the middle of the ring, he was deemed beaten. To ensure compliance with these rules, Broughton provided for the nomination of one umpire by each man, and a referee to settle differences between them. The contribution of these rules to the success of the sport was incalculable.

Two years later, as Bonnie Prince Charlie's Jacobite army menaced London, and the Hanoverian monarchy itself teetered, Broughton's star was still on the rise. He made his second great contribution to boxing with the introduction of boxing gloves, known at the time as muffles or mufflers. It would be a century and a half before they made bare-knuckle fighting obsolete, but their immediate purpose was made clear by Broughton in *The Daily Advertiser* in 1747:

> … and that perſons of quality and diſtinction may not be deterred from entering into a *Courſe of theſe Lectures* they will be given with the utmoſt tenderneſs and regard to the delicacy of the form and conſtitution of the pupil, for which reaſon muffles are provided, that will effectually ſecure them from the inconveniency of black eyes, broken jaws, and bloody noſes.

By this time, Jack Broughton was universally acknowledged to be the master, but, like so many who would follow him, he fought one bout too many. In 1750, he came out of retirement to settle a score with Jack Slack, a Norwich butcher rumoured to be the grandson of James Figg. So confident was Broughton of victory, that, now close on fifty years of age, he scarcely bothered to train.

To make matters worse, his confidence was shared by his patron, who was the King's son and a dangerous man to offend. Four years earlier, at the age of twenty-four, the Duke of Cumberland had earned the nickname Butcher for his ruthless behaviour on the battlefield of Culloden, where his crushing victory over Bonnie Prince Charlie had ended for ever the Jacobite dream.

Slack and Broughton had been fighting only fifteen minutes when a blow between the eyes deprived the champion of sight. 'I am blind but not beat!' he cried desperately, asking only to be placed before his man, 'and he shall not gain the day yet!' But blind was the same as beat, and Cumberland, who had wagered heavily on the fight, was furious.

He immediately dropped the vanquished man and, though with much less enthusiasm, became Slack's patron instead. When his new protégé cost him still more money by throwing a title fight against Bill 'the Nailer' Stevens, he lost all interest in boxing, and the enemies of the sport – always numerous, whatever its popularity – had all amphitheatres closed by 1754.[5]

Still, Broughton continued to coach young boxers, and also went into the antiques business, at which he was highly successful. He was to outlive his royal patron by nearly a quarter of a century, dying a rich man in his mid-eighties in 1789. A tomb in Westminster Abbey testifies to the regard of his contemporaries – though he had to wait two centuries before his wish to have the words 'Champion of England' engraved on his tomb was honoured.

Almost single-handed, he had given boxing its first golden age. Dr Johnson, one of many prominent figures known to box, in later years deplored the decline of the prize ring: 'I am sorry prize-fighting is gone out,' he said. 'Prize-fighting made people accustomed not to be alarmed at seeing their own blood, or feeling a little pain from a wound.'

Boxing imploded. Amongst other things, the fixing of fights now became commonplace. The Nailer, for example, responded to general astonishment at his defeat by the unknown George Meggs by explaining, with endearing frankness, that losing that fight was worth fifty guineas more to him than winning it.

What made this so important was that betting was the life blood of the ring. Although boxers always fought for a purse, side bets, as they were known, accounted for the great bulk of the money that went into the sport. If wealthy men were not prepared to wager money on the outcome of contests, professional prize fighting faced extinction.

As it was, the decline which set in with Broughton's downfall went on for a generation. The lowest ebb was reached in 1780, when Duggan

Fearns, having won the title in a ninety-second fixed fight, simply quit the scene. And then along came Tom Johnson.

———————

Born at about the time that Broughton fell to Slack, Johnson – whose original name was Jackling – convincingly defeated one Jack Jarvis in 1783, and by 1784 was generally considered entitled to the vacant championship. He cemented his claim with victories over the nameless Croydon Drover and over Stephen Oliver (nicknamed Death on account of his pallor), and his attractive personality, together with his refusal to indulge in fixes, restored credibility to the ring. The Bastille fell in Paris, the crew of the *Bounty* mutinied in the south seas, but in England boxing flourished. Tom Johnson's namesake, Samuel, sadly did not live to see the revival of the institution he so much admired: he died just as Tom became champion.

On retirement, the latter set a precedent which was to be followed by many who came after him: he hit skid row. Having brought the wealthy gamblers back, it was a painful irony that, within a year of his retirement, Tom Johnson should gamble away his entire fortune, dying destitute in 1797. But he had served his purpose: by 1791, when he lost the title to Ben Brain, Tom Johnson had brought the prize ring back from the dead.

In fact, it now entered its second golden age. It would never again be truly respectable, but once more it enjoyed the patronage, and thus the protection, of the highest in the land. One of the keenest followers of the prize ring – or the P.R., as it was known to the Fancy – was the Prince of Wales, later to become Prince Regent, and finally to accede to the throne as George IV.

Colours (large patterned handkerchiefs representing each man in a fight), having been popularised by Tom Johnson, now became universal and were eagerly bought by fans anxious to advertise their allegiance. Boxers would wear one set belt-fashion round the waist, and tie another to one of the centre stakes, the winner to take both. As time went on, the wooden rails enclosing the ring became ropes, and the square in the middle of the ring was reduced to a scratch, each man being required to come up to scratch to begin a round.

Sadly, neither Tom Johnson nor his successor as title-holder lived to see very much of it. Ben Brain, nicknamed Big Ben, died suddenly in 1794, and was succeeded by one of the most charismatic of all champions. Brilliantly overcoming the handicaps of being Jewish and only five feet seven inches tall, Daniel Mendoza introduced to the ring technique superior to anything that had been seen before. He lived a chaotic life – in and out of debtor's prison, in and out of work – but he was a genius in the ring.

When he became champion, Mendoza had lost just once, in the first of three famous battles with his former mentor, Richard Humphries. It was his misfortune, however, to be the contemporary of the great, if enigmatic, John 'Gentleman' Jackson. Not only was Jackson a brilliant ring technician, but he came of a higher social class than other boxers, and was at home in the most elevated society in the land, counting Lord Byron among his closest friends.

Strange as it might seem, he only had three formal fights, and lost one of those. His first was in 1788, when, not yet twenty, he overcame the much more experienced and hitherto undefeated William Fewterel. The following year he fought George Ingleston, known as the Brewer. Jackson was well on top when he lost his footing on a slippery surface, damaged his leg and was unable to continue.

Not until 1795 did he return to the ring, when the chance arose to fight the champion himself. Jackson supplemented his advantage in height (four inches) and weight (forty pounds) with a dazzling display of ring craft. But the crucial moment belied his nickname, and had little to do with skill. In the fifth round he seized Mendoza's long hair in one hand and pulped his face with the other. It was a tactic as effective as it was ugly, and although the battle went on for another four rounds, the result was no longer in doubt. Jackson was the victor in little over ten minutes. Thenceforth, boxers wore their hair short.

The patronage of royalty and aristocracy could by now be taken for granted, and the future of the prize ring was assured, at least in the short term. But that attitudes were no longer as easy-going as they had been in Broughton's heyday, is made clear by the report of the Jackson–Mendoza fight printed in *The Times*:

Yesterday a Prize Battle was fought at Hornchurch, in Essex, between Mendoza, the Jew, and one Jackson, a publican, in Gray's-inn-lane, when, as had no doubt been previously settled, after a sharp contest of eleven minutes only, the Jew appeared overpowered by the strength of the Christian...

Among those who disgraced themselves by witnessing, and consequently patronising this exhibition were the Duke of HAMILTON, Colonel HAMILTON, Sir Thomas APREECE, and Colonel DURANT.

Jackson was unconcerned. Though he never fought competitively again, his retirement had nothing to do with the disapproval of the press. He quit the arena in order to cash in on his fame by instructing the richest in the land in the art of self-defence. To this end, he opened in London's Bond Street a gymnasium in which, it was said, one third of England's aristocracy learned to box. Lord Byron certainly did, likewise the Dukes of York and Clarence.

As chaotic as Jackson was organised, Mendoza got little right in the rest of his life. He tried teaching boxing, he tried innkeeping, he worked as a recruiting sergeant in Scotland, he even appeared in pantomime. But he was hopeless with money, and was obliged for financial reasons to return to boxing in his forties and fifties. When he died in 1836, he left his family in poverty.

But in 1795, for all his skill and charisma, the prize ring scarcely missed him. Like Tom Johnson before him, he had served his turn. Even Jackson's retirement was no real setback to the fortunes of the prize ring: he was, even in his mid-twenties, arguably better suited to the role of elder statesman than to that of champion.

In 1800, as the power of Napoleon Bonaparte was approaching its zenith, Jem Belcher of Bristol won the title from Jack Bartholomew, and boxing had its next truly charismatic champion. But Belcher, the grandson of Jack Slack, and thus possibly the great great grandson of James Figg, was unlucky. Three years later – during which time French mining engineer Albert Mathieu presented Napoleon with a scheme for a road tunnel under the Straits of Dover – he lost the sight of one eye. Anxious to retain his title, he managed to avoid defending it for the next two years. And in that time, one very big fight took place without him.

As Lord Nelson chased Admiral Villeneuve across the Atlantic in October 1805, Hen Pearce, nicknamed the Game Chicken, took on John Gully. It was an unlikely contest, because Pearce had to get Gully out of debtor's prison before it could happen. He persuaded a generous sponsor to pay Gully's debts, and the mill came off at Hailsham, north of Eastbourne in Sussex.

High society was there in numbers. The Duke of Clarence, brother of the Prince of Wales, whom he would succeed as William IV, watched the fight from horseback. Also present was Lord Byron, who had dined the night before with two of the other spectators, Gentleman Jackson and Viscount Althorp.

It was a brutal contest. In the early stages, Pearce was on top, then Gully recovered and seemed at one point to be on the verge of victory. But Pearce was famous for bottom, the term favoured by the Fancy for courage and endurance, and he finally emerged the victor after more than sixty rounds.

Jem Belcher could hide no longer. Just a couple of months after defeating Gully, Pearce, who seems to have had almost miraculous powers of recovery, got his shot at the title. In December 1805, by which time Admiral Nelson, in giving his life at Trafalgar, had made England safe from invasion, the Game Chicken beat the one-eyed Belcher in eighteen rounds. Belcher's attempts at a comeback failed, and he died a broken man in 1811.

Even so, he outlived his conqueror. Pearce never fought again, retiring as champion in 1806 in order to spend more time with the bottle. More often drunk than sober, he contracted tuberculosis and died in 1809.

John Gully fared very much better than either. With debtor's prison behind him, he assumed the title for a year after the Chicken's retirement, then himself quit the ring to devote his time to pursuits both more lucrative and less hazardous. He made a fortune from the turf, became a member of parliament, and had the distinction of being portrayed in fiction by the pen of Charles Dickens. He is to be found both in *Sketches by Boz* and in *Nicholas Nickleby*, where he appears as the opinionated and overbearing MP Mr Gregsbury. He died a very wealthy man in 1863, not far short of his eightieth birthday.

As for Hen Pearce, he makes an appearance of sorts in *Dombey & Son*, in which the pugilist friend of Mr Toots is known as the Game Chicken. And for all his fame as a boxer, Hen Pearce is probably best remembered for his nickname. Which is not so surprising, for in the days of the old prize ring, imaginative nicknames were commonplace. In addition to the Game Chicken and Death (Stephen Oliver), there was Young Rump Steak, Old Ruffian (and also Young Ruffian), the Elastic Potboy, the Yokel Jew, Holy Land Pink, Iron-Arm Cabbage, and many others. Sadly, the Flying Tinman of Bath seems to have been apocryphal.

No nickname, however, stuck to John Gully, or to his successor as champion. Tom Cribb, one of the all-time greats of the prize ring, just didn't need one. He was to retire undefeated after a thirteen-year reign as champion, in the course of which he recorded victories over such formidable opponents as Jem Belcher, Bob Gregson and Ikey Pig. He also participated in the first two big international prize fights.

———————

As it happened, he had already fought one black American opponent in Bill Richmond, but Richmond had lived in England from his early teens, and was not considered foreign. Tom Molineaux, who had been born a slave in Virginia and who came to England as an adult, certainly was – though no one, least of all Molineaux himself, would have seen him as representing the United States. Having crossed the Atlantic in the hope of making his fortune in pugilism – the American prize ring had yet to be born – Molineaux soon earned his chance to fight Cribb for the title. Bill Richmond supervised his training.

It was December 1810. Napoleon Bonaparte dominated Europe, George III was hopelessly insane, and the Prince of Wales was about to take over as regent. Jane Austen would shortly publish *Sense and Sensibility*.

After twenty-eight hard-fought rounds, Molineaux had the title in his grasp. Tom Cribb, whose most admired quality was bottom even greater than that of Hen Pearce, was unable to come up for the twenty-ninth. But before the challenger could claim the prize, Cribb's seconds complained that he was fighting with pistol balls in his hands to increase his punching power. The row that followed, during which Molineaux opened his hands to prove the allegation groundless, went on long enough to give Cribb time to recover.

And while the champion rallied, Molineaux, himself in a bad way and suffering much more from the bitter cold, flagged. His plight worsened three rounds later when his head made violent contact with one of the unpadded stakes, and soon the game was up. Tom Molineaux had been robbed.

Still, he had made an impact sufficient to ensure that the rematch nine months later would be the most eagerly-awaited contest the ring had yet seen: on the eve of battle, we are told, not a bed was to be had within twenty miles of the scene of the action at Thistleton Gap in Leicestershire. This time, however, Cribb was trained to the highest degree, while Molineaux had unwisely indulged his considerable appetite for women and food and drink. In front of a crowd variously estimated between twenty and forty thousand the champion won easily in eleven rounds.

Tom Molineaux, lacking the acumen of his mentor Bill Richmond, who became a successful publican when his fighting days were over, did not last long. Within seven years of his second title fight, he died in Galway. His conqueror lived much longer, but was ill-suited to life outside the ring. Retiring as champion in 1822, Tom Cribb became an innkeeper and a coal merchant, but enjoyed little success in either line of business. He died in 1848 at the age of sixty-eight.

It was in Cribb's time that boxing was to find in Pierce Egan its first great chronicler. Born in 1772, Egan began publishing *Boxiana*, his history of the prize ring, in 1812. Issued in monthly instalments, *Boxiana* offered, in Egan's inimitable style, biographical sketches of fighters, and detailed accounts of their battles. Egan knew what his readers wanted, and he gave them it. They would, for instance, have been delighted to read that boxing was both manly and typically English – vastly preferable to the vicious knife-fights common amongst foreigners. And yet, for all his determination to glamorise pugilism, he could be quite hard-headed when he chose:

No men are more subject to the caprice or changes of fortune than the pugilists; *victory* brings them fame, riches and patrons; their bruises are not heeded in the smiles of success; and basking in the sunshine of prosperity, their lives pass on pleasantly, till *defeat* comes and reverses the scene: covered with aches and pains, distressed in mind and body, assailed by poverty, wretchedness and misery,– friends forsake them – their towering fame expired – their characters suspected by losing [a reference to fixed fights] – and no longer the *'plaything of fashion!'* they fly to inebriation for relief, and a premature end puts a period to their misfortunes.

Egan's contribution to the popularity of boxing is hard to exaggerate. But the greatest of all chroniclers of the prize ring described only one battle, the encounter at Hungerford in Berkshire on December 11th, 1821 between Bill Neate and Tom Hickman, known as the Gasman. Despite intense public interest, it was not even a title fight, and we would barely remember it today but for the presence of the fearless radical William Hazlitt, one of the great masters of English prose. He immortalised the contest in an account entitled simply *The Fight*.

Hazlitt does for the prize ring what Homer did for ancient Greek boxing, and what Virgil did for the Roman version. Neate and Hickman might as well be Epeius and Euryalus, or Dares and Entellus. They are similarly heroic figures, mortal men raised above the common mass by strength, skill and courage.

To learn today what a mill felt like in the heyday of the prize ring, we simply have to read *The Fight*. Pierce Egan's idiosyncratic style can be hard going today, but Hazlitt's prose has lost none of its readability. He gives us everything from the arrangement of transport from London, to the return journey the day after the fight. Above all, he gives us atmosphere. Here he describes his coming to the scene of the action:

The crowd was very great when we arrived on the spot; open carriages were coming up, with streamers flying and music playing, and the country-people were pouring in over hedge and ditch in all directions, to see their hero beat or be beaten.

Then he gives us the field itself, and its aspect as the hour of battle drew near:

> The day, as I have said, was fine for a December morning. The grass was wet, and the ground miry, and ploughed up with multitudinous feet, except that, within the ring itself, there was a spot of virgin-green closed in and unprofaned by vulgar tread, that shone with dazzling brightness in the mid-day sun. For it was noon now, and we had an hour to wait. This is the trying time. It is then the heart sickens, as you think what the two champions are about, and how short a time will determine their fate.

He devotes only about one seventh of his account to the fight itself, but his description is memorable, nowhere more so than where he describes the blow which effectively decided the contest:

> Neate just then made a tremendous lunge at him, and hit him full in the face. It was doubtful whether he would fall backwards or forwards; he hung suspended for about a second or two, and then fell back, throwing his hands in the air, and with his face lifted up to the sky. I never saw anything more terrific than his aspect just before he fell. All traces of life, of natural expression, were gone from him. His face was like a human skull, a death's head, spouting blood.

Hazlitt was filled with admiration, but it is scarcely surprising that others reacted with horror. What the admirers of pugilism most loved was what its detractors most loathed. Still, it was only five months since the Prince Regent had been crowned king in the presence of the nineteen prize fighters – Tom Cribb, naturally, was one – recruited by Gentleman Jackson. Boxers were men of substance, whether polite society liked it or not.

———————

But the high noon of the prize ring was nearly over, and the closure in 1820 of the Hyde Park ring which George I had set up nearly a century before was a sign of the times. When Tom Cribb gave up the crown after his thirteen-year reign, a worthy successor appeared in the shape of Tom Spring – who had changed his name from Winter. But when he too retired, after only one year as champion, nothing was quite the same again.

With huge amounts of money being staked on the outcome of fights, the suspicion of fixes had never gone away, and those suspicions were becoming ever more serious. At the same time, boxing now ran counter to the spirit of the age. The Industrial Revolution had given rise to an urban economy in which labour discipline had to be enforced as never before. No longer were working hours and conditions determined by the rising and setting of the sun, and the eternal circle of the seasons. Now people's lives were ruled by the clock, and by the machines whose servants they were.

There was nothing happy-go-lucky about the new economy. For many of the population, it was no longer even possible to live for the moment. Factories, mines and mills enforced deferred gratification, encouraged sobriety and self-control. A puritanical morality grew naturally from such changes, and the captains of industry who formed the new ruling class frowned deeply on such irrational and chaotic spectacles as prize fights. There was something atavistic about the ring, something which cocked a snook at all that the new moralists held dear.

Everything seemed to go wrong at once. Tom Spring, although his nickname, the Light Tapper, says everything about his punching power, was a brilliant boxer, but there was no one quite as good to follow him. When he retired in 1824 – his last fight, watched by some 30,000, was the first in which a grandstand (which collapsed) was used – the title was claimed by Tom Cannon, the Great Gun of Windsor, who was beaten the following year by Jem Ward, the Black Diamond (so-called because he was a coal-heaver to trade, not because he was black).

And there was a problem with Jem Ward. In 1822, he had been banned by Jackson's Pugilistic Club, the ring's governing body, for throwing a fight. But only the following year, he was reinstated, and in 1825 became the first champion to have been convicted of such dishonesty. It was not what the sport needed.

The retirement of Tom Spring had coincided with two other blows to the prize ring. Eighteen twenty-four was the year that Gentleman Jackson finally closed his Bond Street gymnasium, and the year that his Pugilistic Club was dissolved. The loss of Jackson's prestige was a setback from which bare-knuckle fighting never really recovered. There was simply no one to take his place.

He had formed the Pugilistic Club ten years before, noblemen and gentlemen being prominent among its hundred and twenty members. They subscribed an annual sum to ensure purses for fights, they employed an official ring-maker, who became known as the commissary general, and some of the less aristocratic members maintained order at ringside. The Pugilistic Club thus became the governing body of the sport, providing a degree of stability and decorum, and genuinely trying to prevent fixes. Its demise was a serious matter for boxing, because a sport with so many enemies could ill do without reputable centralised administration.

As it turned out, it was quickly succeeded by the Daffy Club, Daffy being the slang term favoured by the Fancy for gin. Pierce Egan was a staunch supporter of the new governing body, but he did not have the prestige of Gentleman Jackson, and the Daffy Club lacked the social distinction which had protected its predecessor. Nor could its members afford to provide purses for fights, and the result was that boxers again had to look for rich patrons. It was inevitable that the number of fixed fights should increase.

Eighteen twenty-four was beyond doubt the annus horribilis of the prize ring. Not only John Jackson, but even his most famous pupil quit the scene. In April of that year, George Gordon, Lord Byron, died of marsh fever at Missolonghi in Greece, where he had gone to fight in the cause of Greek Independence.

Then there was the Elstree murder. It was committed in October 1823, but the scandal reverberated into 1824 and beyond. John Thurtell was a wealthy young man who lost a very large sum of money to solicitor William Weare in a card game. Believing that Weare had cheated, the furious Thurtell plotted revenge, and, having invited Weare to a weekend in the country, murdered him at Elstree in Hertfordshire. He was soon arrested, and was hanged in front of a large and appreciative crowd in January 1824. The problem for the prize ring was that Thurtell had been a prominent ring patron – he features in Hazlitt's famous essay as fight promoter Tom Turtle – and the notoriety of the crime ensured lurid press reports of the evil lives led by the Fancy. Charles Dickens, who had been eleven at the time of the crime, drew on it extensively in describing the murder of Montague Tigg in *Martin Chuzzlewit*.

The scene was set for the enemies of pugilism to strike, and strike they did. In 1824, magistrates stepped in to stop a prize fight between Jem Burns and Ned Neale at Moulsey Hurst (now Molesey) in Surrey. At Kingston Assizes, Mr Justice Burroughs made clear beyond the possibility of doubt that prize fighting was illegal. It was, he said, mercenary in origin, it indulged the propensities of the vicious, and it encouraged gambling. It was a devastating judgement, and, although bare-knuckle fighting staggered on for another half century, it effectively sounded the death knell of the old prize ring.

Royalty and aristocracy now largely withdrew their patronage, and the prize ring went so far downmarket as to become almost invisible to polite society. For the most part, the respectable press simply ignored it unless there was a major scandal to report. It still featured prominently in the sporting newspapers, of which the most significant, *Bell's Life in London*, had only come into being in 1822. Even its editor, Vincent Dowling, made no attempt to disguise boxing's sad decline: 'The Corinthians', he wrote in 1824, 'have ceased to grant either the light of their countenances or the aid of their purses toward the encouragement of the Ring.'

It was just two years before the birth of Tom Sayers.

––––––––––

The lowest point of all was reached in 1845, as Tom was working on the London Road Viaduct outside Brighton, and learning his future trade from Dover's Bob Wade. By this time, Broughton's code, which had served boxing so well for nearly a century, had been superseded by the LPR (London Prize Ring) Rules of 1838. These rules, formulated in response to the death of Bill Phelps in his bout with Owen Swift, were more an extension than a revision of Broughton's – an attempt to define things a little more closely, and to make explicit a number of points which had become matters of usage anyway. Amongst other things, they specified that a fighter should be attended by two seconds, one of whom, the bottle-holder, would provide a knee on which he might rest between rounds. But whatever the hopes of those who framed them, the new rules did little to improve the standing of the prize ring.

One of the first men to win a fight under them – William Thompson, in February 1839 – was also one of the fighters involved in the 1845 debacle.[6] Champion at the time was thirty-year-old Ben Caunt, an undistinguished fighter who, at nearly six feet three inches tall and well over two hundred pounds in weight, just happened to be big enough and strong enough to see off his challengers. Thompson, five inches shorter, forty pounds lighter and three years older, was his main rival. He was also one of the great characters of the prize ring.

William Thompson of Nottingham was the third of triplets who were themselves the last of twenty-one siblings. Although the triplets all had ordinary names, they became known instead as Shadrach, Meshach and Abednego, after the three men in the Book of Daniel who were thrown into the burning fiery furnace. William was Abednego, a corruption of which, Bendigo, was the name by which he became known. There was no doubt as to the origin of his combative spirit, for his mother was the most ferocious woman, once telling her youngest son that if he didn't answer a challenge, she would do so herself.

Bendigo, the first big-name fighter to use the right-fist-foremost southpaw stance, had already had a spell as champion, but had been forced to vacate the title when he damaged his knee in a typical piece of acrobatic clowning. The injury put him out of action for two years, but by 1845 he was ready to fight for the championship again. And the man he would have to beat was Ben Caunt.

Caunt and Bendigo had a history. They had met first in 1835 (when a dirty fight ended with Caunt being disqualified for a foul blow), and again three years later (when a dirty fight ended with Bendigo being disqualified for going down without being hit).[7] Their third meeting, on September 9th, 1845, was always likely to be problematic.

After a long walk necessitated, on a blisteringly hot day, by the difficulty of finding a suitable site, the mill finally came off in mid-afternoon in front of a weary and bad-tempered crowd of some ten thousand, at Lillingstone Lovell on the border between Buckinghamshire and Northamptonshire.

Something of the nature of the crowd, as seen by respectable society, is to be found in *The Reminiscences of Sir Henry Hawkins*. Hawkins, otherwise known as Baron Brampton, was writing of a fight of Ben Caunt's in 1840, while Bendigo was sidelined by his injured knee:

> The sexes were apparently in equal numbers and in equal degrees of ugliness and ferocity. There were faces flat for want of noses, and mouths ghastly for want of teeth; faces scarred, bruised, battered into every shape but what might be called human. There were fighting-men of every species and variety – men whose profession it was to fight, and others whose brutal nature it was; there were women fighters, too, more deadly than the men, because they added cruelty to their ferocity. Innumerable women there were who had lost the very nature of womanhood, and whose mouths were the mere outlet of oaths and filthy language. Their shrill clamours deafened our ears and subdued the deep voices of the men, whom they chaffed, reviled, shrieked at, yelled at, and swore at by way of fun.

(Hawkins might mention their presence, but those who relied on the newspapers for their knowledge of the ring would never have known that women formed part of any fight crowd.)

As *Bell's Life* explained, the few well-to-do spectators at the Caunt–Bendigo fight five years later were to regret their attendance:

> Almost every person having the semblance of respectability was hustled or stopped, and every pocket cleaned out, while some were actually thrown down, and their boots taken off, to ascertain whether they had there concealed their cash.

It was hardly surprising, for a large part of the crowd was made up by the thuggish Nottingham faction known as the Lambs, Bendigo supporters to a man, and no respecters of persons or of property.

Nor was foul play restricted to the spectators. If the previous meetings between the two men had been unsavoury, they were a vicarage tea party compared with what happened on the third occasion. From the very beginning, at three thirty, Caunt was his usual uncultured self, not at all particular as to how, where or when he hit his man, while Bendigo followed his usual tactic of dashing in, throwing a punch, then falling at the least excuse in order to end the round and avoid punishment. Under the new rules, of course, a fighter was not allowed to go down deliberately, but it was a tactic commonly employed by a man overmatched in size, and only in the most obvious cases would the referee award the fight to his opponent. Bendigo was prepared to push his luck.

As long as the ring keepers, whose business was crowd control, succeeded in holding spectators back from the fighting area, a semblance of order prevailed, but in round twenty-four a number of the Nottingham Lambs broke into the inner ring – a roped enclosure just outside the fighting area, where referee, press reporters and other favoured spectators were to be found – and made clear their determination that Bendigo should win. By round fifty, the confusion was extreme, the ring keepers hopelessly outnumbered by the bludgeon-wielding Lambs.

Tom Spring, former champion and one of Caunt's seconds, took a knock; Bendigo himself was hit on the shoulder by a blow aimed at Caunt's head. The referee, Squire Osbaldeston, thought it safer to quit his place outside the ring, and move inside. He was able to resume his correct position only after Jem Ward, seconding Bendigo, had pleaded with the Lambs. The worst moment of a truly dirty fight was when Bendigo clearly punched his opponent in the groin.

The fight went on, but the Lambs had made their point, and Squire Osbaldeston did not care to endanger his health by arguing with them. In round ninety-three, when Bendigo went down for his umpteenth tactical fall, Caunt returned to his corner and sat down. Bendigo, however, rose to continue, and his seconds, Ward and Holy Land Pink (whose name probably refers to the rookery of St Giles, which was nicknamed the Holy Land), appealed to Osbaldeston that Caunt had gone down without being hit. Osbaldeston prudently agreed, the fight and the title went to Bendigo, and nobody was killed.

As *Lloyd's Weekly London Newspaper* put it on September 14th,

> ... and when, at the close of the fight, an appeal was made to the referees and the umpire, to decide who had won, hundreds of ruffians broke through the outer ring, in the most brutal and menacing manner, and thus compelled the judge, out of fear of his life, to give the decision in favour of Bendigo.

And it was not only at the fight that there was trouble. *Bell's Life* reported that toll-keepers, whose job was to sit in a booth and take tolls from road-users, were mobbed and robbed of their takings, even having their houses searched. Almost all publicans in the area were likewise robbed, their upstairs rooms often being ransacked as the mob searched for money.

The same paper, on September 14th, was uncompromising in its judgement of the whole fiasco: 'A more disgraceful and disgusting exhibition never stained the annals of British boxing.' *Lloyd's* was similarly shocked: 'Something must be done, and that instantly, or adieu to the Prize Ring for ever.' *Bell's Life* held out not even that much hope, telling its readers that 'a blow has been given to the boxing school which it can never recover.'

As if to confirm this despairing judgement, Gentleman Jackson, whose unimpeachable character had gained for boxing a prestige now unimaginable, died just three weeks later.

CHAPTER 6

AMERICAN FISTS

JACK HEENAN was just a boy in 1842, the year in which Tom Sayers made his public debut in the ring with his impromptu fight with Haynes near Brighton. On September 20th of that year, during Ben Caunt's reign as British champion, the *New-York Daily Tribune* told its readers that 'we rejoice to know that the originators and fosterers of pugilism in this country are almost entirely foreigners by birth. This species of ruffianism is not native here, nor is our atmosphere congenial to it.' These were the sentiments of the *Tribune*'s high-minded editor Horace Greeley, best known for the injunction – originally coined by another – 'Go West, young man.' And the history of the United States prize ring up to that point bore him out.

Boxing simply had not put down strong roots in the New World, even though the first recognised prize fight had taken place more than a quarter of a century before, and a boxing code of sorts had been in existence at least by the last decade of the eighteenth century. Boxing went on, but only among a very clearly defined section of the population. When Greeley said that boxers and their backers were almost all foreign, what he meant was that they were almost all Irish or English.

By the 1840s immigrants were pouring into the New World from all over Europe, but only the English and the Irish showed any interest in the prize ring. It was in no way surprising that New York and Philadelphia – and to a lesser extent, Boston, Baltimore and New Orleans – were its main centres, for it was there that English and Irish blood ran thickest. There is no record of the involvement of any other nationality. As Elliott Gorn puts it in *The Manly Art*, it was boxers rather than boxing that crossed the Atlantic.

This was only to be expected. Cultural assimilation takes time, and while America may have been a melting pot, it was never a liquidiser. A study of any national group in the United States at the time would reveal that they continued to practise the customs of their native land – and that these customs were not practised by anybody else. The prize ring was a peculiarly Anglo-Irish phenomenon, and the Germans and the Italians and the French were hardly likely to take it up just because the Irish and the English liked it.

More than a century earlier, on March 5th, 1733, *The Boston Gazette* had carried the first mention of the prize ring in an American newspaper. While James Figg was demonstrating the science of self-defence at Tottenham Court Road, Bostonians were reading about the bout at Harrow on the Hill between Jem Faulconer of Brentford and Bob Russel, who kept an alehouse at Paddington:

> There was as great a Concourfe of People as ever was known on fuch an Occafion. The Green was Rop'd round; the Foot were firft and the Horfe kept behind, without creating the leaft Diforder or Difturbance during the whole Engagement, which lafted above eight Minutes: A great deal of Money was laid…

Well, America was a British colony at the time, and *The Boston Gazette* was a British newspaper. A generation would pass before serious talk was heard of American independence. The readers of *The Boston Gazette* in 1733 would have thought of themselves not as American at all, but as British.

How could it have been otherwise? America was England's child, still attached to her mother by the umbilical cord. Had the cord been cut prematurely, the British colonists would have been at the mercy of the French, the dominant European power west of the Alleghenies and to the north in Quebec. They would have had no hope of ever turning the Dutch possession of New Amsterdam into New York, and little chance of ever taking Florida from the Spanish. Boston in 1733 was a British city. It contained no Americans.

Half a century later, it was different: the colonists had cut not only the umbilical cord, but the apron strings with it. In 1788, while Tom

Johnson was rescuing the English prize ring from degradation, the *Register* of Philadelphia reported a charge of assault brought by Silas Freeman against Zachary Thomas Molineaux. Molineaux, whose service in the Revolutionary War against England was clearly taken into account, was released after making an apology. He was, said the *Register*, 'known in Virginia as a Negro whose mauleys [fists] have downed many opponents in fist bouts.'

This was a reference to a type of pugilism now barely visible in the darkness of a distant time. It seems that, on the plantations, slave-owners would sometimes pit their slaves against those of their neighbours. It is said to have been a way in which a number of slaves won their freedom, but what little is known about the practice suggests that it made no contribution to the development of the prize ring as it was to become known in the United States. The American prize ring belongs to the North, not the South, and the idea of a white man facing a black man in the ring was barely acceptable even at the beginning of the twentieth century.

Perhaps the most interesting thing about Zachary Molineaux is that he is said to have been the father of Tom Molineaux, who so nearly overcame the great Tom Cribb when he fought for the championship of England.[8] Tom, like Bill Richmond before him, fought in the English prize ring, and his fame as a pugilist belongs firmly in England, not in America. Whatever his achievements in the ring, they were scarcely reported in his native land, and had no influence on the development of the American prize ring.

––––––––––

To find the origins of American prize fighting, we have to move north. A French traveller, Médéric Louis Élie Moreau de Saint-Méry, writing of his *American Journey, 1793–1798*, said that, in Philadelphia, 'quarrels end in the action known as boxing. Here again the English origin of the Americans is shown.' Contrast his contention with that of Horace Greeley half a century later, and you have a history lesson on the early development of the United States: before 1800, the country, even when independent, was culturally English; by the 1840s, a nation, however disparate, had come into being in its own right.

What Moreau de Saint-Méry witnessed on the streets of Philadelphia was English pugilism. Boxing, he said, 'has its rules and regulations. The two athletes settle on a site for the fight. They strip to their shirts, and roll up their sleeves to the elbows.' Spectators, some of whom would put money on the outcome, formed a ring, and the contest began. It might as well have been London.

But the rules observed were not quite those by which Jackson and Mendoza were fighting on the other side of the Atlantic, for while a man could not be hit while he was down, he was fair game the moment he tried to rise. There were, it seems, no rounds. By the finish, Moreau de Saint-Méry tells us, both men would be very battered, spitting out teeth, and bleeding profusely from nose and mouth.

He notes that, unless they involved drunks or the lowest orders, matches took place by moonlight, which strongly suggests – though he does not actually say so – that boxing was no more respectable in America than it was in England. There was no specific law prohibiting it, but it seems to have been more or less a clandestine activity.

As in England, however, pugilism did have one almost acceptable face. On February 10th, 1798, in the highly respectable *Columbian Centinel*, one G.L. Barrett advertised his services as a fencing and boxing instructor:

FENCING

G.L. Barrett informs the gentlemen of *Boſton* that he propoſes teaching the elegant accompliſhment of FENCING, on the following terms: Entrance, 3 dolls, every 8 leſſons 5 dolls.

Any Gentleman deſirous of receiving leſſons at their own houſes, entrance as above, each leſſon 1 doll.

Mr Barrett likewiſe teaches the Scientific and manly art of BOXING on the above terms. Exactly according to the attitudes of HUMPHRIES or MENDOZA.

Sparring gloves may be had of Mr B. at No 78, State.

Since fencing enjoyed high social regard, boxing could only benefit from being bracketed with it, and Barrett was only the first of many who were to seek to make an American living by teaching the arts of self-defence.

But even if sparring – with gloves, of course – was just about acceptable, bare-knuckle fighting was not. This was certainly the line taken by *The Boston Post* in reporting the fight between Jacob Hyer and Tom Beasley which took place at Hingham, Massachusetts on October 15th, 1816. Under the headline 'Vicious Prize Fight' the *Post* recounted that 'after fighting most viciously and contrary to law for more than an hour, Hyer's arm was broken and he was forced to give up the encounter.' This report, however, while it had the merit of brevity, lacked that of accuracy.

In a contest which soon degenerated into a brawl, Hyer's arm was indeed broken, but, with Beasley also severely punished, friends of the two men finally stepped in to end the fight as a draw. Its main importance lies in the fact that it has gone down in history as America's first genuine boxing match.

Whether it was so in reality is by no means certain. As Nat Fleischer puts it in *A Pictorial History of Boxing*:

> By a sort of traditional consent, the fight between Jacob Hyer and Tom Beasley in New York in 1816 is established as the first ring battle in America in which the public-at-large [*sic*] was represented and in which the rules that governed boxing in England were accepted by the principals.

In truth it was probably not even a genuine prize fight, since there is no record of any stake, and the impact on the public consciousness at the time was minimal. Writing in 1821, the year that William Hazlitt chronicled the Neate–Hickman battle, Pierce Egan could say in *Boxiana* that 'Prize-boxing is unknown in America.' Nor were Hyer's credentials subsequently tested, for he never fought again. Even so, some still accord him the highly dubious title of first heavyweight champion of America.

It was another seven years before a newspaper was to carry a full report of a fight. In the *New-York Evening Post* of July 10th, 1823 an account appeared of a match at Gardner's Wharf on Cherry Street between an unnamed eighteen-year-old butcher and the similarly anonymous 'champion of Hickory Street'. The latter was probably Irish, and tensions between native-born Americans and Irish immigrants may have been an important factor. The contest took place with due formality in front of an orderly crowd, each man having a second in his corner. The young butcher prevailed in eight rounds.

America's first serious public expression of distaste for pugilism followed five days later, when the *New-York Spectator* asked rhetorically

> ... what will become of the morals of the rising generation
> – our apprentices, youth from school, servants, male and
> female, if they have opportunity to mingle in these scenes
> of riot, brutality, and systematic violations of order and
> decency, where customs must be acquired which will not
> bear repetition?

That such a question, however rhetorical, could be posed at all was significant. For all the revulsion which the prize ring so frequently aroused in England, its moral impact, like its very existence, was simply taken for granted. America was different. Not only the ring, but the very moral tenor of the nation, was still in its infancy. It was not at all clear which direction either would take in the years and decades to come.

And there was a back door by which the prize ring might yet come to acceptance, if not respectability, on the western side of the Atlantic. G.L. Barrett had introduced to the United States the sort of gymnasium which Gentleman Jackson ran in England. Many others followed, and none was more influential than William Fuller, who came to America in 1824 just as the prize ring was falling into disrepute in its homeland. Fuller was a Norfolk man who came of boxing stock on both sides of his family. Bill Richmond and Tom Cribb were among his acquaintances.

He had become a middling boxer, good enough to take on (though not to beat) Tom Molineaux, and then had moved to France where he broadened his interests considerably. Fluent in the language, he had been clerk of a racecourse, keeper of a billiard room and master of a sparring school.

His next move was across the Atlantic to America, where his fame soon spread as he travelled the country, giving sparring lessons and exhibitions. In so far as polite society was even aware of the prize ring at this early time, it heartily disapproved, and Fuller did not at first find things easy. But his behaviour was clearly that of a gentleman, and this began to win people over. An early convert was *The Charleston Mercury*, which, on December 12th, 1825, expressed the wish that

> ... the young gentlemen of this city will avail themselves of the present opportunity to acquire a knowledge of Pugilism, and afford that encouragement to Mr Fuller which his conduct, since he has been amongst us, so much deserves.

Fuller was always looking to add strings to his bow. He even appeared on the stage, playing both Cribb and Jackson in an adaptation of Pierce Egan's best-known work, *Life in London*, which introduced Regency bucks Tom and Jerry to the world. In time he built his own gymnasium in New York, and there, not content with sparring alone, he branched out into fencing, gymnastics, quoits and bowling. He was a good businessman, and his elegant manners led some to call him the Jackson of America. Crucially for his chances of social acceptance in the New World, he said that he had no wish to bring the prize ring to America, but wished to teach gentlemen 'a useful, manly, and athletic exercise, at once conducive to health and furnishing the means of self-defense and prompt chastisement to the assaults of ruffians.'

One way or another, pugilism went on, and was, by the 1830s, sufficiently well established for *Porter's Spirit of the Times*, a sporting newspaper based on *Bell's Life in London*, to feel confident enough to give full accounts of fights. And in Gordon Bennett's groundbreaking *New York Herald*, fight reports even found a place in the mainstream press.

As was only to be expected, the American prize ring had by now adopted such British customs as throwing the hat into the ring, tossing a coin for choice of corner, and tying colours to one of the posts. Formal articles of agreement likewise became common.

But the opponents of boxing were as vocal as ever, drawing a stinging riposte from William T. Porter in the *Spirit of the Times* of May 5th, 1832:

> In giving the history of a contest or combat between two men, I am aware of the risk I run of offending the feelings of many a canting, whining swindler and fastidious hypocrite, who will shake the head of disapprobation at the name of a fight, and fleece you at the same instant.

The controversy over pugilism persisted because its cause persisted. It would be nonsense to suggest that boxing had won for itself a place in mainstream American culture, for organised fights were still a great rarity, but it had now gained at least a toe-hold in the New World.

What made that hold more secure was, paradoxically, that the English prize ring, without which pugilism would never have existed in the United States, was in decline. As a result, more and more fighters began crossing the Atlantic to seek their fortunes, most prominent among them being James Burke, commonly known as Deaf Burke because of his impaired hearing. He was English champion, and should have been able to make a living in England better than any of his peers, but he had a problem: he had killed a man in the ring. It was a strange story, involving a bizarre and tragic coincidence.

On June 2nd, 1830, as George IV lay on his deathbed, Simon Byrne, the Irish champion, had been matched against his Scottish counterpart, Sandy Mackay. A savage contest ended with Mackay's death, and led to rioting in Scotland. The trouble was worst in Mackay's home town of Dundee, where three were killed, and in Glasgow, where four died. Religion, as ever, made things much worse, and in Glasgow a Roman Catholic church was destroyed, the rioters taking for granted the religion of the Irishman. In the wake of such mayhem, the last thing the prize ring needed was another fatality. Sadly, another fatality was what it got.

It was almost exactly three years later, on May 30th, 1833, that Byrne took on Deaf Burke. Burke was a particularly tough fighter, and his contests were always likely to be even more brutal than most. This one was no exception, and ended in Byrne's death.

It was all a bit much, and the champion now had difficulty finding opponents. He was not exactly to blame for the tragedy – it was just one of the hazards of the sport – but that did not help. Burke had a living to make, and it was clear that he would have a hard time making it in England. Accordingly, in 1836 he left for America, where the embryonic prize ring might at least yield opponents, and thus purses.

Having given some exhibitions and won a few easy fights, he at last faced real opposition. The successor to Simon Byrne as Irish champion was Sam O'Rourke, and there were issues between him and Burke. When Burke had had such difficulty finding opponents in England, O'Rourke had challenged him to a meeting in Ireland. Unsurprisingly (and bearing in mind, no doubt how the news of Mackay's death had been received in Scotland), Burke thought it safer not to go. But now O'Rourke was also in America, and the two even toured together. Sparring exhibitions, however, were not especially lucrative, and in the absence of worthwhile American opponents, they decided to fight each other for real.

The showdown took place in New Orleans at the forks of the Bayou Road early in the afternoon of Friday, May 5th, 1837. Burke had been wise to avoid fighting O'Rourke in Ireland, but he must have known that there were huge numbers of Irish in America, and should have been aware that there was an especially high concentration in New Orleans.

All was well at first, even if the crowd was overwhelmingly on O'Rourke's side. But in the third round, one of the Irishman's seconds approached Burke who, suspecting a trick, struck at him. Things turned ugly, and in the words of *The Daily Picayune* the following day, 'The Irish handled Burke and his friends with fists and sticks, made of anything but dough or molasses.' The *Picayune*'s rival the *States–Item*, was more explicit: 'Hardly a man was there who had not ruffian stamped on his face... and there was a free and ostentatious display of pistols, bowie knives, bludgeons and sling shots.' Burke was obliged to flee for his life.

One man – presumably not of Irish blood – gave Burke his own bowie knife, and a theatre proprietor by the name of Caldwell gave him a horse. The *Picayune* heard – and thought it might well be true – that the knife donor was beaten and killed by the mob.

Nat Fleischer described the English champion's headlong flight:

> Burke, naked save for his muddy fighting trunks and
> spiked shoes, his brawny torso all stained and streaked
> with blood, his face bruised and swollen, holding the
> bridle of the horse in one hand and waving the bowie
> knife in the other like a Comanche, galloped madly
> toward the distant city. He frightened fashionable
> Creole ladies out for an afternoon drive and threw
> people along the way into panic with the thought that
> a maniac had escaped from the high-walled asylum out
> on the city commons. Burke took refuge in Caldwell's
> St Charles Theater.

Well, perhaps, but Burke was certainly wearing knee-breeches rather
than trunks, and Fleischer's account sounds as if it owes as much to
imagination as to established fact. But that Burke was obliged to flee on
horseback for his life is not in doubt.

Unconcerned by the somewhat unorthodox conclusion to the fight,
O'Rourke's supporters returned in triumph to the city, drawing their
champion on a wagon. But they did not have things all their own way, for
there were enough Anglo-Americans in New Orleans to give them a run
for their money. Fights went on all afternoon, featuring, as the *Picayune*
put it, 'large numbers of malcontents, principally Irishmen'. In the end,
the mayor was obliged to call out the militia to restore order. Burke might
as well have fought O'Rourke in Ireland.

But at least, unlike Mackay and Byrne, he survived. Ultimately he
returned to England, where he fought just once more, losing his title to
Bendigo in a fight held under the new London Prize Ring Rules. Six
years later, a victim of one of the most prolific killers of the age, he would
die penniless of tuberculosis.

That he returned to England at all was significant. However low
it had sunk in the public estimation, in England the prize ring still
had a following sufficient to ensure its survival. The American ring
was different. Supported only by a very narrow section of society, and
universally condemned by everyone else who happened to have heard of

it, its existence was highly tenuous. Somewhat oddly it was to be given its greatest boost by one of its most unsavoury characters.

Yankee Sullivan (who was in fact Irish) was also known by several other names, including Frank Murray and Frank Martin, but his real name seems to have been James Ambrose. He was probably born in Ireland (but possibly in England), 1813 being a fair guess as to the date.

A career criminal as well as a successful prize fighter, he was, in the year that Burke fought O'Rourke, transported to Botany Bay – possibly for larceny or possibly for the drunken killing of his wife. Showing considerable enterprise, he managed to escape to America, and thence back to England, where exposure would certainly have seen him hanged. In the England of Fagin, Bill Sykes and the Artful Dodger, Yankee Sullivan was a good fit.[9]

He fought once in the English ring, defeating the highly-rated Hammer Lane. The unanimous judgement of the Fancy, however, was that Sullivan, who was dreadfully punished, would have had no chance had Lane not broken his right arm in the course of the fight.

With the prize ring at a low ebb in its homeland, and with the ever-present fear of arrest and hanging, Sullivan returned to New York and made his career there, even opening a Bowery saloon called Sawdust House. In the ring, no one could touch him. On September 2nd, 1841, he defeated Englishman Vincent Hammond for $100 (equivalent to £20) a side in a ten-minute contest which made him the hero of New York's huge Irish community.

The only fighter likely to stand a chance against him was the son of one of the men credited with contesting America's first true prize fight a quarter of a century before. Tom Hyer was American-born (as his father Jacob had been), and those who saw themselves as true Americans looked forward keenly to the day that he would defeat the Irish upstart and salvage the honour of his country. That he might be up to the task he had proved just one week after Sullivan's victory over the hapless Vincent Hammond.

Borne along on a wave of Irish patriotic fervour and fortified by the bottle, Sullivan's friend John McCleester (who normally went by

Country McCloskey) had one evening rushed out of Sawdust House and thrown down his own challenge to Tom Hyer. No one was standing on ceremony. The very next day, at Caldwell's Landing on the Hudson, a gruelling three-hour contest ended when McCloskey finally accepted Sullivan's advice to quit before Hyer killed him. Native-born Americans now held Hyer, also known as Young America, in as much regard as Irish Americans did Sullivan. There would have to be a showdown.

But it was not quite that simple. Hyer was happy to fight, but not for less than $3,000 (£600) a side, a sum which the Irishman was unable to raise. Instead, on Staten Island on January 24th, 1842, Sullivan took on another native-born American, Tom Secor, who was available at one tenth of the price. As anyone might have predicted, Sullivan won easily, alternately taunting and pummelling his opponent for sixty one-sided minutes.

His next opponent was Englishman William Bell. Seven months after the Secor fight, on the day that the Treaty of Nanking ended the First Opium War, ensuring that Britain could export opium to China whether the Chinese liked it or not, Sullivan and Bell met in the ring for $300 a side. Ten steamboats took at least six thousand enthusiasts to Hart's Island at the western end of Long Island Sound. There were chaotic scenes among the crowd, but nothing fazed Yankee Sullivan, who was again victorious. The most notable moment was when, locked in a stranglehold against the ropes, he said he wanted to quit. As soon as the trusting Bell loosened his grip, Sullivan walloped him.

The big fight with Hyer was long overdue, and would surely have come soon had it not been for something that happened just two weeks after the Hart's Island mill. In teeming rain on the morning of September 13th, 1842, a crowd of fight-goers, including twenty or thirty women, steamed twenty miles up the Hudson from New York, disembarking at a quiet spot halfway between Yonkers and Hastings in Westchester County. Yankee Sullivan and Country McCloskey were among them.

The fight, which pitted twenty-three-year-old Englishman Christopher Lilly against Irishman Thomas McCoy, three years his junior, was particularly brutal. This was perhaps predictable, for McCoy had chosen for his colours black, signalling his determination to conquer or die. It was even said, though perhaps hindsight was in this case the mother of invention, that his mother had told him to come home victorious or not at all.

Lilly gained the initiative early in the fight, and by round eighty-four it was not looking good for the Irishman. 'As McCoy came up and made a pass', said *The New York Herald* the following day, 'Lilly cried "Ola!" and rushed in, throwing his man, with the blood spouting from him like a harpooned porpoise.'

And it only got worse from there. Two rounds later, McCoy was in a dreadful state. His entire face, the left side especially, was a mess. Even his forehead was black and blue. Both his eyes were black, his lips were swollen to an incredible size, and blood was streaming down his chest. Soon he was obliged to hold his head back just to enable him to see through the narrow slit which remained below one eyelid. Many in the crowd were now calling for his corner to take him out.

But McCoy was having none of it, and was still fighting – just about – more than thirty rounds later. At the end of round one hundred and nineteen, though, he slipped from his second's knee and could not come up to scratch when time was called. Fifteen minutes later, he was dead. His wounds, an autopsy would establish, had drained into his lungs, and he had drowned in his own blood.

It was this tragedy which prompted Horace Greeley to rejoice that at least the prize ring was not native to the United States, nor was the American atmosphere congenial to it.

Lilly swiftly and wisely fled the country for England, but eighteen of those involved in arranging the fight were arrested, Yankee Sullivan and Country McCloskey among them. They came to trial in November, and Justice Charles R. Ruggles left the jury in no doubt as to his opinion of the prize ring:

> A prize fight brings together a vast concourse of people; and I believe it is not speaking improperly to say that the gamblers, and the bullies, and the swearers, and the blacklegs, and the pickpockets, and the thieves, and the burglars, are there. It brings together a large assemblage of the idle, disorderly, vicious, dissolute people – people who

live by violence – people who live by crime – their tastes run that way…

All eighteen defendants were convicted of fourth degree manslaughter, and Sullivan was sentenced to the maximum two years in jail.

The effect of the tragedy on the prize ring was considerable – even though Sullivan, making use of his connections, was pardoned and released after a few months. Just two days after the event, *The New York Herald* predicted that 'The dreadful result of this battle will put an end to prize fighting in this country for years.' And so it did, for the American prize ring was virtually comatose for the next five. But it was not dead.

When it awoke, Yankee Sullivan, who had opened a new Bowery saloon in 1845, was not slow to take advantage. On May 11th, 1847 at Harper's Ferry in Virginia, he defeated Robert Caunt, whose brother Ben had finally lost his long feud with Bendigo in the disgraceful mill at Lillingstone Lovell two years earlier.

But this was not the big one. Everyone knew that there was only one fight that really mattered, and it had been pending for five years. Sooner or later, Yankee Sullivan and Tom Hyer would have to meet. Harsh words passed between them on a regular basis, and when they ran into each other in a New York oyster bar in April 1848, they quickly came to blows. Hyer beat Sullivan senseless, then escaped before a crowd of Irishmen arrived to take revenge.

Feelings on both sides ran so high that gang warfare on a grand scale threatened. That threat, although low-level violence went on constantly, was lifted four months later when articles of agreement were signed for a formal contest between the two principals. Arrangements would have been made sooner but for Hyer's insistence that he would not fight for less than $5,000 a side, a sum which Sullivan had difficulty in raising.

For the first time in the United States, interest in boxing was widespread, for relations between native-born Americans and the invading Irish were now more strained than ever. In 1845, Ireland's potato crop had failed, and it went on failing for several years. With so many of the population largely – in some cases, almost solely – dependent on the potato, the result was famine. And the consequent massive increase in transatlantic migration had serious implications for the young country.

The cultural and ethnic consciousness of the United States was both complex and ill-defined: a first-generation Irish immigrant might, for example, be seen very differently from a second-generation immigrant. Religion was also highly significant, with the powerful if amorphous 'Scotch-Irish' interest (represented, for example, by Andrew Jackson) less anti-English than anti-Catholic.

At street level, resentment was inevitable against incomers who were prepared to work for less than others near the bottom of society, and to live in poorer conditions. There was even a political party, the Native American Party, dedicated to resisting the dilution of Protestant America by the Catholic Irish. Both for personal and for political and social reasons, Hyer–Sullivan was a true grudge match. The colours they chose told the tale: red, white and blue for Hyer, emerald green with white spots for Sullivan. Yet this was the same Sullivan who, to emphasise his loyalty to his new country – or perhaps his hostility to his old one – had willingly embraced his nickname, and had previously worn the stars and stripes around his waist.

While three and a half thousand miles away Tom Sayers was preparing for his prize ring debut against Abe Couch, the fight came off on February 7th, 1849. Hyer and Sullivan, both having narrowly escaped arrest, set sail from Baltimore that day accompanied by some two hundred fans, and closely pursued by a boatload of militia determined to prevent a breach of the peace. When the latter ran aground, the fight party had Chesapeake Bay to themselves, and chose Still Pond Heights, a deserted part of Maryland's eastern coastline, for their venue.

Having put ashore, they brushed a covering of snow from the chosen area, and cut stakes from the woods and ropes from the ship's rigging. Finally, after the contestants had followed their hats into the ring, and all necessary formalities had been observed, they squared up at twenty past four. It hardly looked a fair fight, for Hyer was four inches taller and thirty pounds heavier, but Sullivan's supporters had great faith in their man. Like Hyer's followers, they were more than happy to put their money where their hearts were. An estimated $300,000 was staked in side bets.

The fight was brief but intense. Sullivan set great store by his wrestling ability, and when an early attempt to throw Hyer failed completely, he must have known he was in for a hard time. And so it proved, for within twenty minutes he was finished, unable to come up to scratch for the next round.

Hyer was mobbed in Philadelphia the following day, and on the Wednesday night there was a huge fireworks display at Fountain House in Park Row, the New York bar which had become his headquarters. It culminated in the hanging of a brilliantly-lit transparency with the words 'Tom Hyer, the Champion of America'. The United States prize ring had come of age.

To the despair of Horace Greeley and all who thought like him, there was no stopping it now. It had only taken one big fight to catch the imagination of the nation, and, in spite of continued bitter opposition, the prize ring now gained a firm footing in the New World.

And if Tom Hyer had had his way, the American prize ring would soon have gained its place in the Old World too, but English champion Bill Perry, the Tipton Slasher, was not interested in meeting him. Nor, it seemed, was Hyer interested in meeting anyone else. He would not fight Sullivan again at a price that the Irishman could afford, and the same problem confronted anyone else who coveted his title. One such was John Morrissey of Troy.

———————

Born into a poor and ill-educated family, Morrissey began his working life at the age of twelve in a wallpaper factory. Later he was employed in an iron works, where Jack Heenan may for a time have been one of his workmates. Lacking the latter's formal education, he had sufficient ambition and determination to teach himself the skills of literacy.

Aged seventeen he went to work as barman for a Troy brothel keeper named Alexander Hamilton. He was expected to be able to deal with difficult customers, of whom there would have been many, and his employer was delighted with his performance, for John Morrissey was nothing if not tough.

On a visit to New York City at around this time, Hamilton looked in at the Empire Club of Captain Isaiah Rynders, a sporting man and political fixer without whom James K. Polk would probably never have become president. Located on Park Row, his club, which was part gambling den and part political headquarters, was frequented by some of the toughest and hardest men in America's toughest and hardest city. Having contrived to fall out with one of them, Hamilton told him that he had a bartender who could teach him a lesson.

When he returned to Troy and told his young employee what had happened, Morrissey reacted in an entirely predictable way: he set out for New York City to prove his boss's point. By this time he may already have been working at least some of the time as deckhand on a Hudson River steamboat, so a visit to the metropolis may have been no more than routine anyway.

The sequence of events is not altogether clear, but he went to the Empire Club, where he seems to have insulted the most dangerous of all Rynders's lieutenants, Bill Poole, known as the Butcher. To Poole and his friends, there was no such thing as a fair fight if it could be avoided. They all piled in, and Morrissey, though he fought like a tiger, was finally felled by a tremendous blow from a spittoon. Such was the beating he took that he might well have died had not Rynders himself intervened. Impressed by Morrissey's courage and aggression – and thinking that he could use such a man – he stepped in and called a halt.

He took the young bruiser to an upper room to recuperate, and later offered him a job. Morrissey became an immigrant runner at Castle Garden Wharf in lower Manhattan. His task was to meet immigrants as they disembarked, and direct them to soup kitchens and boarding houses controlled by Rynders. In return, the immigrants would have to pledge political support – which, in mid-nineteenth-century New York, meant much more than simply voting the right way. There was a huge amount of work for the energetic young Morrissey to do, for the famine was raging in Ireland, and Irish immigrants were flooding into the country.

Also entering the northern states as fugitives – though in nothing like the same numbers and of no relevance to John Morrissey – were slaves escaping from the south. They came by the Underground Railroad organised by free blacks and white abolitionists. And the more free people there were, always pushing on the doors to the West, the closer came the doom of the American Indians.

But the worlds of the slaves and the Indians meant nothing to John Morrissey when he came to live in the Five Points district which had so horrified both Davy Crockett and Charles Dickens. The Five Points, which dominated the Sixth Ward at Manhattan's southern tip, was the poorest neighbourhood in all New York, and Morrissey found lodgings at a boarding house on Cherry Street, where, a quarter of a century before, the young butcher had defeated the champion of Hickory Street in the first American boxing bout to be accorded a full newspaper report. His work as immigrant runner may at times have been unsavoury, but a bowl of soup and a roof over the head were worth the world to the pathetic people he greeted on the wharf.

John Morrissey, however, simply couldn't stay out of trouble. There was, for example, the little difficulty he had with Tom McCann. Morrissey was firmly identified as Irish, which ensured the enmity of the native-born Americans, of whom McCann was one. There was always going to be trouble when Morrissey seduced McCann's girlfriend – or perhaps she seduced him. The furious McCann confronted him in the pistol club in the basement of the St Charles Hotel on the corner of Broadway and Leonard Street, and the two men came to blows.

In the course of the battle, a pot-bellied stove was overturned, and McCann managed to force Morrissey's back down on top of it. The air was acrid with the smell of burning cloth and charred skin, but Morrissey would not give in. Ignoring the excruciating pain, he somehow managed to break free and beat his opponent senseless. Ever after, he was known as Old Smoke.

Having thus earned a name for extreme toughness, he began to think of turning that reputation to account. Most boxers began as brawlers, and John Morrissey now saw himself as future American champion, which meant that he was going to have to take on Tom Hyer. The latter, however, wasn't interested. Morrissey simply couldn't raise the sort of stake that might have attracted him, and it was pretty clear that Hyer would fight England's Bill Perry or nobody.

In 1851, at the age of twenty and in company with his friend Dad Cunningham, John Morrissey stowed away on board ship for gold-rush California. It was not an easy passage, but they made it, and Morrissey's energy and restless ambition saw them through their time there. Having failed as gold prospectors, he and Cunningham enjoyed more success with a gambling house. Still he hankered after a prize-fighting career, but still Tom Hyer ignored him. Morrissey settled for the next best thing.

If he could not yet be champion of America, he might at least become champion of California; and if he couldn't fight Tom Hyer, he might still be able to get a shot at the man who had trained him for the Sullivan fight. It so happened that these two roles were combined in the person of George Thompson. Morrissey accordingly issued a challenge, and the fight came off at Mare Island, twenty-odd miles north-east of San Francisco, for $2,000 a side on the last day of August, 1852.

It was a one-sided affair from the first, with Morrissey on the receiving end. This was entirely predictable, because he was not a cultured fighter. He relied, as he had done in the brawl with McCann, on bottom, and bottom alone was not nearly enough against a much more skilful fighter. After ten rounds, the outcome was not in doubt.

But it wasn't quite that simple. The great bulk of the spectators were Morrissey men, and Thompson, a Scot whose real name was Bob McLaren, was placed rather as Deaf Burke had been in his bout with Sam O'Rourke in New Orleans fifteen years before. Appreciating that winning might not be good for his health, he decided that his championship meant less to him than his life, and this he safeguarded by committing a deliberate foul which ensured his disqualification.

The following year, his victorious opponent, still in company with Dad Cunningham, went back east. He did some more political strong-arm work, and resumed his attempts to goad Tom Hyer into fighting him. Hyer was not to be drawn, but Morrissey again found a next-best for which he was prepared to settle. In September 1853, he signed articles of agreement to fight Yankee Sullivan, who had been equally unsuccessful in his attempts to lure Tom Hyer back into the ring. This time, with

Morrissey so clearly identified with Irish interests, it was, bizarrely, Sullivan who donned the mantle of Anglo-American favourite.

There was intense public interest, and in addition to the stake of $1,000 a side, it was reckoned that some $200,000 rested on the outcome in the form of side bets.

The fight came off on October 12th, 1853 at Boston Corners, a little town a hundred miles north of New York City where the Empire State meets Massachusetts and Connecticut. The prize ring being illegal, fight organisers usually adopted the English expedient of maximising their chances of escape in the event of interference, by staging bouts on the borders of local jurisdictions.

A crowd estimated at six thousand saw the two men square up. The twenty-two-year-old Morrissey, though not quite as big as Tom Hyer, still towered over his forty-year-old opponent. But age and size advantage availed him little in the early stages, for he simply did not have Sullivan's ring craft. His powers of endurance, however, stood him in good stead, and he was able to come back strongly after ten rounds of unmerciful punishment. Sullivan, however, still had the whip-hand, and by round thirty-seven Morrissey was a sickening sight, with blood gushing in streams from his nose, his mouth, and half a dozen gashes on his face.

And then something happened. The *New York Clipper*, a recently established rival to the *Spirit of the Times*, reported that Morrissey's bottle-holder, Awful (rightly Orville) Gardner, believing that Sullivan had struck a low blow, rushed in to push him back. A mêlée ensued which involved Sullivan and both sets of seconds.

Morrissey stayed out of it, and was successful in his appeal to the referee to award him the fight because of the supposed foul blow. Such was the confusion, however, that Sullivan was unaware that he had lost until he came out for round thirty-eight. It was all highly unsatisfactory, and the *Clipper*'s reporter made clear that he could not be entirely sure that he had got it right. And since the referee never did go public with a full explanation, no one would ever know for sure. But whatever his reasoning, with Tom Hyer clearly not prepared to fight again, John Morrissey was now generally accepted as American champion.

In the midst of all the excitement over the mill at Boston Corners, another item in the same issue of the *Clipper*, which came out three days after the fight, may not even have been noticed by many of its readers. But they were assured, if they were interested, that the *Clipper* would carry a full report from England of the upcoming fight between Tom Sayers and Nat Langham.

CHAPTER 7

THE CHAMPION

TOM SAYERS could scarcely have timed things worse. He was born shortly after the great decline in the fortunes of the prize ring began – with the Elstree murder, the closure of Gentleman Jackson's gymnasium, and so on – and he made his own entry into the ring in the year of Pierce Egan's death, less than four years after the third Caunt–Bendigo fight, the 'disgraceful and disgusting exhibition' which had dealt 'a blow to the boxing school which it can never recover', as *Bell's Life in London* had put it.

But the prize ring survived, and Tom's impressive victory over Abe Couch got his own career off to a good start. Collyer of Wandsworth was keen to accept the challenge which he issued shortly afterwards, on April 1st, 1849, but defaulted for lack of a sponsor: even £15, the minimum for which Tom would fight, was more than almost any boxer could raise for himself. Unskilled working men, as so many boxers were, might have to work five months to earn £15 – and even then, virtually all of it would have to go on essentials.

Tom was still employed as a bricklayer, almost certainly working on the construction of the Great Northern Line which, at its opening in 1850, ran from Peterborough to the temporary station of Maiden Lane just round the corner from where he lived. But still he wanted to fight, and Mr Viddler, his projected backer against Collyer, was still prepared to sponsor him for up to £25 for any match he chose to make. Accordingly, he issued another challenge, and this time it bore fruit.[10]

———

The retirement of Tom Spring had been one of the events of 1824 which contributed to the swift decline of the prize ring. In one sense, Spring himself had little need to worry: he was out of it. But the truth is that ex-boxers were seldom if ever really out of it. Almost all of them, on retirement if not before, became landlords of sporting taverns frequented by the Fancy, where matches were arranged and fight tickets sold. In the words of ring journalist Henry Downes Miles, 'your pugilist is the publican in chrysalis, so sure as the caddis shall become the May-fly in due season.'[11]

Tom Spring duly became landlord of the Castle Tavern in London's Holborn, perhaps the most prominent of all the sporting houses. And an employee of his, often called 'Tom Spring's waiter', answered the challenge of Tom Sayers. It was Dan Collins, who had been in Tom's corner in the fight with Couch. In late May 1850, each man put down a £2 deposit, and at the Castle a week later, formal articles of agreement were signed for a fight at £25 a side.

It was just what Tom needed, for during that week his first child was born. She was named after her mother – to whom he was still not legally married. With a second Sarah to feed, more money would be more than welcome.

Dan Collins, being roughly the same size and age, looked a good match for Tom in a mill which came off at the Kent village of Edenbridge on October 22nd, 1850. With Alec Keene and Jack Macdonald in Tom's corner, and Jack Grant and Jemmy Welsh in Dan's, all was going well until the ninth round, when a lone magistrate turned up, and – with commendable courage, bearing in mind the notorious volatility of the Fancy – ordered the crowd to disperse. Those in favour of carrying on regardless were overruled, and all reboarded the train which had taken them from London, and travelled some twelve miles to Redhill in Surrey.

There the mill resumed at round ten. But the interruption had cost a good deal of time, and at around twenty to six as darkness was closing, the referee finally called a draw. Tom had not won, but he had learned a valuable lesson. He had used his right fist, his 'auctioneer', too freely, and by the finish it was of little use to him. With unprotected hands, blows to the head could do the giver more harm than the receiver, and many bare-knuckle fights were won and lost because one man could no longer punch effectively. Ever after, Tom credited Dan Collins with teaching him one of the most valuable lessons he ever learned in the ring – that knowing *how* to use the right hand mattered less than knowing *when* to use it.

And Tom Sayers had to do more with his hands than box. Until battle with Collins could be resumed, it was back to the building trade. As a bricklayer, he worked hard for long hours, but while conditions were often dangerous, there were many more hazardous ways to make a living: the following March, a fire-damp explosion killed sixty-one in a pit near Paisley; and two days later in Stockport, twenty died when a boiler blew up. There was a lot to be said for the construction industry.

And whatever might be happening on the railways, easily the most impressive building project of 1850 was the Crystal Palace in Hyde Park. Constructed in five months, a building of glass and steel was a dead loss from a bricklayer's point of view, but it was one of the wonders of the age. By the time the issue between Sayers and Collins was settled, the massive edifice was complete, ready to house one of the defining events of the era, the Great Exhibition of the Works of Industry of all Nations.

And those works were truly astonishing. Along with the railway came the electric telegraph, and as the construction of the Crystal Palace began, seventy miles away in the Straits of Dover the world's first submarine cable was being laid. The initial attempt failed, but the link was still achieved before the Great Exhibition closed the following autumn. With such industry to celebrate, it was little wonder that the Exhibition was a tremendous success.

On April 29th, just two days before Queen Victoria declared it open, Sayers and Collins met again, this time at Long Reach on the south bank of the Thames near Dartford. Tom had been well trained by former heavyweight champion Peter Crawley, but Tom Spring had lost interest in Dan Collins, who consequently was undertrained. With Crawley's help, Tom had in six months improved out of recognition. He won easily in forty-four rounds occupying an hour and twenty-four minutes. The victory over Couch had signalled his arrival in the prize ring; that over Collins made clear that he was a man to reckon with.

But he ran up against the problem which faced all young fighters trying to make their mark. Since the winding up of Jackson's Pugilistic Club in 1824, boxers had had to find their own patrons, and that could be difficult. With a young daughter, and a wife whose expensive tastes were a constant worry, life for Tom Sayers was not easy.

His boxing was not yet bringing in the sort of money that might enable him to give up his day job, and in the latter part of 1851 and the early part of the following year, it is pretty safe to assume that he worked on the massive building project undertaken by the Great Northern Railway to replace their makeshift terminus at Maiden Lane with a permanent station just a little to the south at King's Cross. It was built on the site of the former Smallpox Hospital, and, in the words of *Knight's Cyclopaedia of London* (1851), 'It is at the present time a vast wilderness, with the remains of razed houses strewed around. The destruction of property has been immense.'

Clearly there was no shortage of work for bricklayers, but it was only in the prize ring that Tom had any hope of making big money, and he must have been greatly relieved to find a backer in John Garrett, his old employer from his days at the Copenhagen Grounds. Again he advertised in *Bell's Life*, and on March 24th, 1852, a month after the British troop ship *Birkenhead* sank off Cape Town, drowning some four hundred and fifty, articles were drawn up for a fight with popular East Ender Jack Grant.

The stake this time was £100 a side. This was serious money, and testimony to the high regard in which Tom Sayers was now held. Even so, few expected him be a match for Grant.

Conspicuous in his shabby but rakishly-tilted black-banded white top hat, and seldom seen without a half-smoked cigar in his mouth, Jack Grant, like Dan Collins (whom he had seconded against Tom in 1850), was Tom's size, but he seemed likely to prove a tougher proposition. An impressive record included a win over the highly rated Alec Keene, one of Tom's seconds in the Collins fight, and he was generally expected to have too much fire-power for his less experienced opponent.

The fight came off in June 1852, shortly after three reminders of how cheaply the Industrial Revolution valued the lives of its children. On one day the previous month, a colliery explosion at Aberdare had killed sixty-four, and a pit flood near Llanelli had drowned twenty-seven. Ten days later, thirty-five had died in an explosion in a pit near Preston. What was there to shock in the violence of the prize ring?

For the Sayers–Grant fight, the secrecy required to outwit police and magistrates was pitched still higher than usual. Just before the fight train left Shoreditch Station at half past eight on the morning of June 29th, 1852 – a year and two months since Tom had defeated Dan Collins – the driver was given an envelope secured with sealing wax and not to be opened till Bishop's Stortford. And while he was learning there that his destination was Mildenhall in Suffolk, the authorities received a decoy telegram telling them that the mill would take place at Great Chesterford in Essex, more than twenty miles away.

The ruse worked, and the fight went off without interference. The ring keepers, whose white headbands bore, in bold black letters, the words 'POLICE CONSTABLE OF THE PRIZE RING', were able to devote all their energies to their principal task of preventing the crowd from encroaching on the fighting area. In Jack's corner were Harry Orme and Jemmy Welsh, in Tom's Ned Adams and Bob Fuller – who, unusually for a second, was a pedestrian (foot-racer) rather than a pugilist.

Grant may have been favourite, but his training had not been adequate. After sixty-four rounds occupying two and a half hours, terrible stomach pains made him unable even to stand – though fears of a rupture later proved unfounded. His corner had no option but to throw in the towel – or, in the terminology of the day, throw up the sponge.

It was another big success for Tom Sayers, and was also something of a high point for the embattled prize ring: by this time, any fight which did not culminate in chaos and which was clearly not a fix was worth celebrating. Henry Downes Miles, in *Bell's Life*, contrasted the behaviour of all concerned favourably with 'the disgraceful manner in which the combats of late years have been carried out.'

A week after the fight, Tom received his battle money at a celebration at Jemmy Massey's King's Arms in Compton Street, Soho. He may have decided that he had outgrown the Laurel Tree, his old headquarters, and now began spending more time at the Coach and Horses in St Martin's Lane, the establishment kept by Ben Caunt who, after his epic battles with Bendigo, had retired from the ring and gone the way of all old fighters.

Eighteen months earlier, in January 1851, a pall had been cast over the former champion's life when a fire at his inn had claimed the lives of two of his children. With wood still extensively used in building, and open fires the only way to heat houses, such tragedies were commonplace.

Anyway, Tom Sayers had other things on his mind. Within two months of his destruction of Jack Grant (and just two days before John Morrissey's dubious victory over George Thompson on the other side of the world), Sarah presented him with a second child, a son, who was named after his father. With his wife showing no inclination to restrict her spending, more money was needed, and Tom Sayers was no longer interested in earning it as a bricklayer.

―――――――――――

Once a fighter had turned promise into achievement, sponsors were not quite so hard to find. One of the most prominent members of the Fancy at the time was Jack Atcheler (born Henry Mansfield), who had himself boxed in his youth, and who had now attained a certain celebrity as horse slaughterer to the Queen. In addition to backing Tom for his next fight, he allowed the young pugilist to use his house as a second home.[12]

And Jack Atcheler was not alone, for Alec Keene also put up some money. Tom was able to issue a formal challenge to all comers for up to £100 a side. Mr Lee, landlord of the York Arms, accepted at £50 on behalf of Jack Martin.

Matters, however, did not go smoothly. When Ben Caunt, acting for Tom in arranging the fight, won the toss for selection of venue, he chose Hitchin in Hertfordshire. It was a strange decision, since the Hertfordshire constabulary, ever since the death of Brighton Bill Phelps at the hands of Owen Swift in 1837, had been especially zealous in the suppression of prize fighting, and Caunt was to regret it.

On January 25th, 1853, the fight train arrived at Stevenage Station to find the blues already there in force. Martin's camp were furious, even suggesting that Caunt had never intended that the fight should go ahead, but there was nothing more to be done that day. The stakeholder, a neutral authority who had charge of such matters, decided that they would have to try again the following day, a Wednesday. This was most unusual, since fights almost always took place on a Tuesday, but neither man wanted to wait longer than was absolutely necessary.

Accordingly, at noon the next day, all those who could make it turned up at North Woolwich jetty, from where the Thames steamer *Waterman No. 1* took them through the fog to Long Reach, scene of Tom's victory over Dan Collins, and a favourite spot for prize fights. Commissary General Tom Oliver, assisted by his son Fred, formed the inner and outer rings, where spectators could pay for a better view of the action, and Ned Adams, who had been in Tom's corner against Jack Grant, was appointed inspector of the ring keepers. They numbered seventeen in all, including Con Parker, whom Tom had fought at the Copenhagen Grounds some years previously, and Bendigo, whose interest in the prize ring had not ended with his retirement.

In Tom's corner were Alec Keene and an unidentified 'friend', while Jack was assisted by Tom Paddock and Jerry Noon. For once, the Brighton man faced a smaller opponent, but the fight proved to be his toughest yet. The length of time a contest lasted was not always an indication of its severity, and although Tom won convincingly in little more than a third of the time he had taken to dispose of Jack Grant, he was pushed considerably harder. His cut and battered face told the tale, but at the finish Martin was senseless for five minutes.

Some of the spectators decided against the boat ride back to Woolwich, choosing instead to walk across the marshes and take the North Kent Railway from nearby Dartford. Their enterprise earned an unexpected reward at the station, where the irrepressible Bendigo entertained them with impromptu verses on the day's events, and in praise of himself.

Just six weeks later, Tom finally married Sarah Henderson. They had been living as man and wife for six years, but only now that she had reached twenty-one was Sarah free to wed without the permission of her father. The wedding, a quiet affair conducted by curate John Parr at St Peter's Church, Islington, took place on March 8th, 1853, Tom's sister Eliza being one of the witnesses. Poor illiterate Tom simply made his mark, a cross, but Sarah's name is entered in the same handwriting as the rest of the document.

Both partners were required to be resident in the parish, and Sarah accordingly gave her address as 21 St John Street (now Cruden Street: today's St John Street was not then in Islington), while Tom offered number twenty-four. Since they were definitely still resident in Bayham Street, there was presumably an element of subterfuge in this. Why they did not marry in their parish of residence is now impossible to say.

With two children and a wife, Tom was at last a true family man, and marked the transformation by doing as almost all prize fighters did sooner or later and taking the tenancy of a pub, the aptly-named Bricklayer's Arms in York Street (now Greenland Street). And here his troubles really began. For a start, his lack of business acumen was cruelly exposed in his new venture, and to make things worse there was James Aldridge. A cab driver to trade, Aldridge was a regular at the Bricklayer's Arms, and became a frequent visitor to the Sayers home. And there he caught Sarah's eye.[13]

For the time being, however, things were going well for the young fighter. His record was flawless, and the only problem he seemed likely to face was that of finding opponents good enough to risk themselves against him.

Bigger men might have tested him, but it was generally accepted that boxers fight others of their own size, and Tom's size was unfortunate. Despite the absence of formal weight divisions, a distinction was made between lightweights and heavyweights, leaving men of around eleven stone in a somewhat awkward position – too big for the lightweights, who were under ten stone, and too small for the heavyweights, who were over twelve stone. It was always hard for those informally styled middleweights to get fights at all, but there was nonetheless a widely accepted middleweight champion in the shape of Nat Langham.

Like most pugilists, he had not had an easy life. The victim of a poverty-stricken childhood in Hinckley, Leicestershire, he had a speech impediment which had come upon him in a particularly unpleasant way. When he was still a boy – and undoubtedly a hungry one – a hot potato, forced into his mouth by a furious street vendor from whom he had tried to steal it, had caused permanent tissue damage.

The man Nat Langham most had to thank for his successful boxing career was Ben Caunt, who had spotted his talent early. Six years older than Tom, and markedly taller, he was thin and wiry, and only slightly the heavier. His normal tactic was to throw his favoured left hand, then go down before his opponent could reply. Bendigo had done it against Caunt; Langham did it against everyone.

The Leicestershire man was the only middleweight who now looked a possible match for Tom Sayers, and the mill, for £100 a side and eagerly awaited by the Fancy, came off at Lakenheath in Sussex on October 18th, 1853. On the other side of the Atlantic just six days earlier, John Morrissey had defeated Yankee Sullivan to claim the American championship.

Tom did not look in good condition, and indeed he wasn't: his training had not gone well, and he was suffering from a heavy cold. The ugly eruptions on his face and neck suggested that he might also have picked up a virus. It is unlikely that such problems would have been fatal to his prospects in any of his earlier fights, but this was different. Nat Langham was easily the best man Tom had met, and his seconds Alec Keene and Bob Fuller must have known it would be a hard battle.

The champion, assisted by Jemmy Welsh and Jerry Noon, used his normal tactic, and the constant visitations of his left jab on his opponent's face took due effect. Tom seemed the stronger on his legs, but his eyes were a different matter. It had happened to Jack Broughton when he had fought Jack Slack a hundred years before, it had happened to countless boxers in the interim, and it happened to Tom Sayers now. By round sixty-one the swelling around both eyes had completely blinded him, and his second, Alec Keene, threw up the sponge. Tom was devastated.

Although boxers normally had wealthy sponsors to put up the stake, their habit of betting on themselves meant that defeat usually hit their pockets, and it was normal to take a collection for the beaten man. That taken for Tom at Lakenheath realised the remarkable sum of £50, testimony to the spectators' admiration for the bottom he had shown in adverse circumstances.

As usual, however, the respectable newspapers found other things to write about. That same day, the Australian passenger ship *Dalhousie* had foundered off Beachy Head, leaving one survivor from over sixty on board, and two weeks previously, thirteen had died in a railway collision in Ireland. Coming on top of the loss a fortnight before that of the *Anna Jane* of Liverpool, wrecked in a gale off Barra with nearly four hundred drowned, an illegal contest between two hired fighting men was of little moment.

After all, the worst that had happened at Lakenheath was that Tom Sayers had lost a little pride. True, he had not made as much money as he had hoped, but his reputation was undamaged, and no one suggested that his career was in any danger. Indeed, he had benefited from the experience. Just as he had learned from Dan Collins not to be profligate with his right hand, so he learned from Nat Langham the art of tactical falling, and that a flagging man might still prevail by closing his opponent's eyes. These were lessons he was to turn to good effect later in his career; for now, he had to get on with his life and keep bread on the table.

––––––––––

Leaving the management of the Bricklayer's Arms in the hands of brother Jack, he went into partnership with Alec Keene, who had obtained a contract for two boxers to coach officers at London's Knightsbridge barracks. This went well enough until Tom, tired of being used as a punchbag, flattened one large and bullying officer. The two pugilists were sacked.

Tom was desperate to fight Nat Langham again, but Nat had too much sense. His win against Tom Sayers had been the best of his career, and with it he had confirmed his status as middleweight champion. Having previously kept a tavern in Cambridge, he now moved to London, where he became landlord of the Cambrian Stores near Leicester Square. Outside hung a lantern which proclaimed him 'CHAMPION OF THE MIDDLE WEIGHTS'.

When it became clear beyond doubt that Langham had no intention of fighting again, Tom Sayers was left as middleweight champion by default, but such dubious status did not satisfy him. He challenged the experienced Harry Orme, who had seconded Jack Grant against him, but Orme, who did not like the Brighton boy, gave his reaction in *Bell's Life*: 'I have given up, but if Sayers wants a fight, my haddock smoker will fight him if Sayers will stake £50 to £25'.

The insult could hardly have been lost on Tom, but his tavern was not doing well, and he was prepared to swallow it: with a high-maintenance wife and two children to support, even £25 was a lot of money. The so-called haddock smoker was George Sims, who, like Nat Langham, was taller than Tom but not much heavier. He had no form in the ring, but was, to quote Henry Downes Miles, a 'supposed professor of boxing'. Whether or not he was also a haddock smoker is uncertain.

The mill came off on February 28th, 1854, ten days after a colliery explosion at Wigan had killed eighty-nine.

On the day of the fight, Queen Victoria wrote to her uncle, King Leopold of Belgium, a letter in which she described the scene she had witnessed from the balcony of Buckingham Palace early that morning: 'an immense crowd collected to see these fine men, and cheering them immensely as they with difficulty marched along... It was a touching and beautiful sight...' The men were the Scots Guards, and they were on their way to the Crimea.

The whole country was suffering badly from war fever, but another conflict entirely was on the minds of those who gathered at mid-morning twenty miles away at Long Reach on the Thames, a happy hunting ground for Tom Sayers since his victories there over Dan Collins in 1851 and Jack Martin in 1853. He and George Sims entered the ring at half past eleven, with Tom firm favourite. In fact, despite his defeat against Nat Langham, most of the Fancy regarded it as a sure thing. They were right: in five minutes, Sims was unconscious.

Tom was an exceptionally hard hitter, and the decisive blow was devastating. A doctor was in attendance to staunch the blood pumping from the resulting cut above the left eye as the 'supposed professor' lay inert. Tom himself was one of those seriously concerned that he might have killed his man. But Sims came round a few minutes later, and, his memory of the contest sadly unimpaired, expressed, as Miles put it, 'a strong wish to be thrown into the river'.

At least he did not take to the water with the steamship *City of Glasgow*, which left Liverpool for Philadelphia the following day. Neither she nor the four hundred and eighty people on board were ever seen again. It was altogether a bad winter for shipping. In the month of January alone, Lloyd's of London had recorded three hundred wrecks, with the loss of seven hundred lives.

Such things may have meant more to Tom Sayers than to most, since his days on Brighton beach must have given him a healthy respect for the power of the sea, but he had other things to think about. With the Bricklayer's Arms losing money under Jack's management, he could not afford to be idle, and he now went off on tour, taking part in exhibition bouts. This was the accepted means for a boxer to maintain some income between fights, but it left Sarah alone with the children, and free to indulge her liking for James Aldridge.

It seems that Jack Sayers, having discovered what was going on, threw Aldridge out of the house and informed his brother. Tom returned to have it out with Sarah, who told him defiantly that she would do as she pleased. The marriage – which had probably been under strain anyway – was now effectively over, but Tom was determined to keep up a pretence for the sake of the children. Sarah, old enough at four to understand something at least of what was happening, was sent away to school, while a nursemaid was hired for the infant Tom.

Their father went on with his tour of the provinces, but his difficulties went beyond his marriage. His reputation was now such that no one of his own size cared to take him on, and he was simply unable to find an opponent. In despair, he sold the Bricklayer's Arms, and seriously considered emigrating to Australia, where his chances might have been better, but he finally elected to remain in England and try his luck against bigger men. Accordingly, he issued a challenge to one of the leading heavyweights, Tom Paddock, offering to stake £200 against £100. But it was not to be: his friends were horrified at such temerity – none believed that he would have any chance against so much bigger a man – and he had to withdraw the offer for lack of a sponsor.

When one of his most significant supporters, Captain Webster of the 79th Highlanders, had to go to the Crimea, Tom's prospects in England looked bleak. In fact, he was not to enter the ring even once while the fighting with Russia was on. The Light Brigade charged, the thin red line stood firm, Florence Nightingale wielded her lamp, but Tom Sayers struck not one blow in anger.

Not until Sebastopol had fallen in September 1855 did his luck look up. Unwilling to see such a man leave the country, Nat Langham managed to persuade wealthy Corinthian Sir Edward Kent to back him. The consequence was that a match was finally arranged with Nottingham's Harry Paulson. That the stakes were only £50 a side and Paulson was a heavyweight hardly mattered. Tom said he would have fought an elephant for fifty quid.

Again the fight coincided with a dark mystery of the ocean. When it came off, a search was underway in the north Atlantic for the steamship *Pacific,* which, with nearly two hundred passengers and crew, had sailed from Liverpool for New York five weeks previously. Like the *City of Glasgow* a couple of years before, she was never seen again. And just to underline the dangers of the ocean, HM steam-sloop *Polyphemus* was, on the very day of the fight, wrecked off Jutland, with the loss of fourteen crew.

And while there was fog in the North Sea that day – January 29th, 1856 – there was frost in London. The necessity of roughing horses' hooves to give grip on the ice on an unexpectedly cold morning caused many people to miss the train hired to take them to Appledore in Kent. Tom himself barely made it to the station.

When the men were stripped, his condition did not inspire confidence. In the words of *Bell's Life*, 'he was as fat as a pig, and altogether out of health'. This was most unusual in a man who, unlike most pugilists, actually enjoyed training, but marital difficulties coming on top of a long period of enforced idleness may have made it hard for him to focus on his task.

Whatever the cause, Tom seems to have been unconcerned. He made merry till midnight the night before the fight, saying that he was waiting for his fighting boots to arrive. His airy confidence was not widely shared. Few gave him a serious chance against Paulson, who, seven years Tom's senior, was a top-ranking heavyweight. For a man who stood only five feet seven, he was remarkably powerfully built, weighing one hundred and seventy pounds. He looked indestructible, and hardly anyone thought that he could be beaten by a man twenty pounds lighter.

Tom, however, had other ideas. Whatever the inadequacy of his training, he gave no sign of concern as he faced up to his formidable antagonist that icy morning. His self-belief was justified. Putting to good use the lesson taught him by one of his seconds, Nat Langham – another great faller, Bendigo, was in Paulson's corner – he stayed out of trouble by going down whenever danger threatened. After three hours and eight minutes, his right hand, the auctioneer, made firm contact with Harry Paulson's jaw, and the fight was over. He took some criticism for the falling tactic, but it was the only way for a half-trained middleweight – even one with the remarkable bottom of Tom Sayers – to hope to succeed against such a heavyweight as Harry Paulson.

All of Tom's fights so far – even the one defeat by Nat Langham – had enhanced his reputation. But now he had moved into a different league altogether. In thrashing one of the top heavyweights of the day, he had himself become a heavyweight in all but the literal sense. No middleweight wanted to have anything to do with him: he was just too dangerous. And his new standing created an interesting possibility.

In 1855, some wealthy members of the Fancy had come up with the notion of a new championship belt. It would not be the first trophy of its kind, but it was to be intrinsically more valuable than any earlier belt had been, and was to be contested according to strict rules. Was it possible that a middleweight could challenge the heavyweights for its possession?

At the time, however, Tom Sayers had other things on his mind. The sporting press, though well aware of his marital problems, never wrote about them. Henry Downes Miles, however, was prepared at least to acknowledge their existence. 'We are aware', he wrote, 'that since the present match [with Paulson] has been made, many things have occurred to harass Tom's mind, and that he had difficulties to contend with which, we trust, will not exist in future matches.' But the difficulties predated the arranging of the Paulson fight, and, despite Miles's wish, were not to end with it.

But for Kent's backing he might have left the country, and emigration was still a possibility. It did not help that, quite apart from his domestic difficulties, Tom was, at the time of the Appledore mill, in the midst of a harrowing professional experience. Just six weeks after his victory, he stood accused as an accessory to manslaughter.

On Tuesday, December 11th at Long Reach, he had seconded Mike Madden against John Jones. The latter had seemed to be well on top when he fell heavily and was knocked out. He had in fact suffered a serious head injury, and died during the night. Following an inquest, Madden was indicted for manslaughter, with both sets of seconds as accessories. The acquittal of all defendants was predictable – it was in the nature of the offence that witnesses were unlikely to be helpful to the prosecution – but the experience can only have been wounding for all involved.

Still, not all of Tom's luck was bad. He had always found friends when he really needed them, and he found another now. His co-workers had put up the £5 that got his career started, Mr Viddler had stood by him even when the Collyer fight fell through, John Garrett had backed him against Jack Grant, Jack Atcheler and Alec Keene had come forward at the right moment, Nat Langham had persuaded Sir Edward Kent to sponsor him against Harry Paulson.

The man who kept his career on the rails this time, and finally persuaded him against emigrating, was John Gideon. Businessman, sportsman and entrepreneur, Gideon had lost money backing Harry Paulson, but saw in Paulson's conqueror a way of recouping his loss and more. He had all the sophistication that the Brighton boy, five years his junior, lacked, and he would be the most significant sponsor Tom Sayers would ever know.

Gideon it was who matched him against his next opponent, Aaron Jones of Shropshire. Comparable in standing to Paulson, Jones was five years younger than Tom, and much bigger. The stakes were a healthy £100 a side, and whatever doubts his friends might have had about his meeting with Paulson, this time no one thought Tom Sayers would be out of his depth.

But the need for secrecy ensured that fight arrangements were never straightforward. Fearing he might have given too much away in handbills advertising a special excursion from King's Cross, Gideon, the night before the fight, changed the departure point to Fenchurch Street. Inevitably, many prospective fight-goers went to the wrong station.

Even so, everyone turned up whose presence was essential, and the mill took place on Canvey Island in the Thames estuary on January 6th, 1857. It was a savage day, with sleet and snow, driven by a biting wind, making the event almost as much of a trial for the spectators as for the principals. After three hours, with no decision in sight, the referee called a draw.

Not surprisingly, there was fury among those who had missed the fight through ignorance of the last-minute change of departure point, and *Bell's Life* was inundated with letters of complaint. There was also bitterness on the part of Aaron Jones, who felt that John Gideon had behaved churlishly in refusing him some of the tea and brandy with which he had kept his own man going in the dreadful conditions. Gideon's response was hard to fault. He explained that he was a businessman, that his money was on Sayers, and he was under no obligation to make up for the oversights of Jones's corner.

The rematch came off at the same place a little over a month later, on February 10th, and Aaron Jones discovered, as Dan Collins had six years previously, that Tom made no mistakes the second time. The smaller man won, almost unscathed, in eighty-five rounds.

The way was now prepared for a challenge for the belt itself, and on March 3rd, 1857 articles of agreement were drawn up at Nat Langham's Cambrian Stores for a match between Tom Sayers and the redoubtable Bill Perry of Birmingham, the Tipton Slasher. No one was quite sure at the time who England's heavyweight champion was, but Perry was widely regarded as the most credible. The stakes were £200 a side, and the new championship belt.

By his own account, Perry was now thirty-eight years of age, but he was probably forty or more. He had not fought for years – back in 1850 he had shown no interest in answering the transatlantic challenge of Tom Hyer – but he was tempted out of retirement by the chance of winning the new trophy. Considering that he was over six feet tall and weighed around two hundred pounds, it is scarcely surprising that he was confident that he would beat a man the size of Tom Sayers. He staked all he had on the fight, even his inn.

His confidence was widely shared, for despite Tom's successes against Paulson and Jones, most thought that this time he really was taking on too much. The Tipton Slasher – called for short the Tipton rather than the Slasher, much as the Artful Dodger was known as the Artful – was firm favourite.

The match attracted more attention than any since the third Caunt–Bendigo clash of 1845, but still the prize ring was a minority interest, and the attention of the newspapers was on other matters entirely. By the day of the fight in June 1857, twenty-one-year-old Madeleine Smith, in a sensational trial in Edinburgh, stood accused of the murder by poison of her lover Emile L'Angelier; and four thousand miles away in hellish heat, five hundred British men, women and children were surrounded by a vastly more powerful enemy at Cawnpore on the Ganges.

There was little that England's police and magistrates could do about the Indian Mutiny, but it was their responsibility to prevent breaches of the peace at home. Accordingly, as the day of the contest drew near, Sayers had to adopt disguises and move from county to county, covering his tracks. As for Perry, when he travelled from Fenchurch Street to Southend on the appointed day of June 16th, 1857, he was so heavily disguised that his own friends failed to recognise him.

Even so, the two fighters and their supporters got to Southend successfully – and then their troubles began. They had to board the waiting steamer in a roaring gale, and it was over an hour before Tom Oliver, with the ropes and stakes, was safely on board. A small flotilla accompanied them to the designated scene of the action, across water so rough that, in the words of Henry Downes Miles, 'many offered their contributions to Neptune in the most liberal manner.' Even when they disembarked, their troubles were not over, for just when all was in readiness, a substantial number of police appeared. There was a rush back to the boats, many boarding the wrong vessel in the confusion.

Some miles further on, they put ashore and tried again, and on the Isle of Grain at half past four in the afternoon the two men entered the ring. Such was Perry's advantage in size that many in the crowd of three thousand must have been convinced this was a mismatch. The only thing that spoiled the Tipton's appearance was his legs which, due to the rickets which he had suffered in childhood, formed a letter K. It had never bothered him before.

His opponent's stature was of no concern to Tom Sayers. He used the same hit-and-fall tactics which he had adopted against Harry Paulson a year and a half previously, and with the same result. Perry, abandoning his pre-match plan to let Sayers come to him, pursued him in rage, hitting out wildly and to little effect. It was over in ten one-sided rounds occupying an hour and a quarter. Tom Sayers, just over five feet eight inches tall and little more than a hundred and fifty pounds in weight, was the heavyweight champion of Great Britain.

It was an astonishing achievement, but scarcely noticed in the respectable newspapers, which would soon have much more serious matters to report. Within a month, Madeleine Smith would walk free from court in Edinburgh, the case against her found not proven; and in Cawnpore, all but seven of the five hundred Britons would be dead, the massacre of the women in particular being one of the most horrible incidents of the Mutiny.

Things were going on even under the sea, for the summer of 1857 saw the first gallant but unsuccessful attempt to lay a telegraph cable under the Atlantic. There was even, for those who took an interest in such things, a new scheme for a tunnel under the Straits of Dover. Following in the footsteps of Albert Mathieu, who had first proposed such an undertaking in 1802, French engineer Thomé de Gamond went so far as to make a number of hazardous dives to check the suitability of the sea bed. It just didn't quite happen.

But for Tom Sayers, things were looking up. Whatever the heartache caused by family relations, at least he was now comfortably off. With John Gideon to advise him, he was unlikely to squander his money, and his future was assured. Even so, at the age of thirty-two he was still in excellent condition, and there was every reason to suppose that he had years ahead of him in the prize ring.

This was of great significance, for the belt was to become the permanent property of the man who could defend it successfully against all comers for three years. With no one in sight who might reasonably hope to defeat him, Tom Sayers could look forward to a very comfortable retirement from June 1860 if he could only remain focused till then. In the meantime, he could make more money off anyone so foolhardy as to take him on.

His first challenger was Tom Paddock of Redditch, against whom, three years previously, no one had been prepared to back him. Two years older than Tom, two inches taller and nearly twenty pounds heavier, Paddock, who had come out on top in two of three bitter battles with Harry Paulson, looked a formidable antagonist. Tom was happy to accept the challenge, but then Paddock contracted rheumatic fever, and, far from being able to fight, looked as if he might even die. The challenge came to nothing.

Tom did not have to worry. He could afford to be easy-going about things now, and to take pleasure in life outside the prize ring. Thus it was that, on Friday, September 18th, three months after he had defeated the Tipton Slasher, he went to the races at Doncaster. While British soldiers four thousand miles away fought ferociously to retake Delhi from the mutineers, Tom Sayers was in for a livelier day than he had expected in Yorkshire.

The trouble started when Mr W. I'Anson's *Blink Bonny* cantered to victory in one of the day's events. The same horse had disappointed backers shortly before in the St Leger, and her impressive win persuaded many that she had been pulled in the big race. Things began to look nasty for Mr I'Anson and for jockey Jack Charlton, and they were lucky that Tom Sayers, in company with fellow-pugilist Jem Ward, stepped in. In the words of *The Times*, 'Tom Sayers, the "Champion of England" deserves special praise for the promptitude with which he went to the rescue of Charlton and Mr I'Anson and for the effectual efforts which he made to protect them from ill-usage.'

As a prize fighter, Tom Sayers may have been of dubious repute, but he could be a hero when he chose. In recognition of his conduct, Mr I'Anson and others came together to present him with a silver tea service engraved with his initials. Things were going well for the new champion.

His next foray into the prize ring was to be perhaps the strangest of his career. Bill Perry's predecessor as champion had been Harry Broome, now retired from the ring but, like all former pugilists, still a part of it. There was considerable interest in the latter part of 1857 when, for £200 a side, he issued a challenge to Tom Sayers on behalf of an Unknown. Great was the speculation as to the identity of the mystery man, the names of Bendigo, Ben Caunt and Nat Langham all being suggested. But whatever the surprise occasioned by the initial challenge, it was as nothing to the general amazement when the name of the Unknown was revealed.

Bill Benjamin (whose real name was Bainge) was unknown in more ways than one, for nobody had ever heard of him. He was a novice with no form at all, and although he was the same size as Tom Paddock and Aaron Jones, and some years younger than the champion, no one gave him a prayer. Except for one thing. Nobody really trusted Harry Broome, and many suspected a cross, or fix. Tom Sayers, they feared, might have been bribed to lose. They were to be comprehensively disabused.

The fight came off on the fifth day of January 1858. By this time, Delhi had long been retaken, and the Mutiny still raging in India – with British troops taking horrific and often indiscriminate reprisals for such atrocities as the Cawnpore massacre – was losing its grip on the public imagination. Still more distant from the thoughts of the Fancy was the fighting in China, where the British and French had decided to improve on the trading concessions won in the First Opium War of the early 1840s. Sayers and Benjamin met on the very day that Lord Elgin's completion of the capture of Canton made clear that European military supremacy was beyond challenge.

On a piercingly cold day on the Isle of Grain, those prepared to ignore suspicions and bet on the champion had to take odds of five to two. Their money was safe. Benjamin looked all right until Sayers hit him just once, at which point he folded.

It was George Sims all over again. In his despair, Miles tells us, Benjamin 'could not use his legs and his arms flew about like the sails of a windmill.' Jemmy Massey, who assisted Harry Broome in Benjamin's corner, showed his contempt quite openly. Three farcical rounds took less than seven minutes. It was the easiest £200 Tom Sayers had ever earned, and he had no doubt wagered heavily on himself to augment his winnings.

By this time Tom Paddock, having recovered from his near-fatal bout of rheumatic fever, had issued another challenge. Just ten days after the fiasco on the Isle of Grain, articles of agreement for Sayers–Paddock were signed for £150 a side. In fact, the champion was not obliged to defend the belt for less than £200, but Paddock could afford no more, and Tom was prepared to be generous.

Paddock's main backer had been Alec Keene, but when the notoriously hot-tempered Paddock fell out with him, the consequences were grave. Keene went to stakeholder Frank Dowling, who had succeeded his late father Vincent as editor of *Bell's Life*, and demanded the return of his deposit. This was a serious blow for Paddock, who desperately needed the money, and he was very lucky that Lord Drumlanrig, heir of the Marquess of Queensberry, stepped in to take Keene's place.

The mill came off – but only because the crushers narrowly failed to arrest the two pugilists – at Canvey Island on the eve of the first anniversary of the Perry fight. With Paddock on the receiving end from the first, the outcome was never in much doubt, and what many spectators most remembered later was not the fight itself but the moment when, twenty minutes in and to general astonishment, Alec Keene turned up.

He forced his way through the crowd to Paddock's corner, determined, in spite of everything, to do all he could for his former protégé. Paddock, greatly moved by his generosity, shook his hand warmly, and Keene gave him what help he could for the rest of the fight. It was to no avail. Paddock was not the man he had been, and was beaten in twenty-one rounds which took an hour and twenty minutes.

The fight took place at the height of the Great Stink, when, in unusually hot weather, the use of the Thames as a sewer led to a stench so dreadful that everyone stayed away from the river if they possibly could. The fight-goers were lucky that the smell was much less offensive out of town.

In conditions perfect for the spread of cholera, it was ironic that Dr John Snow, the man most responsible for the eventual defeat of the killer, was lying on his deathbed at the age of forty-five. He would die the following day, the day on which, four thousand miles away in Illinois, Abraham Lincoln, identifying slavery as the issue which would decide the fate of the Union, would warn America that 'A house divided against itself cannot stand.'

And no one, it seemed, could stand against Tom Sayers. But if Keene's arrival on Canvey Island had caused amazement, the next development was greeted with disbelief. Harry Broome challenged yet again on behalf of Bill Benjamin. The latter used every excuse in the book – and a few of his own invention – to explain his miserable showing in the earlier fight, but the truth was that he simply wanted a chance to redeem himself. No one could believe that he had found a sponsor, until it was revealed that he had persuaded his own father to back him for another £200. Again some feared a cross, but most knew now that Tom Sayers was incapable of such a thing.

Like everyone else, the champion simply could not take Benjamin's second challenge seriously. In December 1858 he took a holiday in St Helier, Jersey, where his old friend and first boxing coach Harry Phelps now kept a boarding house. A Mr Brown, who was there at the same time, recounted in a letter an incident which took place during Tom's stay on the island.

One evening a party including Brown and a Captain Smith got into an altercation with a group of drunken sailors. The sailors had numbers on their side, and things were looking bad for Brown's group when Captain Smith stepped forward. Superior force notwithstanding, the sailors took a beating, and it was only after the Captain had left the island that Mr Brown was told that he was in fact England's champion, travelling incognito. Like William I'Anson, Mr Brown discovered that Tom Sayers was a good man to have on your side in a tight spot.

When he returned from Jersey shortly before the new year, Tom found that he had a great deal more on his plate than just a second meeting with Bill Benjamin.

First he had to consider the challenge of Bob Brettle, a Scottish fighter long resident in Birmingham. It was a move which surprised everyone, since no one had thought that a smaller man would dare take on a champion who had proved too much even for the heavyweights. Brettle, however, had an excellent record, and had done well against Tom in gloved sparring. The champion accepted the challenge, but insisted on putting up £400 to Brettle's £200. This meant that the belt would not be at stake, since it could only be contested for even money. The fight was arranged for September.

And just a few weeks later, a further challenge came in when a gentleman visited *Bell's Life* to lay a first deposit of £10 on behalf of another Unknown. The champion, it seemed, was in for a busy time in 1859.

Nevertheless, he began the year in relaxed manner, going to stay at the Plough Inn, Rottingdean near Brighton, where he took to riding with the Brighton Harriers. With a match coming up, it was not a clever thing to do, for Tom was no more a horseman than Benjamin had been a boxer, and he was lucky to suffer no serious injuries from the many tumbles he took. His reckless behaviour, however, may have been attributable at least in part to two heavy blows which had hit him almost simultaneously.

First he heard that Sarah was now pregnant by James Aldridge, and then his mother, having suffered from cancer of the womb for the past year, died on February 16th. It cannot have been a happy time for England's champion.

After the funeral, he travelled the country giving sparring exhibitions and receiving the acclaim of the Fancy. This was profitable, and must have been a welcome distraction from his troubles, but with the Benjamin fight fixed for early April he might have been wiser to have been in training. And even when he did belatedly begin his preparations, a further call was made on his attention.

It came in the form of yet another challenge, but a rather more intriguing one. In March, Frank Dowling received a letter from George Wilkes, editor of *Porter's Spirit of the Times*, challenging the British champion on behalf of his American counterpart John Camel Heenan.

CHAPTER 8

THE CHALLENGER

IN THE United States in the 1850s, the lot of the American Indians was scarcely a matter of controversy: everybody, even those among the invaders who defended them, knew they had to go. The lot of the slaves of the South was another matter entirely. Two million at the time of Jack Heenan's birth, they numbered over three million by 1850: far from diminishing, the problem was growing.

As the nation pushed westward, it became ever more intractable. The South always wanted slavery in states newly admitted to the Union, if only to strengthen their own position against those who would deprive them of the labour needed for the plantations. But the abolitionists were implacable. The great bone of contention was the territory which came to be known as Bleeding Kansas: would it enter the Union slave or free?

In the Senate in May 1856, Congressman Preston Brooks savagely beat Senator Charles Sumner of Massachusetts in retaliation for the latter's uncompromising speech holding pro-slavery Southerners responsible for violence in Kansas Territory. Days later, John Brown was inspired to lead an assault on the settlement at Pottawatomie Creek. His group dragged five pro-slavery men from their homes and hacked them to death.

———————

Yankee Sullivan would survive Brown's victims by only a week.

He had not stayed long in the East after his defeat by John Morrissey in October 1853. By the end of the year, he was in California, where his presence had a galvanising effect on pugilism.

Certainly it helped Jack Heenan, who, by participating in a sparring exhibition organised by Sullivan, was able to augment the reputation he had made with his victories over Sam Banta and the 'powerful desperado' named Gallagher. Guided by Jim Cusick, he was anxious to go still further by pitting himself against Sullivan in a real contest, but it came to nothing.

And anyway, time was running out for Yankee Sullivan. California was a lawless place in the 1850s, and in both 1851 and 1856 committees of vigilance were set up in San Francisco to clean up the town. Sullivan, whose presence was never good for law and order, fell foul of the 1856 committee and was jailed. Under the threat of deportation or even hanging, he was found dead in his cell one day, his wrists slit. Whether it was suicide or murder has never been established. Exactly one week had passed since the slaughter at Pottawatomie Creek.

Sullivan's removal from the scene had a devastating effect on the Californian prize ring, partly because there was no one to take his place, and partly because all prize fighters, fearing the same fate, now found it expedient to lie low. Seeing how things stood, and knowing that if Jack Heenan was ever to enter the big time he would have to go back east anyway, Jim Cusick took his young protégé to New York. In autumn 1857, not long after the British recapture of Delhi on the other side of the world, John Camel Heenan arrived in the city which would become his home.

It was a bad time for New York, still harder hit than most of the country by the panic consequent on the failure in August of its branch of the Ohio Life Insurance and Trust Company. And an already dire situation had been exacerbated the following month when some two million dollars' worth of gold had accompanied more than four hundred passengers to the bottom of the Atlantic in the sinking of the SS *Central America*.

But the young boxer came to the big city anyway, and his reputation was there before him. Left to his own devices, he might have done almost anything, but Jim Cusick was taking good care of him. His much-anticipated first appearance in the New York ring was to be in an exhibition bout which might whet the appetite of fight fans without entailing the danger of a damaging reverse.

On the evening of Thursday, December 10th, 1857, the Benicia Boy – which is what everyone was now calling him – entered the ring at the

Born into poverty in Brighton in 1826, Tom Sayers became the greatest prize fighter of his day. A small man, he defeated all the best heavyweights in England. And then John Camel Heenan challenged him from across the Atlantic. (*Getty Images*)

John Camel Heenan, the Benicia Boy, was beaten by John Morrissey in his first formal fight, but became US champion by default on Morrissey's retirement. Unable to find a suitable opponent in America, he caused a sensation by challenging Tom Sayers. (*Getty Images*)

JAMES FIGG,

(Prize Fighter.)

In the early eighteenth century, all-round martial arts expert James Figg was England's first boxing champion. He was also a promoter, and the shows which he staged in London's Tottenham Court Road were patronised by the highest in the land. (*Mary Evans Picture Library*)

In the 1740s and 50s, Jack Broughton dominated boxing both as performer and as promoter. He drew up the sport's first rules and invented boxing gloves, which he called mufflers. Later generations would style him the Father of Boxing. (*Getty Images*)

Tom Cribb owed his victory over black American Tom Molineaux in December 1810 to sharp practice on the part of his corner. Never again did he come so close to losing a fight. He retired undefeated as champion in 1822. (*Getty Images*)

Bendigo was the nickname of William Thompson. An early southpaw and one of the great characters of the prize ring, he defeated much bigger men to become champion. The last of his three fights against Ben Caunt was considered a disgrace. (*Getty Images*)

Ben Caunt was not a cultured fighter, but his size and strength helped him become champion. Having lost two of his three notorious battles with Bendigo, he retired to become landlord of the Coach and Horses in London's St Martin's Lane. (*Getty Images*)

From a Painting by A. P. de Horace.

NAT LANGHAM.

CHAMPION OF THE MIDDLE WEIGHTS.
The Only Man who ever Beat TOM SAYERS.

Born at Hinckley, Leicestershire, February 18th, 1820.   Died, 1st September, 1871.

Height, 5 feet 10 inches.   Weight 11 Stone.

Discovered by fellow-midlander Ben Caunt, Nat Langham became middleweight champion, and was the only man ever to beat Tom Sayers. By the time Sayers fought Heenan, he was landlord of the Cambrian Stores off London's Leicester Square. (*Mary Evans Picture Library*)

At a time of great prejudice against the Irish Catholics pouring into the United States, Tom Hyer was the idol of the native-born Americans. Victory over Irishman Yankee Sullivan saw him enthroned as America's first champion. (*Getty Images*)

In 1858, John Morrissey and Jack Heenan, who had inherited their fathers' bitter enmity, fought for the American championship. Ill-health had disrupted Heenan's training, and he damaged a hand early in the fight. Morrissey emerged a somewhat lucky winner. (*Getty Images*)

Adah Menken's acting career was not harmed by the scandal caused by the revelation that her 1859 marriage to Jack Heenan was bigamous. She became notorious as the Naked Lady of Mazeppa, but her relationship with the Benicia Boy was short-lived. (*Getty Images*)

In Tom Sayers's corner when he fought Jack Heenan was Harry Brunton, his favourite second. Brunton's own ring career had been blighted by easily-damaged hands, but he went on to enjoy success as trainer and as publican. (*Getty Images*)

Sayers and Heenan meet for the first time at London Bridge Station. Moments later, they were on their way to Farnborough. Fearing arrest if he were recognised, Heenan is wearing a false beard, but Sayers thought disguise unnecessary. (*Getty Images*)

Heenan rushed away from the Ring.

The ring makers calmly gather up the ropes and stakes amidst the chaos which followed the fight, Heenan lashing out wildly in his fury at being, as he saw it, cheated of victory. Relations between the two camps remained sour for some weeks. (*Getty Images*)

Jack Heenan greets American illustrator Thomas Nast at his headquarters in Salisbury. The young cartoonist was one of many visitors to Salisbury after Heenan's whereabouts had been revealed. (*Getty Images*)

When the two men were reconciled, elaborate plans were made for them to tour the country. Sadly, there were empty seats at the first venue, London's Alhambra Palace, and a dismal tour of England was redeemed only by success in Ireland. (*Mary Evans Picture Library*)

Jem Mace was one of the pivotal figures in boxing history. His career was well under way before Tom Sayers retired, and he would become one of the great bare-knuckle champions, fighting on into the Queensberry era. (*Getty Images*)

In front of the tomb of Tom Sayers in Highgate Cemetery, north London, lies an effigy of his mastiff, Lion. At his master's funeral, Lion was given pride of place as the sole occupant of Tom's phaeton, which followed first after the hearse.

National Hall, 31 Canal Street near Broadway. His opponent was the highly-rated Joe Coburn, himself seen by many as a potential national champion. Expectations were high and the hall was full.

Jim Cusick himself took part in one of the supporting bouts before introducing his man to the expectant crowd. The *New York Clipper's* reporter was impressed with the newcomer, but recorded the general disappointment at the one thing that failed to materialise in the course of the evening: 'there was no intimation made of Mr Heenan's intentions of competing for the Championship of America, as was generally anticipated.' Here it was in black and white. The Benicia Boy had not yet had a single official contest, but already he was expected to challenge the champion himself. And the champion was already well known to him.

In many ways, John Morrissey was an unlikely title-holder. Both George Thompson and Yankee Sullivan had outclassed him, and no one would have given him a prayer against Tom Hyer, but still he wore the crown. He was the man to beat.

He was also incredibly violent. Frustrated by his continued failure, even after beating Yankee Sullivan in 1853, to goad Tom Hyer out of retirement, he managed to fall out with Hyer's friend Bill Poole. Poole, one of the men who had nearly beaten him to death on his visit to the Empire Club back in 1849, was a prominent member of the anti-Irish Native American Party, now popularly called the Know-Nothings because of their policy of answering queries as to the party's activities with a protestation of ignorance. Morrissey, by contrast, was closely identified with the Irish-dominated Tammany Hall, their bitter enemies.

In such circumstances, Morrissey was ill-advised to agree to meet Poole in a no-holds-barred fight at Amos Street dock on Poole's home ground. When, on the appointed day in July 1854, Poole turned up with a large retinue of thugs, Morrissey must have known he was in trouble. Within minutes, Poole had him down and the two men were struggling on the ground, with Morrissey underneath. The crowd surged forward, making it impossible for those further back to see what was going on, and it is not clear whether or not Poole's friends joined in. Whatever happened, after a few frantic minutes of bared teeth and flailing limbs, Morrissey had had enough. He was badly hurt, but his opponent bore only one injury worth noting: his cheek was scarred where Morrissey had bitten him.

The subsequent low-level gang warfare between their partisans reached its climax in February 1855, when a number of Morrissey's friends confronted Poole in a gaudy Broadway saloon known as Stanwix Hall. Among them were Jim Turner and Lew Baker, who had recently combined in a farcical attempt to murder Tom Hyer. After a heated exchange of words, Jim Turner drew his gun on Poole, but contrived to shoot himself in the arm. He did manage, perhaps accidentally, to shoot Poole in the leg as he fell, and in the ensuing mêlée, Baker was still more successful; Poole received a pistol ball in the chest.

Within two weeks, he was dead, and his reported last words, 'Goodbye boys, I die a true American', became a rallying cry for the Know-Nothings. His funeral was a huge event for lower Broadway, with many thousands of mourners and several brass bands. Attempts to hold John Morrissey to account for the murder – to prove at least that he was behind it – came to nothing: he remained at liberty, and he remained champion.

It was undoubtedly Jim Cusick who was responsible for the widespread expectation at the end of 1857 that Jack Heenan would challenge Morrissey, for it is by no means clear that the Benicia Boy himself was persuaded. Not only was no challenge issued on the night that he fought his exhibition bout with Joe Coburn, but none was forthcoming for some time thereafter.

One problem may have been that his performance against Coburn had not engendered sufficient confidence among those who might have considered backing him. The *Clipper*'s report of the bout had spoken well of him, but ten months later, on October 30th, the same source said that his showing had not matched expectations.

There was, however, no doubting the animosity between Morrissey and Heenan, and only police intervention prevented a brawl between them just ten days after the exhibition at the National Hall. No one doubted that they would meet in the ring before long.

Certainly, both men were adamant that they wanted to fight, but money was a contentious issue. Morrissey was not happy to settle for less than $5,000 a side, while Heenan could promise only $2,500. The wrangling went on, trying the patience of all those who were desperate to see the promised contest.

The *Clipper*, finger as ever on the pulse, had something of significance to report on May 15th, 1858. At 474 Broadway, the saloon-cum-brothel kept by John Allen (reputedly the wickedest man in New York), an overheated Morrissey supporter had offered a $25 deposit on a Heenan–Morrissey fight at $2,500 a side, and a Heenan acolyte had swiftly covered it. Allen himself had taken both deposits as stakeholder, and although neither of the two principals was personally involved, everyone expected them to go along with this arrangement.

As ever, and however little the Fancy might care, there were more important things going on in the world. Just three days before the unofficial transaction at John Allen's, a hundred Texas Rangers, together with a similar number of their Tonkawa allies, had killed scores of Comanches at the Battle of Little Robe Creek in today's Oklahoma. Reports of the action had nothing to say of the Tonkawa victory banquet that night, the menu for which included body parts of the slain enemy. The American Indians might stand in the way of the achievement of Manifest Destiny, but little was said publicly against those who would join the colonists in dealing with the more intractable of them.

Anyway, it was of no interest to the Fancy. All that they cared about was the Heenan–Morrissey showdown. But it just wouldn't happen. The two men taunted each other through the newspapers, but came to no agreement. The general opinion – that the Benicia Boy was not as keen on the fight as had been supposed – was not far off the mark.

New York politics in the mid-nineteenth century was murky in the extreme. Officials were expected to loot public funds, politicians were expected to buy election, and all parties made considerable use of 'shoulder-hitters', professional strong-arm men who could act as enforcers. Jack

Heenan, being one of the most effective, was rewarded with a sinecure in the New York Customs House. He was now well paid for doing very little, and the prospect of a prize fight, which would entail both a considerable period of uncharacteristic self-denial while in training and the risk of serious damage in the ring, lost its appeal for him.

But he found that there was a price to be paid for disappointing the expectations of the Fancy. The only reason that most could think of for the cooling of his enthusiasm was that his nerve had failed, and it was the stigma of cowardice which made him decide that he had better fight Morrissey after all. On July 19th, 1858 (a month after Tom Sayers had brushed aside the challenge of Tom Paddock), the match was made at the offices of the *Clipper*, Morrissey being prepared by this time to fight for half of the $5,000 he had originally demanded. The fight would come off in late October.

Public interest was intense. To the horror of Horace Greeley's *New-York Daily Tribune* and other high-minded publications, it eclipsed even the enthusiasm for the Sullivan–Hyer or Sullivan–Morrissey fights. By those not naturally committed to either side, it was generally seen in black and white: whatever his activities as shoulder-hitter, Heenan had generally behaved well in New York, and had become very popular; Morrissey, by contrast, had a well-earned reputation as a thug. Press and public made the Benicia Boy the hero, and his opponent the villain.

Both men quickly went into training – Morrissey at Lansingburg near Troy, and Heenan on Manhattan's Bloomingdale Road, to be swallowed up in time by Broadway. Morrissey's camp had chosen better: he was sufficiently isolated to ensure peace and quiet, while his opponent's preparations, only half an hour from New York City, were disturbed by a constant stream of visitors.

Training was a serious business, as was witnessed by *The New York Herald*'s reporter when he visited Morrissey. The boxer rose at five every day, and, under the supervision of Englishman Jack 'Shepherd' Hamilton, followed a strict diet and gruelling exercise régime. Food and drink included sherry, eggs, broiled chicken, unseasoned mutton, tea, toast, beefsteak and currant bread. Strictly no spices or seasoning. Three times daily, he went for long walks, covering extraordinary distances – up to an improbable-sounding forty miles a day at the beginning, reduced by half later on.

In the gym, aside from sparring, two of the favoured exercises were rowing and skipping. Equipment included weights and pulleys, dumb-bells and a punchbag. In the boxer's room there were blankets for sweating the body, even a mask for sweating the face. The régime included induced vomiting, and rubbing down several times a day 'until the flesh is in a glow'. At nine every evening he retired, ready to rise eight hours later and go through the same thing all over again.

In charge of Jack Heenan's training, which would have been very similar – the overall system never varied greatly – was another Englishman. It was Tom Sayers's old adversary, Aaron Jones, who had recently crossed the Atlantic in the hope of improving his career prospects.

That both men should look across the ocean for trainers was not especially surprising, for England, despite the dramatic decline in the popularity of the prize ring, remained its heartland. English boxers and trainers had been crossing the Atlantic for decades.

And it was now that two countries which had never really been far apart suddenly moved dramatically closer. As Heenan and Morrissey prepared for their showdown, Brunel's *Great Eastern*, a failure as a passenger vessel, successfully laid a cable under the Atlantic – a cable one hundred times the length and lying at one hundred times the depth of the one which had forged the telegraphic link between England and France less than seven years previously. On August 16th, Queen Victoria and President Buchanan exchanged greetings by telegraph.

There was tremendous enthusiasm on both sides of the Atlantic, but Jack Heenan had little to celebrate, for his training was not going nearly as well as Morrissey's. Apart from the unwise choice of headquarters, it cannot have helped that Jim Cusick – who, together with Joe Coburn, assisted Aaron Jones – resented not being in overall charge. Then there was the fact that Jones was drunk much of the time. But most serious of all, an old wound in Jack's ankle broke out again during training, and severely curtailed the work he could do. For a full week, he was confined indoors, leaving him no chance of reaching peak condition.

As the day drew near, both men had to be increasingly careful, since warrants were out for their arrest. Prize fighting might have become ever more popular in the United States, but the authorities were no less keen than before to put a stop to it. Heenan and Morrissey were both obliged on occasion to cross the border into Pennsylvania, where New York State's arrest warrants were not valid.

Fixing the venue of the fight took some time, but it was finally agreed that it would take place in Canada, where official interference was much less likely. Accordingly, as the day approached, fight fans began pouring into Buffalo, the western terminus of the Erie Canal. The fight would come off somewhere on Lake Erie's northern (Canadian) shore, with Buffalo, where the American Express Company had been established eight years before, as jumping-off point.

The respectable press decided they had no option but to report an event which excited so much public interest, but they felt no obligation to alter their opinions. The *New-York Daily Tribune* called the fight fans assembled in Buffalo 'the most vicious congregation of roughs that was ever witnessed in a Christian City.' *Frank Leslie's Illustrated Newspaper* said that 'a worse set of scapegallowses... could scarcely be collected; low, filthy, brutal, bludgeon bearing scoundrels'. Even *The New York Herald*, normally a friend of the prize ring, was in agreement: 'It would be difficult... to select a crowd in any part of the world whose features were more deeply seethed with every bad and foul passion that belongs to man.'

The roughs, the scapegallowses and the scoundrels were unconcerned. They had come to see the fight they had so long anticipated, and they had a lot of money riding on its outcome. It was estimated that in New York state alone, three quarters of a million dollars had been wagered. Interest in the fight was all-consuming.

———

The moon was bright and the weather fine on the night of Tuesday, October 19th, 1858 when Morrissey's boat, the *Galena*, set off from the foot of Michigan Street, followed by the *Kaloolah* and a flotilla of other vessels all carrying the champion's faction. Heenan's *Globe*, which set sail from the foot of Commercial Street, was accompanied by a rather smaller flotilla: for all the Benicia Boy's popularity with the wider public, his opponent had more friends in New York's prize ring. The fight-goers were all in possession of tickets marked 'Excursion' or 'Pic-nic'. The ring was fond of euphemism.

The boats had to cover some seventy miles across the placid waters of the great lake to anchor off Long Point, a thin spit of barren sand stretching out twenty-five miles almost due east from the Canadian shore, and pointing like a dagger at New York state. The American authorities could not intervene, and the chances of problems with the Canadians were minimal.

First to reach Long Point, at about four in the morning, was the *Galena*. Disembarkation began at eight, by which time *Kaloolah* and *Globe* had joined her some three quarters of a mile from the shore. It took three hours to land the passengers, who waded ashore, rowed, or even paid sailors to carry them.

So barren was the chosen spot that some stray tufts of grass had to be transplanted inside the ring in order to satisfy the requirement that the fighting area should be of turf. At twenty past one, Heenan threw his hat into the ring, and Morrissey followed suit. All was ready.

The crowd – scoundrels, roughs and scapegallowses – were to be kept in check by no fewer than fifty ring keepers, half of whom were appointed by each side. The organisers did not want a repeat of the sort of scenes which had marred Morrissey's fights with Thompson and Sullivan. Even so the crowd, if the December 1858 issue of *Harper's New Monthly Magazine* was to be trusted, made an intimidating spectacle:

> Round about is a bestial crowd
> Heavily-jawed and beetle-browed;
> Concave faces trampled in,
> As if with the iron hoof of Sin!
> Blasphemies dripping from off their lips,
> Pistols bulging behind their hips…

Among this appetising crowd, Morrissey supporters were much in the ascendancy, and their man's appearance gave them every cause for confidence. He might be conceding three inches in height and twenty pounds in weight, but he was trained to the highest pitch. He said he felt like a race horse.

And the sight of Jack Heenan could only have increased the confidence of the champion's supporters. The Benicia Boy's interrupted training had left him overweight and clearly not in peak condition. He limped across the sand to the ring, pained by the rubbing of his shoe against the still unhealed wound which had caused him so much trouble. Offers of $100 to $50 on Morrissey found few takers.

There were the usual formalities to observe. Colours were tied to one of the stakes – red, white and blue stripes for Heenan, who was the favourite of the Native American faction; blue with white spots for Morrissey. The seconds helped their men strip for action and lace up their spiked fighting boots.

All was in order, but the appointment of the referee who would arbitrate between Heenan's umpire and Morrissey's in the event of disagreement did not go so smoothly. Two hours were wasted before a compromise was reached with the naming of two referees. It was gone half past three when the two boxers came to the scratch in the middle of the ring to shake hands.

The fight was as fierce as everyone had expected. The champion came out fast for the first round, but Heenan countered well, drawing first blood. Five minutes later, he threw Morrissey to end the round. The *Clipper* was enthusiastic: 'Never before in this and perhaps in any other country was there witnessed such a terrific fight as the present. The hitting was tremendous...' Heenan had unquestionably had the better of round one, but he had missed Morrissey with a left hand and hit one of the unpadded stakes, damaging two knuckles. On top of his other problems, it was a handicap he could not afford.

Still, he had the better of the next round also, again ending it by throwing his man. But the one quality which John Morrissey possessed in abundance was bottom, and as the contest went on he seemed only to gather strength as Heenan weakened. By round eleven both men were severely battered, and had to be led up to scratch, but it was Heenan who was at the end of his tether. He swung wildly and missed, Morrissey replied with a powerful blow to the jugular, and it was over. Like the

Atlantic cable, which had failed in a few weeks, Jack Heenan had been unable to last the course. A year of anticipation had culminated in twenty-one minutes of boxing.

In New York, the telegraph and newspaper offices were under siege from crowds desperate for the earliest possible news. It was the same elsewhere. The day after the battle, the *Herald* carried a report from Albany: 'The greatest excitement exists here to know the result of the fight... Some five hundred 'gentlemen', mostly with short hair, broken noses and thick boots, are gathered round the telegraph office...'

And of course, once the outcome of the fight was known, it had to be discussed. On October 30th, *Harper's Weekly* told its readers – though they already knew it well enough – that 'On Thursday, especially, there was nothing heard of – up town, down town, and in the country – but the great prize-fight'. By this time, the prize ring had ceased to be a fringe interest, and had taken its place among the principal entertainments of the young nation. As *Harper's* put it, 'a report of a prize-fight will sell a newspaper more widely than the news of a Presidential election'.

The prize ring might have been in terminal decline in its country of origin, but it was in rude health in the new world.

Defeat rankled with the Benicia Boy. He had every reason to think he might have won had his training gone smoothly, and he was anxious for a rematch to prove his point. Morrissey, however, was not interested, and Heenan was left to recover from his drubbing and to brood. But it was not long before a welcome distraction came along.

On the evening of Christmas Day 1858, he was in Cincinnati, Ohio, giving a sparring exhibition at the New National Theater. The principal entertainment of the evening had been a stage adaptation of Sir Walter Scott's *Ivanhoe*, and he had been so taken by the actress who had played the part of the Jewess Rebecca that he visited her dressing room after his bout was over.

Her name was Adah Isaacs Menken, though she was probably born Ada C. McCord – or just possibly Ada Bertha Theodore, or Dolores

Adios Fuertes (or perhaps Fiertes). Like her real name, her parentage and her date and place of birth will never be known for certain, for Adah Isaacs Menken could not quite make up her own mind who she was, when or where she had been born, or to whom. For her father, she gave the world a choice of Josiah Campbell, Ricardo La Fiertes (or Fuertes), James McCord or Richard Spencer. To these possibilities, later researchers have added the name of August Theodore.

She was probably born in 1835, most likely in Memphis – though she preferred 1841 and New Orleans. Early in life – not long after she had been kidnapped by Indians and rescued by Texas Rangers, apparently – she took to the stage, but made no great impact till she reached her mid-twenties.

She was probably the Miss Adda [*sic*] Theodore who, in 1854, married W.H. Kneass, a musician from her touring company, and she certainly married Alexander Isaac Menken, another pit musician, on April 3rd, 1856. Whether this second marriage was legal, though, is open to doubt, since no record exists of a divorce from Kneass. (And if her father really was August Theodore, then even her marriage to Kneass was illegal, since Theodore was a free black man, and marriage between blacks and whites was not permitted.)

Alexander Menken came of a prominent Cincinnati Jewish family, and the couple moved there, almost certainly to heal family rifts and ensure that the family fortune was not entirely lost to him. There Ada added an 'h' to her own name, an 's' to her husband's middle name, and assumed Jewish identity. Her motive may have been to ingratiate herself with her in-laws, or perhaps to create her own identity, or perhaps both. There too, she began to write, having some success with newspaper articles and poetry.

Cincinnati was at the time the fourth largest American city and a significant centre of drama, but it was never big enough or important enough to contain an ego the size of Adah Menken's. By the summer of 1859 she was estranged from Alexander and living in New York. There, at the offices of the *New York Clipper*, she met Jack Heenan again.

Her stage career was not going well, and she had gone to seek comfort from two influential friends, *Clipper* editor Frank Queen, and reporter Ed James.[14] There was nothing unusual in this: sport and the theatre were closely linked in the public mind, and the *Clipper*, like *Porter's Spirit of the Times*, gave full reports of both. In Queen's office at the same time – for he, too, regarded the *Clipper* as an ally – was Jack Heenan.

Adah and Jack did not appear a likely match, for the two could hardly have had less in common. She was intelligent and even intellectual, fluent in several languages, temperamental, ambitious and artistic. He, though not stupid, had no interest in the arts, was easy-going, and took little care for the future. He was also about a foot taller than her.

It mattered not. Both were smitten, and before the summer was out it was public knowledge that they were living together. Jim Cusick never took to Menken, nor she to him, but it made no difference. No one came between Adah and her desires, and Jack Heenan was not the man to let the chance of an easy and agreeable life pass him by. Jack lived in the present, and his new lover was for the time being of much greater interest to him than the ongoing efforts of his manager to arrange his next fight.

But what Cusick had in mind was something special. When it became clear that Morrissey would not fight again, the Benicia Boy was widely accepted as American champion, much as Morrissey had been when Tom Hyer had retired. Cusick now wanted to pit his man against England's Tom Sayers in what would be effectively a world championship bout.

CHAPTER 9

JOHN BULL AND BROTHER JONATHAN

In the mid-1850s, Nathaniel Hawthorne was American consul in Liverpool, the main port for transatlantic crossings. His feelings towards his hosts were not always congenial: 'There is an account to be settled between us and them for the contemptuous jealousy with which (since it has ceased to be unmitigated contempt) they regard us ...' Perhaps Hawthorne – an aesthete, after all – was a little oversensitive.

And then again, perhaps he wasn't. The opinion entertained of Americans by his opposite number in Boston, Thomas Colley Grattan, is worth considering: 'They have no resemblance but to Englishmen, and their inferiority to these is undoubted ... They can bear no comparison with the stock from which they sprang ... The Anglo-Saxon deteriorates with transplantation.'

With such attitudes commonplace, it was small wonder that the coming contest between Tom Sayers and John Camel Heenan excited extraordinary interest on both sides of the Atlantic.

———

The nineteenth century belonged to Great Britain, with the result that Victoria's England was as widely loved as Bush's America – too rich, too powerful, too proud. And nowhere was resentment stronger than in the United States.

It was only natural. The States had been a British colony until the last quarter of the eighteenth century, and the War of Independence had left scars which were reopened within a generation. The War of 1812 had been the making of Andrew Jackson, whose triumph at New Orleans had helped forge the myth which all countries need to underpin their humdrum reality. It had also given the young nation an anthem, even if it was not yet official. Francis Scott Key's 'Star-Spangled Banner' (originally and more prosaically 'The Defence of Fort McHenry') celebrated the repulse of a British naval force at Baltimore in 1814. And when Key wrote 'Their blood has washed out their foul footsteps' pollution', he was writing of British blood and British footsteps.

The young America, personified as Brother Jonathan, was painfully conscious of being overshadowed by its former colonial master. It was not only that England was incomparably more powerful than America; it was the attitudes which accompanied this disparity. Everything about England was of intense interest to the United States, but very little about the United States was of any concern to England.

Nathaniel Willis, an American visitor to Britain in the 1830s, expressed it clearly in *Pencillings by the Way*, which appeared when Tom Sayers was a small child, and around the time Jack Heenan was born:

> America is far further off from England than England from America. You in New York read the periodicals of this country, and know everything that is done or written here, as if you heard it within the sound of Bow-bell [*sic*]. The English, however, just know of our existence; and if they get a general idea twice a year of our progress in politics, they are comparatively well informed.

All of the world's major powers were European, and events in Paris and Vienna and Moscow mattered far more to England than anything that happened on the other side of the Atlantic. For the most part, Brother Jonathan could be left to do as he pleased.

Americans were ambivalent about England. On the one hand, they wanted to be accepted as the equals of the old colonial power; on the other they wanted nothing to do with her. As Philip Freneau expressed it as far back as 1788: 'Can we never be thought / To have learning or grace / Unless it be brought/From that damnable place... ?'

Still, it was not all bad. Those English people who did show an interest in the United States were not uniformly negative. William Cobbett, for example, writing in 1828 of the country in which he had lived ten years earlier:

> The American labourers, like the tavern keepers, are never servile, but always civil. Neither *boobishness* nor *meanness* mark their character. They never *creep* and *fawn*, and are never rude... Full pocket or empty pocket, these American labourers are always *the same man*: no saucy cunning in the one case, and no base crawling in the other. This, too arises from the free institutions of government. A man has a voice *because he is a man*, and not because he is the *possessor of money*.

But Cobbett was not typical. In 1832, another English visitor really ruffled the eagle's feathers. Fanny Trollope's distaste for slavery was not a crime in all eyes, but in *Domestic Manners of the Americans* she had one big issue with the people of the United States: their domestic manners were appalling.

'I hardly know of any annoyance so deeply repugnant to English feelings,' wrote Mrs Trollope, 'as the incessant, remorseless spitting of Americans.' Nor, she thought, did they have any idea of table manners. As well as spitting at the table, they put their knives into their mouths when they ate, and cleaned their teeth with penknives. And they contrived to offend her ears almost as much as her eyes:

> I very seldom, during my whole stay in the country, heard a sentence elegantly turned, and correctly pronounced from the lips of an American. There is always something in the expression or the accent that jars the feelings and shocks the taste.

Had Mrs Trollope been alone in her opinions, Brother Jonathan might have been able to shrug them off, but she wasn't. There was Thomas Hamilton, for example, who published *Men and Manners in America* in 1833. Of a trip on an Ohio river steamboat, he wrote: 'In regard to the passengers, truth compels me to say that anything so disgusting in human shape I have never seen. Their morals and their manners are alike detestable.'

From the western side of the Atlantic, baiting the Americans seemed like one of those blood sports of which the English had always been so fond. Canadian author Thomas Chandler Haliburton, writing as Sam Slick, offered in 1840 his recipe for a successful book about America and the Americans. In *The Letter-Bag of the Great Western*, he recommended the inclusion of accounts of 'Lynching – spitting – gouging – steam-boats blown up – slavery… licentious manners of the South… ignorance of the fine arts – bank frauds – land frauds – stabbing with knives… ravenous eating – vulgar familiarity…'

But was there not more to life than polished manners dictated by an effete English upper class? Just as English visitors to America were horrified by vulgarity, so American visitors to England were horrified by poverty.

There was, for example, Mrs Fanny Hall, who, in *Rambles in Europe*, had the temerity to ask 'in what respect the condition of the Irish peasant is superior to that of our African slaves for whom the English profess so much sympathy'.

And when Massachusetts statesman and historian George Bancroft came to London twelve years later, he was horrified by the condition of society's outcasts. To William Cullen Bryant he wrote: 'The general poverty here is appalling… There is no hope for the poor. Their youth is dreary and doleful; their prospect of age horrible.' And in 1848, when half of Europe was in a ferment of popular insurrection, he saw no danger of revolution in England, because 'habits of subserviency to the aristocracy are so bonded into the national character.'

———————

Of course, there were plenty of English people who saw the evils of poverty clearly, none more so than Charles Dickens, whose diatribes were planting in a nation the germ of a social conscience. When he went to America in 1842, he hoped to see a future worth fighting for. He was to be disappointed.

He wrote to his English actor friend William Charles Macready that while he liked many Americans and admired some of their institutions, he was deeply disappointed in the country as a whole. No one, he said, was allowed to utter a word of criticism, and 'In respect of not being left alone, and of being horribly disgusted by tobacco chewing and tobacco spittle, I have suffered considerably.'

In *American Notes*, which offended his hosts as much as Mrs Trollope's work of ten years earlier, he had more to say on the subject of spitting. When he visited Congress, he found it to be practised as enthusiastically by the highest in the land as it was by the lowest:

> Both Houses are handsomely carpeted; but the state to which these carpets are reduced by the universal disregard of the spittoon with which every honourable member is accommodated, and the extraordinary improvements on the pattern which are squirted and dabbled upon it in every direction, do not admit of being described.

He was also vexed by the American habit of pressing visitors to give their opinion of all things American – and reacting very badly if that opinion was less than ecstatic. He was, for instance, unable to show the enthusiasm for Congress which he felt was demanded of him:

> In the first place – it may be from some imperfect development of my organ of veneration – I do not ever remember having fainted away, or having even been moved to tears of joyful pride, at the sight of any legislative body. I have borne the House of Commons like a man, and have yielded to no weakness, but slumber, in the House of Lords.

To make things worse, Dickens would not shut up about copyright. American copyright law was notoriously weak, and gave no protection at all to foreign writers. His hosts, with the resentment characteristic of all who are presented with an unanswerable case against them, felt that his insistence on the matter constituted a breach of etiquette.

His impassioned condemnation of slavery, in what is easily the most powerful chapter of perhaps his weakest book, allowed no compromise. Other English commentators had been prepared to see some good in the institution, but Dickens saw none. And his denunciation seemed to implicate in the great evil all Americans bar those who actively and energetically strove to end it.

It got worse. Dickens was, if anything, still more censorious in his next book, *Martin Chuzzlewit*, part of which is set in the United States. Everyone is out to fleece Martin, his worst experience being the purchase of real estate in the new city of Eden, which turns out to be a malarial swamp. Martin is 'battered and bamboozled by the relentless fire of Yankee verbosity, pomposity, chicanery and chauvinism.'

Between *American Notes* and *Martin Chuzzlewit*, Dickens succeeded in offending just about everyone on the other side of the Atlantic.

And if Britons could easily make themselves unpopular in America, so could Americans make a bad impression in England. While Dickens was at work on *Martin Chuzzlewit*, Thomas Carlyle's friendship with Ralph Waldo Emerson was bringing to Chelsea more American visitors than he liked. In November 1843, Jane Welsh Carlyle expressed her exasperation in a letter: 'I counted lately fourteen of them in one fortnight of whom Dr Russel was the only one that you did not feel tempted to take the poker to.'

And Americans didn't like Britain any more than the Brits liked America. As United States consul in Liverpool in the 1850s, Nathaniel Hawthorne never felt at home. 'There are some Englishmen whom I like,' he wrote, '… but still there is not the same union between us, as if they were Americans… in this foreign land, I can never forget the distinction between English and American.'

The thing that struck him most about England, as it had George Bancroft and Fanny Hall, was the wretched condition of the lowest in the land. In the poorer parts of Liverpool he found filthy people in ragged clothes, their lives made bearable only by the gin shops 'every two or three steps'. He gazed with horror on 'women, nursing their babies at dirty bosoms; men haggard, drunken, care-worn, hopeless, but with a kind of patience, as if all this were the rule of their life ...'

Begging, which English people took for granted, shocked and unsettled him:

> It is strange to see how many people are aiming at the small change in your pocket; in every square, a beggar-woman meets you, and turns back to follow your steps with her miserable murmur; at the street-crossings, there are old men or little girls with their brooms; urchins propose to brush your boots; if you get into a cab, a man runs to open the door for you, and touches his hat for a fee, as he closes it again.

Another thing which struck Hawthorne was the ugliness of so many English people. One day he saw a crowd of girls who had been taken from the workhouse and educated at some charity school. They were, he said 'without a single trace of beauty, or scarcely of intelligence, in so much as one individual; such mean, coarse, vulgar features, betraying unmistakably a low origin, and ignorant and brutal parents.'

And it was no better among the higher orders. In September 1854, he attended a meeting of the British Scientific Association, and was horrified by

> ... the lack of beauty in the women, and the horrible ugliness of not a few of them... I really pitied the respectable elderly gentlemen whom I saw walking about with such atrocities hanging on their arms – the grim, red-faced monsters! Surely a man would be justified in... taking a sharp knife and cutting away their mountainous flesh, until he had brought them into reasonable shape, as a sculptor seeks for the beautiful form of woman in a shapeless block of marble. The husband must feel that something alien has grown

over and encrusted the slender creature whom he married, and he is horribly wronged by having all this flabby flesh imposed upon him as his wife.

Here surely Hawthorne demeans himself more than he does the objects of his scorn. Can we trust any of the observations of one so manifestly biased?

At his best, though, he is a most perceptive observer. No one captured the difference between British and American class attitudes better than Hawthorne in his comments on a visit to the House of Commons in April 1856, as a guest of Boston MP Mr Ingram. Ingram's aspect and manner immediately betrayed his lowly origins, wrote Hawthorne, whereas his American equivalent would have become just as refined as the company he now kept. Americans, wrote Hawthorne, accepted success as their due, but Mr Ingram took a naïve delight in his position, and was openly astonished that he had achieved it.

But there was more to the transatlantic tensions of the mid-nineteenth century than the attitudes of the well-to-do. Above all there was Ireland. Mass immigration into America from the impoverished island began in the 1820s, and between then and 1860 the Irish never made up less than one third of all immigrants.

A peak was reached with the devastating potato famine of the late 1840s, when they poured across the Atlantic at a rate of two hundred thousand a year. By 1860, the Irish, at over one and a half million, made up the largest foreign-born group in the United States. Hundreds of thousands more of Irish blood had been born there, and almost to a man, woman and child, they harboured a visceral hatred of England. For centuries they had struggled to throw off the foreign yoke, and the untold misery of the famine was just too much. The sheer numbers of Irish Americans in the mid-nineteenth century ensured a healthy level of Anglophobia in the New World.

And it was not only the Irish who felt they had good practical reasons to detest the English. On September 6th, 1851, the *New-York Daily Tribune* railed against the iniquities of the free trade which, with her huge wealth and her mighty navy, Great Britain could so easily enforce. 'Such is British free trade', said the Tribune, warming to its theme. 'It closes our mills and our furnaces, and compels men to remain idle when they would desire to work.' And so on.

Great Britain was just too powerful to be popular. There was even a break in diplomatic relations in 1856, when the British Minister to Washington was dismissed in a row about the unlawful enlistment of Americans into the British army during the Crimean War. In June of that year, the crisis inspired the satirical magazine *Punch* to verse:

> How can you think, you Yankee fellows,
> That of your progress we are jealous?
> Why, Middlesex as well might worry
> Herself because of thriving Surrey.
>
> We know the spread of your dominion
> Is likewise that of free opinion,
> Which, bowie-knife, revolver, rifle,
> And Lynch-law but in small part stifle …
>
> Against us why are you so bitter?
> Because we sometimes grin and titter
> A little at your speech and manners?
> Therefore must ours be hostile banners?
>
> Don't we ourselves laugh at each other?
> Consider, Jonathan, my brother,
> Laugh at our beadles and our flunkeys
> Caparisoned like fools and monkeys? …
>
> Say is it your intent to wallop
> Us on account of Mrs Trollope?
> Or are we by you to be smitten
> For something Dickens may have written? …

Brother Jonathan would have required the patience of a saint not to be offended by this patronising drivel.

One American who was in fact endowed with that rare quality was Ralph Waldo Emerson. Unconcerned by the changing currents of fashion and by attitudes which he knew would pass soon enough, Emerson wrote from England that, although he could never help being impressed by all things English, he would, as soon as he returned to Massachusetts,

> ... lapse into the feeling, which the geography of America inevitably inspires, that we play the game with immense advantage; that there and not here is the seat and centre of the British race; and that no skill or activity can long compete with the prodigious natural advantages of that country, in the hands of the same race; and that England, an old and exhausted island, must one day be contented, like other parents, to be strong only in her children.

It was one of the more perceptive comments to pass across the Atlantic in the middle of the nineteenth century. If more Americans, and more English people, had been so philosophical, there would have been much less interest in the great prize fight of 1860.

CHAPTER 10

SET-UP

ON SUNDAY, March 27th, 1859, *Bell's Life in London* carried the following announcement:

> CHALLENGE TO THE CHAMPION OF ENGLAND. —
> John C. Heenan, otherwise known as the Benicia Boy,
> who recently fought John Morrissey at Long Point,
> Canada, being unsuccessful in getting a match in this
> country, desires us to announce for him that he will fight
> Tom Sayers, the present Champion of England, for £200
> and the champion's belt...

Jim Cusick had been at work.

It was an exciting time for the world's greatest city, even if very few of the population knew it. At the end of January, work had begun on Joseph Bazalgette's sewage system, the upshot of Dr Snow's identification of contaminated water as the cause of cholera. Opened in the year that Tom Sayers died (though not completed for another ten), it would end for ever the reign of King Cholera in London.

As for the reign of Tom Sayers, it seemed that only foreign intervention could pose any threat. That the challenge should have appeared where it did was to be expected. While *Bell's Life in London and Sporting Chronicle*, launched by John Bell in 1822, covered the theatre and more general news – Charles Dickens had been on the payroll in the 1830s – it was known principally as the doyenne of British sporting newspapers. Serving a two-hundred-mile radius of London, it came out every Saturday evening for distribution on Sunday. Before the appearance in 1859 of *The Sporting Life*, it was the only place where you could find full reports of the battles of Tom Sayers.

It had long been essentially a family concern, the late Vincent Dowling having been succeeded as editor in 1851 by his son Frank, whose monocle and vast Dundreary sidewhiskers conveyed an impression of eccentricity bordering on madness. From his office in Norfolk Street, which ran from The Strand at Aldwych down to the river, Frank Dowling was easily the most influential figure in the English prize ring. Matches – especially big ones – were more often arranged at *Bell's Life* than anywhere else, Dowling being entrusted to hold the stakes, and he was frequently called on to act as referee for major fights.

Heenan's challenge, however, was not published first in London, but in New York, where it had appeared in *Porter's Spirit of the Times*.

In 1831, the Porter brothers had launched a weekly newspaper, *Spirit of the Times*, modelled closely on *Bell's Life*. Aiming at those interested in sport and the theatre, the *Spirit of the Times* steered clear of political comment which might unnecessarily alienate readers. The wave of Anglophobe articles which followed the publication of Dickens's *American Notes* in 1842 did not constitute an infringement of this policy, Americans being virtually unanimous in their outrage. No newspaper was likely to lose readers by lashing out at the old colonial power.

When the *Spirit* carried Heenan's challenge to Sayers, it had no hesitation in making clear its own feelings on the matter: 'should he win, we shall look upon him as having done the country a good service by vindicating its climate from the British sneer that the human race upon this continent is suffering a constant and rapid deterioration.'

By 1859, the *Spirit of the Times* had split, and confusingly, two papers existed side by side – the *Spirit of the Times* and *Porter's Spirit of the Times*. The latter had been edited by shaggy-haired and bearded William Trotter Porter until his death in 1858, and by 1859 George Wilkes was at the helm. Wilkes was to the American prize ring what Dowling was to the British, and Heenan's challenge had crossed the Atlantic covered by a letter from Wilkes to his British counterpart.

By the time it was published in *Bell's Life*, Dowling had already taken the short walk up Norfolk Street and along the Strand to Adam Street, where John Gideon was staying at Osborne's Hotel, once a haunt of Mr Pickwick. Tom Sayers, now known to all the Fancy as Gideon's protégé, was at Tonbridge, where he was belatedly getting himself into shape – more or less – for his second meeting with Bill Benjamin. Gideon undertook to inform him without delay.

The champion was happy to accept the American challenge – indeed, if he wished to keep the belt in perpetuity, he had no choice – and took no more seriously than anyone else the rider that, in the event of his losing any of his three upcoming fights, his conqueror would then be Heenan's opponent. It was all quite clear: after defeating Benjamin, Brettle and the Unknown, his next fight would be against Heenan.

And then everything changed. Just two days after the publication of Heenan's challenge in *Bell's Life*, George Wilkes wrote Frank Dowling a letter which would complicate matters greatly. He enclosed a draft of £200 to cover a challenge for the belt by Aaron Jones, who had remained in America after training Heenan for the Morrissey fight. Acknowledging that he had already written on behalf of Heenan, Wilkes put the ball firmly in Dowling's court: 'Your sense of propriety will find a law for the matter.'

In fact, the position was clear: no challenge was official until a deposit had been laid, and Heenan's failure to arrange one immediately had allowed Jones to jump the queue. Dowling was excited at the prospect of a match between the English and American champions, but he had no choice in the matter.

For the rest of the Fancy the possibility of an international contest for the belt was as yet too remote to be of much interest. For the time being, their attention was occupied by the prospect of the second meeting between the champion and Bill Benjamin.

And so, at last, was that of Tom Sayers. He had by now engaged as trainer the squat and bull-necked Harry Brunton, born the same year as Tom, and known for his naïve pride in the arm and leg muscles which he would invite others to feel and admire. His own career in the prize ring had been curtailed by easily-damaged hands, and he was now landlord of the George and Dragon at London's Barbican.

If Tom had been lax in his preparations, the same could not be said of Bill Benjamin. Bitterly ashamed of his performance on the Isle of Grain a year earlier, he was ready to do anything to redeem himself, and attempted to engage Nat Langham – Ould Nat, as he had come to be known – as trainer. The former champion, however, while prepared to visit and advise, could not spare the necessary time.

He recommended instead the irrepressible Bendigo, who had by this time managed to control the heavy drinking which had threatened to destroy him, and was now, astonishingly, devoting himself to preaching the gospel. Seeing nothing in the prize ring incompatible with the word of God, he found in Bill Benjamin as keen a pupil as any boxing coach had known.

The results were seen at Ashford in Kent on Tuesday, April 5th, 1859, when it was clear from the first that Benjamin had been transformed in the fifteen months since his humiliation on the Isle of Grain. And, it being equally clear that the champion was not as thoroughly trained as he should have been, the odds of four to one began to look unrealistic. The mill was ferocious, and the seventh round in particular was probably the fiercest that Tom Sayers had known. He threw everything he had at this dangerous opponent, but, in the words of Henry Downes Miles, 'The fighting was tremendous, and the way Benjamin stood to his man was beyond all praise.' There were even moments when it seemed that the champion might be beaten.

Almost inevitably, however, he came through in the end. Because of Benjamin's determination to go forward, the fight took only twenty-two minutes, but it was a twenty-two minutes Tom Sayers would not forget. Benjamin fought like a wounded lion, and even when his seconds finally threw up the sponge to save him from further punishment, they had no easy time restraining him from battling on. The champion had come uncomfortably close to paying the full price for going into a fight inadequately prepared.

———————

Meanwhile Jack Heenan, under the guidance of Jim Cusick, was getting on with his own career three and a half thousand miles away. The day before Sayers disposed of the spirited challenge of the transformed Benjamin, he stepped into the ring with John Morrissey for the second time. The latter, with an eye to his political ambitions, had arranged a benefit for the wife of former prize fighter Boss Harrington, who had disappeared a few weeks previously and was now presumed dead. The benefit took the form of a sparring exhibition at Hoym's Theater on the Bowery, and the main attraction was three rounds between Morrissey and the Benicia Boy. It was only for show, but at least it constituted some sort of payday for Jack Heenan.

This had nothing to do with his now somewhat tenuous transatlantic challenge, but there was in England an issue which had to be taken into account. Sayers was now committed to fighting Bob Brettle in September, but what of the mysterious Unknown who was next on the list? There was widespread scepticism about this challenge, many believing it to be a ruse to use up time in which other potential opponents might compete for the belt before it became the property of Tom Sayers in perpetuity.

Though he did not say so explicitly, it is clear that Frank Dowling himself was suspicious, but the Unknown's representative, Mr C – who was, Dowling said, a former backer of Harry Orme – insisted when challenged that his man, though he had not yet fought in the prize ring, was 'a well-tried man in private'.

The matter was still in doubt when Dowling received Wilkes's letter of March 29th, enclosing £200 to back the challenge of Aaron Jones. This he made public in the next issue of *Bell's Life*. With the challenge of the Unknown to take into account as well as the upcoming Brettle contest, there would be time for only one more fight before Tom Sayers could take permanent possession of the belt. Jack Heenan might not get his chance at all.

And whatever the suspicions, the Unknown was not going to disappear in a hurry. On Thursday, April 21st, Gideon and Sayers turned up at *Bell's Life* to meet the enigmatic C. Challenged to produce the mystery fighter, C brought in a tall, slim young man who looked nothing like a pugilist. To make his challenge still less likely, it was fixed for the middle of November, less than two months after Tom was due to fight Bob

Brettle. By this time, even Frank Dowling was prepared to acknowledge his suspicions – though he was careful to say he did not believe that the champion himself would have been party to such a fraud.

The latter's acceptance of Heenan's challenge, written just before the Benjamin match, had by now reached New York. The trouble was that, although the world was shrinking fast – work began on the Suez Canal just days after the appearance of C's Unknown – England and America were still not linked by telegraph. The Atlantic cable of 1858 having succeeded only briefly, even the swiftest reply to a letter from the other side of the Atlantic was most unlikely to arrive within three weeks of the dispatch of the original, and might well take much longer. Sayers might have accepted Heenan's challenge, but Aaron Jones, whose deposit gave him precedence, had yet to receive a reply to his. It was all very complicated.

Still, the correspondence was at least getting through. Not all letters made it across the Atlantic at all, and neither did all passengers. On the stormy night of Thursday, April 28th, just a week after Sayers and Gideon got what was (at least officially) their first sight of the Unknown, the emigrant ship *Pomona*, bound for New York from Liverpool, ran aground on a sandbank off the coast of Ireland. After a terrifying night and day, she went down the following evening, taking with her all but a handful of her three hundred and seventy-five passengers and thirty-two crew. She had flown the colours of the unfortunately named Dramatic line.

Tragic as this was, George Wilkes and Frank Dowling had other things on their minds. Nine days after the loss of the *Pomona*, Dowling published a letter from Wilkes saying that the sum of £50 was on its way from Jack Heenan, as first deposit for his challenge for the championship. This, however, changed nothing: Heenan might have made the first challenge, but Jones had laid the first deposit.

The Benicia Boy, it seemed, was too late. In the next issue of *Bell's Life*, Tom made clear that he could not at that moment accept the American's challenge, since, after Brettle, he was engaged already to fight first the Unknown, then Aaron Jones. But Frank Dowling knew a good match even before he saw it, and expressed the wish that Sayers would nonetheless fight Heenan if at all possible. 'The match,' he said, 'cannot fail to create the greatest excitement on both sides of the Atlantic.'

His opinion was shared in New York. In the words of the great rival of *Porter's Spirit of the Times*, the *New York Clipper*, 'the United States has been plunged into a state of the deepest excitement… an immense amount of interest not only among the "fancy" but throughout all classes of the community.' The paper acknowledged, however, that Jones's challenge had to take priority, since he had laid the first deposit. The only problem that Jones now had was that everyone wanted Sayers–Heenan, and no one wanted Sayers–Jones. Efforts were soon being made in America to get the Shropshire man to stand down.

In England at the same time, by contrast, no one was trying to persuade the Unknown to stand down. After all, no one really believed that he existed, except in the unlikely form of the young man whom C had produced at *Bell's Life* – and no one seriously thought that *he* would ever be seen in the ring with Tom Sayers. There was, accordingly, very little interest when, on June 7th, C turned up again at *Bell's Life* to place a further deposit of £25.

But if no one cared about the Unknown, everyone cared about the Benicia Boy who, on July 1st, around the time of his second meeting with Adah Menken, was injured in a brawl in Boston. It turned out to be nothing serious, but concern was widespread, for the projected international fight had truly captured the American imagination.

For Tom Sayers, however, there was at least one more matter to be attended to before the way ahead was clear. On July 12th he went to Tonbridge to begin preparations for the Brettle fight, fixed for mid-September. He would not repeat the mistake of neglecting his training. Tom was hot favourite, but some thought that Brettle, who had looked more than a match for him when they had sparred with gloves, had a real chance.

By this time, the obstinate figure of the Unknown was beginning to get on everybody's nerves. On July 24th, *Bell's Life* published a letter from 'Athlete', who wanted the Pugilistic Benevolent Association to look into the matter. Many, said Athlete, believed the Unknown to be a myth, 'and the only object of the business is to wear away a few months of the time, at the expiration of which Sayers may "according to the articles under which the Champion's belt was raised," claim it as his own for ever.'

Tom Sayers showed no concern. On August 3rd he went to Brighton to continue his training. He was a busy man. Only four months had passed since his second encounter with Bill Benjamin, in less than two months he would face Bob Brettle, then (theoretically) the Unknown, and after that there was Jones, and Heenan too if there was time.

The idea was floated in America that there might be an eliminator between Jones and Heenan, but neither man showed much enthusiasm. And then another time-killing possibility was mooted. On August 7th, *Bell's Life* reported that John Morrissey's former trainer Jack Hamilton, judging that it would be some time before Sayers could accommodate Jones, was prepared to match the latter with Harry Paulson for between £100 and £200 a side. A deposit of only £5 or £10 left at Alec Keene's Three Tuns tavern at Moor Street, Soho, would ensure the match.

But Aaron Jones wasn't that stupid. The almost universal opinion among the Fancy was that the Unknown was a fiction, albeit a stubborn one – on August 18th, his sponsor put down a further £25 deposit – and the champion might be available much sooner than was officially admitted. Jones was not about to commit himself to fighting anyone but Sayers.

The problem remained that his challenge simply didn't capture the imagination on either side of the Atlantic, whereas that of Heenan did. And on August 27th, the *Clipper* carried the news that the Jones–Sayers fight was off. Jones, it seemed, had somehow upset his sponsor, identified simply as a 'New Orleans gentleman'. This gentleman, who had backed Jones's challenge with the full stake, to be drawn as deposits fell due, now elected to forfeit the initial deposit of £50, have £100 transferred to the Sayers–Heenan account, and the remaining £50 given to Jones to cover the cost of his return to England when he chose to make it.

Tom Sayers, of course, knew nothing of this at the end of August when he went to Newmarket to complete his training before he faced Bob Brettle. What mattered to him was that no one should defeat him before midday on June 16th, 1860 when, according to the rules established five years earlier, the champion's belt would become his in perpetuity. For the time being, he was interested only in Bob Brettle.

Across the Atlantic, Jack Heenan, though he knew all about Jones's withdrawal, also had other things on his mind. By now, in spite of Jim Cusick's strong disapproval, he had moved in with Adah Menken, and on September 3rd they went through a marriage ceremony at Rockaway Cottage, Bloomingdale Road. Now Rockaway Cottage was not a church, the louche reputation of Bloomingdale Road was known to all, and it is not certain that the ceremony had any legal force. Still, it clearly indicated that actress and boxer took their relationship seriously, even though, as later transpired, very few people so much as knew that the wedding had taken place.

Tom Sayers was certainly unaware, but he did learn just eight days later that the Jones fight was off. During training, he always liked to have the ring news read to him, and on September 11th, *Bell's Life* told how Jones had lost his sponsor. It seemed, however, that this might not be the end of the matter, since Jones was now saying that he would find the money himself. It was still impossible to know what might happen.

Another Anglo-American sporting contest had proved much less problematic to arrange. On September 7th, a cricket eleven, including one Julius Caesar, had set sail for Canada and the United States on the first overseas tour by an English cricket team.

They were still at sea when, at Ashford in Kent on Tuesday, September 20th, Tom Sayers met his latest challenge. There had been doubters – including some who thought, inexplicably, that Sayers might find it harder to fight a smaller than a bigger man – but the champion did what almost everyone had expected of him, and won easily. His only problem was a nasty gash on the leg from Brettle's spikes, which were longer than strictly permitted. The wound was to give him trouble for some weeks.

It was one down and, theoretically, three to go, but this did not long remain the case. Just after Brettle's downfall, the Unknown surrendered rather more ignominiously. As *Bell's Life* put it on September 25th:

> This match, as we have all along anticipated, has ended in smoke. On Thursday last the backer of the Unknown called at our office and intimated that that individual had not been going on at all to his satisfaction, and that, therefore,

he should make Sayers a present of the money down! Our readers can draw their own conclusions.

One conclusion drawn by *Bell's Life* was that Aaron Jones, with his determination not to be deprived of his shot at the title, was likely to fight the champion in early February.

As for Jack Heenan, he would have to wait and see. In the meantime, he could find other ways of amusing himself. On October 6th, the day after the English cricketers had completed a crushing victory over the United States in New Jersey, he attended a fight at Point Abino, Canada, some twelve miles from Buffalo. The mill, at which John Morrissey was also present, saw Ed Price of Boston defeat Jem 'Australian' Kelly of New York. Kelly's lack of bottom annoyed his backers and made for a poor contest. But it passed the time.

The very next day, George Wilkes wrote to Frank Dowling to tell him that Aaron Jones had finally decided to withdraw, 'conceding to the common desire on this side of the Atlantic to see Heenan have the first chance...' It had all happened in less than three weeks. Brettle was beaten, the Unknown had evaporated, and Jones had stepped aside. Suddenly the way was clear for the Benicia Boy to face the English champion.

The *Spirit* must already have gone to press before Wilkes wrote to Dowling, for its subscribers were to read the following day that Jones seemed *likely* to give way because he recognised the strength of feeling in America: 'We hope Jones will take the liberal view of this matter, and let us have the great international Fight for the Championship of the two hemispheres.' And should that fight come off, Wilkes had no doubt as to whose side he was on: 'If Heenan can win, the British sneer at our physical inferiority will be pretty well upset.'

He would have been horrified to know that, even as he was writing, many in England thought there would be no fight, since Tom Sayers was now dead. This was in fact an exaggeration. All that was wrong was that the leg wound which he had sustained against Brettle was taking time to heal. Even so, the rumour gained such currency nationwide that Dowling found it necessary to set the record straight in the next issue of *Bell's Life*.

None of this was known on the other side of the Atlantic, and little over a week later, the *Spirit* and all other American newspapers had something very different to write about anyway. Late on the night of October 16th, in an attempt to foment slave rebellion, John Brown captured the armoury and arsenal at Harper's Ferry in Virginia – where, twelve years before, Yankee Sullivan had defeated Robert Caunt. On the morning of October 18th, the insurrection was crushed by a force led by Brevet Colonel Robert E. Lee. Ten of Brown's twenty-one men were killed, and he himself taken prisoner. With everyone nervous about a possible confrontation between North and South, this was news powerful enough to distract attention even from the big fight.

But not for long even in America, and in England hardly at all. By the time the news of Jones's withdrawal had crossed the Atlantic, Tom had made a full recovery from his injury, and was at Newmarket races where he was a very familiar figure. Not for another two weeks and more would he come to London for the drawing up of preliminary articles for the international contest. There was no great urgency now, since only one fight was on the agenda.

By this time, Julius Caesar and his team-mates were on their way home. They had had five matches in all, against various representative American and Canadian sides, and, despite playing eleven against twenty-two each time, had won them all. It was pretty clear that cricket was going nowhere in the New World.

On November 3rd when the articles for Sayers– Heenan were signed, John Gideon wrote to *Clipper* editor Frank Queen, telling him that '£50 a side are deposited now in the hands of the stakeholder, the Editor of *Bell's Life*, and the next deposit of £50 a side to be made at Mr. Owen Swift's... on Thursday, December 15.' The fight, he said, would come off in February.

Owen Swift was the man who had killed Bill Phelps, brother of Joe and Harry, in the ring in 1837. Curiously, Brighton Bill was his second victim, for Anthony Noon had suffered a similar fate at his hands three years earlier. Both times, Swift had escaped the most serious repercussions, and was now, like almost all old fighters, a publican – landlord of the Horse

Shoe tavern in Tichborne Street off Haymarket. It was one of London's premier sporting houses, and was the venue at which Tom, having missed an earlier date because of his injury, received his battle money for the Brettle fight on the evening of Friday, November 4th.

By this time, the sporting fraternity on both sides of the Atlantic were becoming genuinely excited by the prospect of the great international match. As *The Sporting Life*, established only that year as a rival to *Bell's Life*, put it on November 2nd:

> It is really creating a positive furore in P.R. circles, not only in London, but amongst the habitués of every sporting hostelry in the kingdom... It is upon the tongue of thousands, and the common type of conversation in camp, crib, and cottage.

Since the fight was to be in England, all arrangements had to be made on the eastern side of the Atlantic, and the Americans were consequently always a couple of weeks behind the times. By the first week of November, however, everybody on both sides of the ocean knew that the big fight was on. The *Clipper* told its readers that 'We have recently been overwhelmed with enquiries from every quarter.' Many of these concerned the rules laid down for the defence of the belt, and these the *Clipper* set out in full.

Heenan, *Clipper* readers learned, was already training daily at the gym, and would doubtless give sparring exhibitions in the principal cities of the Union before he sailed for England. This would at least keep him away from his supposed wife, which was probably a relief to both, for the differences between them were by now making themselves felt. She spent her time at the theatre and socialising with her theatrical friends; he went to saloons and came back drunk. Whether he used to beat her or she him – he had certainly given her sparring lessons – is not entirely clear, but in truth their union had been doomed from the first.

In England meanwhile, *Bell's Life* told its readers that Tom wanted the fight to be no later than February, and proposed meeting his challenger at Owen Swift's on Thursday, December 15th to settle final articles and make the necessary arrangements. 'The match', said *Bell's Life*, 'will doubtless create more interest than any similar affair in modern times.'

But it was not all going to be straightforward, and the champion could not take for granted the dates he favoured. For the fight itself he thought February fair, since that was when he would have met Jones. But when this became known in America, there was trouble. On November 23rd, Wilkes wrote to Dowling outlining Heenan's – or more likely Cusick's – objections.

The nub of the matter was that, far from taking Jones's slot, Heenan was issuing his own challenge, and was, according to normal procedure, entitled to six months from the moment the fight was arranged. This, Wilkes said, might be considered to be either October 20th, when Sayers had covered Heenan's £50 deposit, or November 3rd, when the preliminary articles were signed. Whatever happened, Heenan would not be ready in February.

Three days later, the point was emphasised in the *Clipper*, where Frank Queen published Gideon's letter of November 3rd. February, said the *Clipper*, was far too early for the Benicia Boy, who needed time not only to get to England, but to acclimatise once he was there. And he was clearly not planning to cross the Atlantic in the very near future, since he had a benefit already arranged for Tuesday, November 29th, at Hoym's Theatre.

And then another potential difficulty arose. The better part of two months had passed since the Kelly–Price fight of early October, but only now did the Buffalo authorities issue warrants for the arrest of a number of those who had been involved. Among them were John Morrissey and Jack Heenan, who gave a surety of $100 that he would go to Buffalo on January 3rd to stand trial. Since no one had been killed, and since the Benicia Boy was not one of the principals, it seemed a trivial matter, and *Porter's Spirit of the Times* predicted that it would all come to nothing.

No one could be sure of that, but the *Spirit* was far more interested in the Benicia Boy's sparring benefit at Hoym's Theatre:

> Rarely has so large or respectable an audience been witnessed in this popular place of public resort, as on this present occasion. Every available seat was occupied, and numbers were obliged to stand the whole time, to witness the pugilistic displays. The price of admission was fixed at

one dollar per head, and there must have been over 1200 persons in the house.

—————

By this time, it was clear that Heenan really needed his own representative on the spot in England. Everyone there now expected the fight to take place in February, and Heenan's objections would not be known for some days. There would then be the usual delay of three or four weeks before Dowling received a reply to his own response to Wilkes. The only way to sort things out was for someone to go to London with full power to act for the Benicia Boy.

Enter Frederick Falkland, New York solicitor and proprietor of one of the more salubrious of New York's sporting saloons. He was booked to sail for England on the last day of November (the day after Heenan's appearance at Hoym's), and, having no doubt been briefed at length by Jim Cusick, was just the man to act as the Boy's agent in England. Now at last the two sides could meet face to face and sort things out.

Outside the prize ring, life went on, and so did death. With Falkland's ship two days out, John Brown was hanged for the Harper's Ferry raid. One of the soldiers on duty at his execution, Major Thomas Jackson, known to history as Stonewall, wrote of his 'unflinching firmness'.

It would be some time before Fred Falkland heard the news. For now, what concerned him was the date of the big fight. If he proved unable to arrange it for later than March, then the Boy would have to leave for England very soon. The *Clipper* reported on December 17th that he now meant to sail on Christmas Eve, but thought this mistaken. Why not wait for word from Falkland, which might be expected by the end of the month?

The *Clipper* was right, for the matter had already been settled in London. Fred Falkland had paid his respects at *Bell's Life* when he had arrived in the capital in early December, but in the absence of anyone to speak for the champion, a decision as to the date of the fight had to wait until the middle of the month.

On December 15th, by which time everyone knew that Heenan's representative was in town though few had yet met him, there was great excitement at Owen Swift's, where the second £50 deposit was to be paid.

(The laying of the deposit was, on Heenan's side, a pure formality, since Frank Dowling by now had the entire £200.)

English curiosity was finally satisfied when, immediately after Sayers's money was handed over, Fred Falkland stood up. Having introduced himself, he addressed the issue that most concerned the Americans. By this time, Heenan's objections to fighting in February were known in England, and John Gideon had written to Frank Queen saying that March would be acceptable. This, however, Falkland explained, was still earlier than Heenan wanted. There was no problem. Tom Sayers, who was there in person, immediately offered to give way, and the battle was set for Monday, April 16th. Everyone would have understood that this might change – for a start, fights almost always came off on a Tuesday – but a date in mid-April at least, was now guaranteed.

But then a second issue arose. John Gideon had already written to Frank Queen, expressing his surprise that Heenan had made no effort to raise the stakes above the £200 minimum for which the title could be contested. With his man almost certain to be clear favourite, in England at least, there was no advantage to Gideon in placing additional money in side bets. From his point of view, the higher the stake the better. And after all, in his original challenge, issued all of nine months previously, Heenan had expressed his willingness to add £600 or £800 to the required £200.

As Falkland explained, however, for the same reason that it was likely to be more profitable for Gideon to invest his money in the stake, so it would be better for the American sponsors to put their money into side bets. Although Gideon was to make one more despairing plea to Frank Queen, he had no option but to accept £200 a side.

Everything was falling into place, but Aaron Jones just wouldn't go away. In early December, he wrote to *The New York Herald*, alleging that he had been drugged before his second fight with Tom Sayers. This had taken place nearly three years previously, and yet he had hitherto made no complaint. On December 17th the *Clipper* told its readers that it was Jack Macdonald, Jones's second on the day, who had written to Jones telling him what had happened, and even identifying the culprits – whose names, however, the boxer had not divulged. No one knew what to make of it.

With the usual transatlantic time-lag, *Bell's Life* did not catch up with this extraordinary turn of events until January 8th, when its readers learned the full story. Macdonald had written to *Bell's Life* to deny the *Clipper*'s allegation that the suggestion of doping originated with him, though he said he did think that Jones might have eaten something that disagreed with him on the day of the fight. Dowling considered the whole story absurd, and said that he reported it only in order to pour scorn on a notion so potentially damaging to the prize ring.

Other things, too, were happening on the unpredictable Jones front. Jack Hamilton's challenge on behalf of Harry Paulson had come to nothing, but just as Jones was crying foul over his defeat by Sayers, another challenge came, this time from Paulson's old adversary Tom Paddock. He wanted to fight Jones in the same ring as Sayers would fight Heenan. Two days after Christmas, *The New York Herald* carried a letter from Aaron Jones accepting the match for £200 a side. This would ultimately come to nothing, but for the time being April 16th looked like being a busy day.

Meanwhile, Jack Heenan, perhaps taking the *Clipper*'s (or more likely Cusick's) advice to wait for word from Falkland before booking his passage to England, had been giving sparring exhibitions in Philadelphia and Baltimore. On the last day of the year, the *Clipper* said that he had now firmly decided to sail from New York on the *Asia* on the fourth day of January. No reference was made to the fact that he was bailed to appear in court in Buffalo the previous day, in connection with the Price–Kelly fight.

On Wednesday, January 4th, 1860, the Cunard steamship *Asia*, a wooden vessel two hundred and sixty-six feet long by forty feet in the beam – four of her could have fitted inside the hull of the *Great Eastern* – was berthed at New York, ready to leave for Liverpool. Provided that engine failure did not render necessary the three masts which supplemented her funnel, her two paddle wheels could propel her through the water at twelve knots, and get her across the Atlantic in ten days. But to Jack Heenan, hidden below deck some hours before she was due to sail, all that immediately concerned him was that he should not be found by the Buffalo detectives searching the ship in order to execute the warrant for his arrest.

He was lucky. Had the officers waited just a little longer they might have had him, for with sailing postponed due to a snowstorm, the young boxer went ashore in the evening. In company with the many well-wishers who had turned up to see him off, he had, in the words of the *Clipper*, a 'jolly time at a hotel not far distant.' Adah Menken was not among those present.

At four o'clock in the morning, in company as ever with Jim Cusick, he boarded again unmolested, and the *Asia* finally weighed anchor at five thirty. Nothing in America could now prevent the big fight.

In *American Notes*, Charles Dickens had given a typically graphic description of the beginning of a transatlantic voyage in the middle of the nineteenth century:

> ...the vessel throbs like a strong giant that has just received the breath of life; the two great wheels turn fiercely round for the first time; and the noble ship, with wind and tide astern, breaks proudly through the lashed and foaming water.

To Dickens also we are indebted for an account of life aboard: the unbelievably tiny cabin which he shared with his wife, the violent winter seas which threw the ship about like a cork, the seasickness so dreadful that he ceased to care whether he lived or died. More reassuringly, he gives us a night-time description of how things were when the sea was placid:

> The gloom through which the great black mass holds its direct and certain course; the rushing water, plainly heard, but dimly seen; the broad, white, glistening track, that follows in the vessel's wake; the men on the look-out forward, who would be scarcely visible against the dark sky, but for their blotting out some score of glistening stars; the helmsman at the wheel, with the illuminated card before him... the melancholy sighing of the wind through block, and rope, and chain...

CHAPTER 11

IN TRAINING

ON SUNDAY, January 15th, Jack Heenan and Jim Cusick saw land for the first time in ten days. Crossing the Atlantic nine years later, Henry James wrote of being greeted by 'the sight, as one looked across the wintry ocean, of the strange, dark, lonely freshness of the coast of Ireland.' And the following day, he described 'the black steamers knocking about the yellow Mersey, under a sky so low that they seemed to touch it with their funnels.' The sun could not be seen, only 'the gray mildness, shading away into black at every pretext.'

Early on the foggy morning of Monday, January 16th, the *Asia* docked at Liverpool. Waiting to meet them were Fred Falkland and Jack Macdonald, who had seconded Tom against Dan Collins nine years before, and had more recently been at the centre of the controversy over Aaron Jones's alleged doping. Jim Cusick had engaged him to help with the training of the Benicia Boy. Cusick himself was now home, but with the dubious exception of his brief foray into Canadian territory to fight John Morrissey in 1858, it was Jack Heenan's first experience of a foreign country.

When he had landed at Liverpool some months before, American traveller Edward Hale, as he wrote in *Ninety Days Worth of Europe*, had noted with fascination the 'shrimps, Spanish grapes, beggars playing at coach-wheel, red-coated post boys, police-men with shiny hats...' (Police headgear at the time was a tall top hat.) All of this was waiting for Jack Heenan.

Also waiting, as if to dispel any doubts he might have had as to the interest the coming match had aroused in England, was an excited crowd. As *Bell's Life in London* put it on January 22nd, the scene was 'something extraordinary, the landing stage and the street adjoining resembling a fair for hours before the steamer reached her berth.' Fortunately for Heenan and Cusick, Falkland and Macdonald had expected this, and sent them word to come off with the mail bags as soon as the vessel reached the river. The expectant crowd thus missed their man completely, but they were in no mood to give up without a fight. *Bell's Life* explained:

> At length a gentleman of commanding height, wearing moustaches and closely muffled, was by general consent pitched upon, and a rush was made on all sides to shake hands and congratulate him on his safe arrival. Cheer followed cheer in rapid succession, and the scene for a time was very exciting. The passenger (who turned out to be a German businessman) was naturally taken aback at his warm reception, and, after numerous struggles to get free, at length found temporary safety in a cab. The driver attempted to drive him to his hotel, but was peremptorily ordered to stop. This he declined, until his horse was seized upon, and the crowd then manned the doors of the vehicle, opening the windows, and very nearly upsetting the ill-fated passenger in their attempts to get a peep at him.

When it was established that he was not Jack Heenan, the poor man was, said *Bell's Life*, lucky that the angry mob did not inflict on him any punishment for this shortcoming.

Thanks to the foresight of Falkland and Macdonald, the Benicia Boy had escaped a riotous welcome at St George's Dock, but the crowds were always going to catch up with him sooner or later. He reached Lime Street Station without incident, but there large numbers rushed the platform and cheered him as he and his companions waited for the London train. They travelled first-class and, news having been telegraphed ahead, found people gathered at all stops – Crewe, Tamworth, Rugby and so on – just to catch a glimpse of the American hero.

Again we have Edward Hale to thank for telling us what sort of things were likely to make an impact on American visitors to England at the time. When he left the city, he was amused by a Staffordshire hamlet's 'droll squeezing together of half a dozen brick houses as close as if they were in North Street in Boston, while all around there was plenty of room.' Remembering the only images of England which he had seen, he was forever exclaiming 'How like *Punch*!' when he saw, for instance, an unfamiliar pattern of cab, or a crossing sweeper holding out his hand for a penny. And he would exclaim 'How like the theatre!' on seeing high brick walls and garden gates in the midst of the country, and little wayside inns with projecting signs and names like Royal Oak.

This (and the ubiquitous poverty, so readily accepted by poor as well as rich) was the England to which John Camel Heenan came in 1860. But London itself was something else. The Boy and his friends arrived at Euston Station at ten in the evening, and took a cab straight to the Saracen's Head hotel, Snow Hill – the London base from which Wackford Squeers took his unfortunate charges to Dotheboys Hall in *Nicholas Nickleby*.

Henry James recorded his impressions on coming to the 'murky modern Babylon' nine years later. Like Jack Heenan, he arrived in Liverpool and took the train to Euston. Then he took a cab to Morley's Hotel in Trafalgar Square.

> It was not lovely – it was in fact rather horrible; but as I move again through the dusky, tortuous miles, in the greasy four-wheeler to which my luggage had compelled me to commit myself... The immensity was the great fact, and that was a charm; the miles of housetops and viaducts, the complication of junction and signals through which the train made its way to the station had already given me the scale. The weather had turned to wet, and we went deeper and deeper into the Sunday night... The low black houses were as inanimate as so many rows of coal-scuttles, save where at frequent corners, from a gin-shop, there was a flare of light more brutal still than the darkness.

From his base at the Saracen's Head, Jack Heenan had chance to absorb London's sheer size – three times as big as New York – by daylight the following day. In company with Jim Cusick, he visited *Bell's Life*, noticing

159

as he walked down the Strand that his picture was prominently featured in every cookshop window. That he was not recognised had something at least to do with the fact that he had had his moustache shaved off at the start of the day.

Much had been made of the assertion that the Benicia Boy would shun the metropolis before his job was done. His minders, it was said, feared that the temptations of such a city could prove irresistible, and that indulgence might ruin his chances in the big fight. In fact, as he wrote to George Wilkes later, he and Jim Cusick spent all of six days there, leaving for Salisbury to begin training only on the following Monday.

A boxer would spend up to three months training for a fight, and nothing was left to luck. If anything went wrong – as when Jack Heenan's old leg wound erupted before the Morrissey match, or when Tom Sayers was unwell during training for the fight with Nat Langham – his chances might be fatally damaged.

Frank Dowling, in *Fistiana*, devoted a good deal of space to the subject. Whoever was in charge – a whole team, including sparring partners, would be involved in preparation for a big fight – would be answerable to the boxer's sponsors. A good trainer, said Dowling, was invaluable, and potential backers should not waste their money on a boxer who was not prepared to work hard to get into condition.

The two main aspects of training were diet and exercise. The latter was built up steadily as the day of the fight wore on, but the correct diet was mandatory from the first. 'Spirits, porter, gross feeding, stimulants, tobacco, onions, pepper, and the sexual intercourse must vanish, and be no more heard of within the first week.' Dowling felt that the ban on sex required explanation: 'Indulgence with women is every bit as bad as indulgence with wine. Indeed, one leads to the other; both enfeeble, undermine, and at last prostrate the constitution.'

No women, then. Alcohol, however, was not altogether prohibited. Beer and port, said Dowling, might be taken in moderation, and were indeed preferable to hot tea and coffee, both of which were to be avoided as being 'in all cases enervating'. For liquid sustenance, nothing could match the mix of oatmeal, salt and water known as gruel.

As for solid food, 'all young meat, such as veal and lamb, all white flesh, whether game or poultry, are good for nothing.' Beef and mutton were the best meat, but all fat should be trimmed off. No mustard, pepper or spice of any kind was permitted, and vegetables, with the exception of potatoes, were to be avoided. Bread was to be stale.

Dowling shared the almost unquestioning faith in medicines which was a characteristic of the golden age of the quack and the unscrupulous hawker of patent remedies. People, it seemed, would believe anything. The entirely respectable Holloway's Pills and Ointment, for example, were said by the manufacturers to be effective in combination against

> Bad Legs, Bad Breasts, Burns, Bunions, Bite of Moschetoes and Sand-Flies, Coco-bay, Chiego-feet, Chilblains, Chapped Hands, Corns (Soft), Cancers, Contracted and Stiff Joints, Elephantiasis, Fistulas, Gout, Glandular Swellings, Lumbago, Piles, Rheumatism, Scalds, Sore Nipples, Scurvy, Sore-heads, Tumours, Ulcers, Wounds, Yaws.

Of all the medications which Dowling commended to boxers in training, his favourite was the famous 'blue pill', a laxative which was to be taken in a mild infusion of senna. He also believed in the use of emetics, and, on occasion, bleeding.

Walking and running were the principal forms of exercise, to be replaced by skipping in bad weather. Sparring was, of course, vital, and should take place daily at the time of the projected fight, the sparring partner being required to imitate as far as possible the style and mannerisms of the intended opponent.

Beginning in the second week of training, sweating was necessary, achieved by hard exercise in flannel clothing or, at night, by warm wraps and possets – drinks of hot milk curdled with ale. The boxer was to be kept scrupulously clean, his skin after washing being rubbed with coarse linen till it glowed.

It was universally accepted that a fighter should go to bed early, but care had to be taken, said Dowling, over the sort of air he breathed at night, since 'if he has been stove-bred in the populous purlieus of a large town, he may find the rare air of the country overpower the compass of his lungs – if let in upon him at once.' For the town-bred boxer, said Dowling, windows should not be opened wide at night straight away. Dowling was generally regarded as a reliable authority, and few boxers would have deviated greatly from the regimen he recommended.

In early February, Tom went to Brighton for his preliminary training. As *Bell's Life* put it on February 12th, 'Sayers has not gone into strict training, but has been taking a few refreshers at his old quarters in Brighton.' His opponent, too, was said to have 'gone into gentle work in country quarters'.

For the champion, problems with the police were unlikely. Prize fighting might be against the law, but he had long established by precedent the right to train at his favourite locations. Jack Heenan, however, was in a different position entirely. He was new to England, and his lack of regular quarters where he might train in peace was potentially serious. Although training was not illegal, many anti-fight campaigners were of the belief that a boxer preparing for a fight was clearly intent on committing a felony, and might therefore be apprehended.

The best policy for the Heenan camp was, therefore, to choose an out-of-the-way spot, and to keep a low profile. Sadly, their man had scarcely begun his training when his cover was blown. It was on Thursday, February 16th that the following announcement appeared in *The Times*:

> THE AMERICAN PUGILIST.–Mr. Heenan, the American pugilist, better known in the professional world as the 'Benicia Boy,' has established himself at East Harnham, adjoining the City of Salisbury, where he is undergoing the necessary training for the forthcoming contest with Sayers for the championship of England.

It was the last thing that Jack Heenan needed.

Two days later, a lengthy article by 'Childers' appeared in *The Field*. The author did not specify where the Benicia Boy was, but, thanks to *The Times*, everybody knew that anyway. His quarters, said Childers, were 'a fortified farm, within a high wall of flint and clay like the squares of a chess-board.' Also present was 'a small man who walked as though he could never tire' – clearly Jim Cusick. The gym was in a barn where,

> ... he had weights and pulleys to get him into wind; he had no boat to pull to get him into the water, although he sat at his work as do the gentlemen who start from Putney; there he had a swinging sack to practice at, and fancy he was engaging the renowned Tom Sayers; there he had some very pretty clubs, which he called his dumb-bells, of about the same size as one imagines that of Hercules to have been when he tamed the Nemean lion. With these toys he played as would a small boy with a battledore.

Childers was impressed. 'I must,' he said, 'yield to the notion that if he be not too much of a gentleman for the work he has set himself, he will achieve it.' And, even writing as an Englishman, he thought this might be no bad thing, since it would 'also teach Americans that a man may defend himself without pistol-ball or bowie-knife.'

It was all very complimentary, but the trouble was that, for the Benicia Boy in England, any publicity was dangerous. Salisbury being a cathedral city, there was no lack of opposition to such lawless and godless activities as prize fighting, and the Heenan camp soon found it advisable to up sticks and move – in the first instance to London, where they took up residence at the Round Table, St Martin's Close, near Ben Caunt's Coach and Horses.

It was while they were there that Jim Cusick decided it might be a good idea for his protégé to attend an English prize fight. Nothing could rival public interest in the coming Sayers–Heenan battle, but Jem Mace, a discovery of Nat Langham's, and the black fighter Bob Travers were both highly regarded, and the meeting between them, scheduled for Tuesday, 21st February, certainly caught the imagination of the Fancy.

Accordingly, the Boy and his minders set off that day for Long Reach on the Thames. It was chilly, and Jack, who was wearing an astrakhan-trimmed overcoat, was more conspicuous than was good for him. There was a police ambush, and the American would have been taken had not Jem Mace himself dragged him aboard one of the fight boats at the last instant. Everyone now crossed the river, but the blues again intervened, and proceedings finally had to be abandoned. The two pugilists met again the following day, when a disappointing fight, which the Benicia Boy did not attend, was awarded to Mace, Travers having gone down too easily and too often.

But at least the American had escaped arrest, and despite the vexations, Frank Dowling reported that his training was going well. In company with Jim Cusick, the Boy had visited *Bell's Life* two days after his brush with the police, and Dowling was impressed with his condition – though he said he was 'hunted almost beyond endurance by the curious, who would hardly allow him even to have his meals in peace.' Dowling thought he might have to move again.

———————

By law, of course, the Travers–Mace match should never have taken place. And even when police failed in their attempt to prevent it, they might still, after the event, have arrested anyone known to have been present. This was, after all, what the Buffalo authorities had done after the Price–Kelly battle. As was usually the case with prize fights, however, no action was taken.

One of the main reasons for this inactivity was that the jurisdiction of magistrates did not extend beyond the borders of their own counties, and many, whatever their personal feelings, must have thought it futile to attempt to enforce locally a law which might be ignored just a few miles away.

In the case of the Sayers–Heenan fight, such was the interest nationwide that the only way that it might have been prevented was for central government to have taken the matter in hand. With this in mind, two days after Mace had defeated Travers, Sheffield MP Mr Hadfield asked Home Secretary Sir George Cornewall Lewis what he intended to do to prevent a breach of the peace. Lewis replied that he was confident that Sir Richard Mayne, Commissioner of the Metropolitan Police, would see to it that the fight did not come off in his area.

Far from being evidence of determination to uphold the law, this sounded suspiciously like dereliction of duty. After all, the Home Office was responsible for keeping the peace throughout the land, not only in the London area. The Home Secretary's statement amounted to little less than official permission to stage the fight, provided only that it took place outside London.

The truth was that nobody really expected the mill to be prevented, and preparations went on unhindered. By early March, both men were training in full earnest. Tom had moved to the Brown Jug at Tonbridge in Kent, where he did mostly road work. For this he was in good hands, for in addition to his chief trainers Harry Brunton and Jemmy Welsh, he was now assisted by his old pedestrian friend Bob Fuller.

For the most part, Tom followed the training recommendations of Frank Dowling, but, like all fighters, he had his individual preferences. He had, for example, nothing against white meat, and regularly ate chicken and fish. And although he had lived in towns all his life, he always kept his window open at night. Dowling, however, would have approved of most of his programme, especially his regular ingestion of the blue pill.

That the contest might be prevented seemed most improbable, but the anti-fight campaigners were not giving up, and their efforts became the more determined as the day drew near. On March 28th, Samuel Godfrey of 35 Park Street, Islington wrote to his MP Sir Fitzroy Kelly, enclosing information from *The Globe* on the forthcoming battle, and asking what would be done to prevent it. The following day, Kelly wrote to H. Waddington at the Home Office on Godfrey's behalf. Nothing was done.

By now the champion, who liked to be around horses, had moved to Newmarket to complete his training, an essential part of which was the toughening – and incidental darkening – of the skin of hands, neck and face by the process known as pickling. Five or six times daily they were rubbed with a tepid solution of essence of turpentine, saltpetre, lemon juice, scraped horse-radish, bay salt, vinegar and whisky. And on the final three days, a solution of dissolved hydrated sulphate was added for the hands. Well-pickled knuckles were rough and sharp, while the pickled skin of the face stood up much better to punishment.

The champion was untroubled by the crushers, and was even able to visit Newmarket races quite openly in company with Bob Fuller and Harry Brunton. There were those, however, who would have liked to take action. On the last day of March, *The Times* reported that the chief constable of the Isle of Ely (only twelve miles from Newmarket, but, crucially, in a different county) had obtained warrants for the apprehension of both fighters, 'with a view to their being bound over to keep the peace for twelve months.'

For those who wanted to see the fight prevented, the problem was that so many people felt differently. Bar the odd concerned private citizen, a magistrate here and there, and perhaps a chief constable or two, everyone seemed caught up in the excitement.

Still, sporadic efforts to prevent the anticipated breach of the peace went on. On April 2nd, just two weeks before the appointed date, *The Times* reported that Colonel Archibald Robinson, chief constable of Hertfordshire, had applied for warrants to arrest both Sayers and Heenan. Robinson claimed to have reliable information that the fight would come off within his jurisdiction, and while his force could normally cope with such an event on the day, in this case a crowd of perhaps eight thousand might give real problems. The warrants were immediately granted.

At about the same time, Captain Forrest, chief constable of Hampshire, wrote to his opposite numbers in adjacent counties requesting their cooperation in preventing the fight. They replied favourably.

On April 7th, Mr Godfrey of Islington, despairing of any action being taken in response to his earlier letter to his MP, wrote to Sir George Cornewall Lewis directly, asking him to take steps to prevent the fight. He said that he had had no help in such matters from Sir George's predecessors at the Home Office, Sir George Grey having been especially unsympathetic.

And on the same day, according to *The Times*,

> Articles of the peace were exhibited before the Warwickshire
> magistrates against Sayers and Heenan, the chief constable

having received information which led him to suppose that it was intended that the fight between them would take place on the borders of that county.

With so much zeal, however sporadic, to prevent the fight, it seems barely credible that nothing really effective was done. But Mr Godfrey had the right idea. It was all very well for local magistrates and police to take action, but when there was no knowing where an anticipated breach of the peace might occur, what was really needed was action on the part of the Home Office. And the Home Office was clearly not interested.

Local opposition, however, was making life difficult for the challenger. Chased from Salisbury to London, where he had no chance of being left in peace, his next move was to Jack Macdonald's home at Frome in Somerset. Then it was off to the village of Box near Bath, and so it went on. The training of the Benicia Boy took place in Wiltshire and in Somerset and in Cambridgeshire and in Northamptonshire and in Leicestershire and in Derbyshire. It was all highly unsatisfactory.

To make matters worse, there was disturbing news from home. Shortly after the Boy's departure for England, Adah Menken had discovered that she was pregnant. Whether it was to assert her child's legitimacy or to boost her career by claiming the link with a man who had suddenly become as famous as any in America, she now let it be known that she and Jack Heenan were married.

When George Wilkes, in what was now *Wilkes' Spirit of the Times* – a court injunction had forbidden him to go on using Porter's name – told his readers that she was lying, Adah angrily reasserted her claim. By this time, anything to do with the Benicia Boy was of the greatest interest to Americans generally, and the controversy became big news.

On February 18th, it took a positively scandalous turn when the *Spirit* published a letter from Alexander Menken, informing readers that:

> On the third day of April, 1856, in the town of Livingston, in the county of Polk, and the state of Texas, I had the

misfortune to be married, by a Justice of the peace, to this adventuress, since which time I have never been divorced from her...

Alexander was accusing Adah of bigamy.

Lest there should be any doubt as to his feelings, he wielded his pen as he might have a bludgeon:

> ...a woman calling herself Adah Isaacs Menken Heenan... The effrontery and nonchalance with which she sentimentalizes... this incubus... I have borne disgrace for this woman... her superlative impudence and brazenness... I would much prefer she would make use of his [Heenan's] name and discontinue mine...

Adah had previously claimed to have been divorced from Alexander, so that – always assuming that her marriage to W.H. Kneass had been legally dissolved, and that her father had not been black – her marriage to Jack Heenan was fully legal. She may even have believed it, but if so she was wrong. It must have been a relief to her when, having unburdened himself to the press, Alexander set about obtaining the divorce which she had always wanted.

She must surely have been in need of comfort, because her baby was stillborn. Perhaps, as the offspring of such an ill-matched couple, he was lucky. But if Adah was deeply upset by her loss, she did not let it show. Billing herself as the wife of the Benicia Boy, she took full advantage of a blaze of reflected glory, becoming a regular at Pfaff's fashionable restaurant, and an intimate of Walt Whitman and other bohemian figures. Her union with a pugilist bordered on the scandalous, but for an actress, notoriety could be a marketable commodity.

None of this, however, was calculated to improve the mood of Jack Heenan, already tested by the frequent changes of training location. His reaction to the news is not recorded, but, with his supposed marriage over anyway in all but name, he would presumably have been happier if his supposed wife had stayed quiet.

There was to be a further twist to the tale – though news of it could not have reached him till after the fight – when a woman came forward calling herself Josephine Heenan, and claiming to be the lawful wife of the Benicia Boy. Shortly before the fight, *Wilkes' Spirit of the Times* published a letter from Josephine to Alexander Menken, dated February 27th, saying that she had married Jack Heenan in Boston on November 14th, 1859 and that they had lived together from then until Heenan sailed for England. She claimed that Adah had effectively stalked Jack Heenan for a year, but had never been married to him.

It was a bizarre intervention, and has never been satisfactorily explained. No one has ever established who Josephine Heenan was, and no certificate of her supposed marriage to the Benicia Boy has ever been found.

In any case, none of this would become known in England until after the fight. Which was just as well, because the Benicia Boy had quite enough to contend with when, having chased him over half of England, the authorities finally caught up with him.

———

On April 5th, the chief constable of Leicestershire informed his opposite number in Derbyshire that he had received information that John Camel Heenan was now to be found at Mr H. Rice's Navigation Inn at Trent Lock, Long Eaton.

Just after dawn the following day, Good Friday, three officers of Derbyshire constabulary made their move. Jack got out of the inn just in time, and took refuge in the nearby lock house, where the lock keeper refused to allow the crushers to enter. While one of the officers went off to get a search warrant, the boxer tired of the siege and made his escape through a back window. He might have got away but for the fact that he had had no time to put anything on his feet when he ran from the inn. The handicap was too great, and he was caught.

The following morning – the day that Mr Godfrey wrote to the Home Secretary – he was brought up before Dr Heygate in Derby, where a great crowd had assembled as soon as the news got out that the American champion had been taken. His counsel, Mr Leech, apologised for the harsh language his client had used when arrested, but said that it was understandable in the heat of the moment. He complained bitterly about the constant hue and cry after his client, while Sayers was allowed to go on 'with the greatest impunity'. In the end, the Boy was bound over to keep the peace on his own recognisance of £50, plus two sureties of £25 each put down by others. He could not have wished for a better outcome.

To save the harassed American from still more unwanted attention, a decoy wearing some of his clothes left the court by the front door and entered a cab which was instantly mobbed. The man himself left quietly through the rear.

The Sporting Life was horrified at the treatment that he was receiving, and was in no doubt as to where the blame lay:

> Those who have had the management of his training have certainly bungled matters in the most abominable manner. Could anything be more absurd than to take up his training quarters in the first instance within a mile of a cathedral city, where saintly feelings and opposition were certain?… writers of the press were admitted to his presence to give him greater notoriety, and he may thank these 'friends' for being chivied all over the country.

While all this was happening, Tom Sayers was having it easy. A warrant for his arrest did come to Newmarket magistrate Mr Benyon, but he refused to sign it on the grounds that Sayers had committed no offence. It was entirely predictable. The champion was well known in Newmarket, where he had trained many times, and it was never likely that a magistrate who had not previously taken action against him would suddenly do so now.

From the point of view of the many opponents of prize fighting, this was the fundamental difference between Sayers and Heenan. Sayers had, over many years, established his right to train in certain locations, and, no one ever having tried to prevent him, it was a bit late to start now. Heenan, by contrast, had set no such precedent, and with so much discretion in the hands of local magistrates, his was always the more vulnerable position.

The point has to be made, because he and his supporters were not alone in believing that his harassment was a deliberate ploy to lessen his chances of winning. The possibility certainly exists that some of those with money on Sayers might have been happy enough to see his opponent's training disrupted, but it seems clear that almost everyone interested in the contest really was determined that the American should have fair play – provided that, on the day, he did not actually look like winning. They wanted his training to go well so that, when Tom Sayers won his inevitable victory, there could be no complaints from the loser. Those who harassed Jack Heenan, far from being fight fans, were anti-fight activists.

It was *The Liverpool Telegraph* which pointed out the paradox in the behaviour of those activists. Public interest on both sides of the Atlantic was intense and increasing. The more attention that was drawn to either of the two principals, the greater the fascination, and consequently, the poorer the chances of stopping the event. 'If the magistrates and police are trying to prevent this,' said the *Telegraph*, 'they are trying in the wrong way.'

But the circus went on, futile attempts still being made to attack the fire-proof champion. On April 12th, just four days before the fight was due, the Deputy Chief Clerk of Assize of the Norfolk Circuit, replying to a letter which has not survived, wrote to Mr Waddington at the Home Office, saying that Sayers was bailed to appear in court in Norfolk (this for participation in an earlier fight), but had not yet been called.

The following day, the indefatigable Mr Godfrey also wrote to Waddington, asking why Sayers had not been arrested, when he was clearly planning to repeat the offence for which he was presently bailed. Taking refuge behind the local organisation of the magistracy, Mr Waddington replied that only the competent court could act in such a matter, and then only if the man in question failed to appear when summonsed.

It was all quite pointless. From the moment that Jack Heenan had walked free from his court appearance in Derby, if not before, it was clear to all that the fight would not be prevented, and Mr Godfrey and others were fighting a battle already lost.

Certainly the sporting journals were not greatly concerned. Readers of *Bell's Life* and *The Sporting Life* would scarcely have known that there was any controversy. As the day of battle drew near, the latter reported enthusiastically on the champion:

> Tom Sayers's condition is perfection. During the week he has been taking his breathings on Newmarket Heath, where the indefatigable Bob Fuller never loses sight of him. Harry Brunton has, as usual, been with the champion, giving him the finishing touches. Tom looks superb. His eye is as bright as a star; his complexion as clear as alabaster.

There was, however, one more charade to be gone through before all was in readiness. The articles of agreement, in specifying that the two men must be in London by Sunday, April 15th, created certain problems. Boxers who were clearly on their way to a fight were normally in danger of arrest, and Scotland Yard sent men to Newmarket to apprehend the champion if he tried to get to the capital. Knowing he was being watched, Tom sought the aid of his horse-racing friend Sam Rogers.

On the Sunday morning, Jem Handley, a training team member of roughly the champion's build, donned Tom's flannels and cap and strolled on Newmarket Heath with Harry Brunton. The detectives followed at a distance while the man himself, having weighed in at Rogers's stables, went for lunch with Rogers, John Gideon, and another backer, Farmer Bennett – who, despite his nickname, was a well-known bookie.

In the early evening, disguised by a heavy beard and moustache, Tom travelled by horse van to a station down the line from Newmarket, and there, along with one of Sam Rogers's stable lads, he was secreted in a horsebox and dispatched to London as a racehorse. Police on watch at every station from Newmarket to the capital failed to find him, and he arrived safely at Shoreditch. The discretion with which all this was accomplished may be gauged from the fact that a large crowd, including a number of policemen in plain clothes, was waiting at the station. But the champion was nowhere to be seen, and in the early hours of Monday morning the stationmaster, who was in on the plan, released him from his hiding place.

Waiting to greet him were Nat Langham and Robert Ware, who took him by brougham to spend the night at Ware's Castle Tavern, Hampstead Heath. Theoretically, the fight might still be prevented, but in practice everyone knew it was on.

CHAPTER 12

BUILD-UP

BY THE time Jack Heenan arrived in England, the coming fight was the talk not only of the town, but of the whole country. For decades, the respectable newspapers had ignored the prize ring almost completely: occasional prosecutions of boxers and their seconds might be reported, but the fights themselves were shunned. It was different now.

Not everyone, however, was prepared to come onside. *The Daily Telegraph*, for one, resolutely refused to compromise, condemning the prize ring in the strongest terms it could command. Nor was it slow to attack those of its rivals who had suddenly taken a friendly interest in pugilism. The very day that Heenan and Cusick called on Frank Dowling, the *Telegraph* took *The Observer* to task for having carried two days earlier a 'nauseous homage to pugilism' which had already appeared in *Bell's Life in London*. The *Observer*, said its rival, carried the piece only because it and *Bell's Life* had the same owner. *The Sporting Life* was outraged, saying that the *Telegraph* had behaved disgracefully in revealing this trade secret.

The *Telegraph* had no such scruples and the following day asked a question which went to the heart of society's strangely ambivalent attitude to the prize ring. Prize fights being illegal, the *Telegraph* said,

> how is it that they are regularly advertised in a sporting print, the editor of which is not only a faithful and unctuous chronicler of the most revolting incidents which mark the encounters, but is also the stakeholder and referee for the majority of the pugilistic combats which take place in this country?

Anyone might have been puzzled. Little more than a year previously, the day after the Heenan–Morrissey fight had confirmed the rising interest in pugilism in America, *The New York Herald* had noted that 'Prize-fighting has in England sunk so low in the scale of national amusements, that nobody but the dregs of the grog-shops knows anything about the ring, or takes any interest in it.'

The prize ring in England, it seemed, was a bit like prostitution. All decent people condemned it, but no one quite knew what to do about it. Writing at this time, J. Ewing Ritchie, in *The Night Side of London*, talked of 'the beastly prize-fights which still disgrace the land.' Whatever the line taken by local authorities, the will to stamp it out nationally simply wasn't there.

And with Jack Heenan's arrival in England, boxing suddenly regained something like the status it had enjoyed in the palmy days of the Regency. Pierce Egan, dead more than a decade, would have loved it. As *The Sporting Life* put it on January 21st, in terms which seemed to confuse the heroism of antiquity with the chivalry of the Middle Ages:

> The coming to the old country of the Yankee Ajax to throw down the gauntlet to the redoubtable Sir Thomas de Sayers, the Champion of England, has been noticed and commented on by all the papers, whether daily or weekly, in town or country.

As for the *Telegraph*'s obstinate refusal to share in the general enthusiasm, its attack on Frank Dowling was, according to *The Sporting Life*, 'unmitigated twaddle':

> We have been vastly amused by the Wednesday's number of the 'Daily Telegraph,' and might, perhaps, be almost inclined to be angry with the scribe of the daily Tel-a-crammer, only we know that his puny efforts to put down the prize ring are as futile as his arguments are false and strained.

Whatever the merits of its case the *Telegraph* was, for the time being, swimming against an irresistible tide. It was not only that people were gripped by the unfolding drama as they might be by the serialised instalments of a Dickens novel, but their fascination was in many cases taking the tangible form of wagers. Betting had always been the life blood of the prize ring, the stakes making up only a very small part of the money riding on any contest, and betting on the big fight dwarfed anything hitherto seen.

Sayers–Heenan was the first contest to be heavily wagered on in America as well as in England. As the Benicia Boy was setting sail, *Wilkes' Spirit of the Times* expressed surprise that even in England, odds of one hundred to eighty were being offered in Heenan's favour. It was more than just surprising. In England, Tom Sayers was widely considered invincible, and that he should not start as favourite was unimaginable.

In fact, as the *Spirit* was forced to admit on January 25th, it had been duped. In America, where Heenan was favourite, anything which tended to increase the odds against Sayers – such as the news that even his own countrymen thought him unlikely to prevail – was of course good news for those who wished to back the English champion.

There were, however, genuine reasons to fear that he might be a bad risk. Although in early February *The Sporting Life* rubbished the claim made in the *Spirit* by one J.A.D. that Sayers was drinking heavily and could sometimes be found carousing at four in the morning, *Bell's Life* would later support the American assertion: 'It is to be regretted that... he has paid so much devotion to the shrine of Bacchus, and has consumed the midnight oil so profusely...'

The fascination with the coming fight never flagged. On February 5th, *Bell's Life* said it was 'every week inundated with letters from all quarters.' And on the other side of the Atlantic, the *Spirit* explained what it was that made the contest of such absorbing interest to Americans, including those who normally disdained the prize ring:

> ... and it has for years been an established assumption with
> the bold inhabitants of Britain that physical vigour of all
> kinds deteriorates upon this continent, and year by year

this disparaging reflection is repeated in leading English journals.

The *Spirit* looked to the Benicia Boy to give England the lie, but was clear as to the magnitude of the task he faced, warning him that 'Sir Thomas de Sayers is a mighty man of war.'

So much for the patriotic view from the western side of the Atlantic. Three days later, a letter published in *The Sporting Life* under the title 'American Boasting' gave the view from the other side. 'How these Americans do talk!' exclaimed Young John Bull. 'If the championship and the Derby [in which the American horse *Umpire* was due to run] are to be won by talking, they are the boys to do it.'

But there was still plenty of good feeling between the old country and the new. In that same issue, *The Sporting Life* quoted a letter which Fred Falkland had written to George Wilkes for publication in the *Spirit*:

> I can hardly describe what a gentlemanly friend I found in Mr Dowling, of 'Bell's Life'. You would be delighted with him if you could but know him, for his just nature and pleasant manners make him a favourite with everybody.

In any case, patriotic feeling, however strong, mattered less than money, and the news of the Benicia Boy's safe arrival in England had brought a huge increase in betting on both sides of the Atlantic. One English resident of New York, according to *The Sporting Life* of February 18th, had entrusted George Wilkes with a barely-credible £10,000 to be wagered on Tom Sayers when the price was right. For those in America wishing to place a bet on the English champion, however, it was hard to get odds as favourable as they might have hoped: the attempts to persuade Americans that Sayers had little chance had not been very effective.

In England, of course, the vast bulk of the betting was on Sayers, which made it hard to dismiss out of hand *The Globe*'s report that 'there is a rumour in sporting circles that the 'roughs' will not allow the American to win, and that if he should get the advantage, there will be a wrangle with a view to deprive him of his honours.' Many could vividly recall the Caunt–Bendigo fight of 1845, when the Nottingham lambs had used their considerable muscle to ensure that the result went their way.

If such a thing were to happen, though, there were going to be plenty of Americans there to cry foul. Content hitherto to reprint *Bell's Life*'s reports of the English prize ring, some American papers were prepared this time to shoulder the considerable expense of sending their own men. First to go was William T. Bryant of the *Clipper*, who left New York on February 11th on the *City of Baltimore*. Others followed, but only, said the *Clipper*, because they had been given a lead.

It seems highly unlikely, though, that George Wilkes, in deciding to attend the fight in person, needed a lead from anybody. Only a few days behind Bryant, he arrived in Liverpool on February 29th, and visited *The Sporting Life* two days later. As well as going to the big fight, he intended to watch *Umpire* run in the Derby.[15]

As yet, whatever the tensions generated by national rivalry, the American press showed the greatest respect for Sayers, as did the British for Heenan. The Boy had omitted to pay a call on *The Sporting Life* when in London, but the Fancy saw him at the Travers–Mace fight on February 21st, and *The Sporting Life* was favourably impressed: '... he is of quiet, gentlemanly bearing and exterior, and a perfect model of a man... and we can speak with confidence that he is well worthy the warm reception he has received at our hands.'

While *The Daily Telegraph* was certainly not alone in fulminating against the prize ring, press coverage of the big fight was in general a bitter disappointment to the enemies of pugilism. The ultimate endorsement came from the most unexpected quarter. No journal in the land was more exalted than *The Saturday Review*, and it was remarkable that such an august organ should deign to mention the disreputable prize ring at all. But on February 25th, even the *Review* threw its hat into the boxing ring. 'We can venture to speak of the great event fixed for the 16 of April,' said the *Review*, 'without any danger of not being understood.'

The *Review*, as befitted so elevated a publication, soared high above the noise of battle to enquire into the causes of the extraordinary revival of interest in the prize ring. The international nature of the event was clearly significant, said the *Review*, but there was a deeper explanation, having to do with a crisis in relations with France which some thought might even lead to armed conflict. Pugilism had achieved its highest popularity in time of war – that is, during the Revolutionary and Napoleonic Wars – and now again war threatened. The prize ring was the arena which exhibited to best advantage those qualities of which England stood most in need at such times.

That prize fighters could be aggressive was not to be doubted, and it was not unusual for them to be involved in violence even outside the ring. On Monday, March 5th, for example, Tom Paddock was the main witness at a hearing at Marlborough Street Police Court. The Redditch fighter, whose temper was notorious, had been drinking at Nat Langham's at lunchtime two days earlier when, in the course of a quarrel over a few shillings, twenty-nine-year-old Thomas Spencer (nicknamed Smash) had pulled a knife on him. Stabbed several times about the face and head, Paddock was horribly disfigured. Part of the blade had even broken off in one of the wounds. Spencer was committed for trial at the Old Bailey.

It was all very nasty, but few wanted to dwell on the seamy side of prize fighting, or the often chaotic lives of pugilists outside the ring. For the time being it was the acceptable face of boxing which every-one wanted to see, the colourful face. And nothing in prize fighting was more colourful than the colours themselves, effectively the flags of the two fighters.

For the Sayers–Heenan fight, these, as might have been expected, emphasised the international nature of the battle. Those of England's champion, designed and printed as ever by David Evans & Co. of Wood Street, Cheapside, featured an abbreviated royal standard guarded by four lions, one at each corner. Pride of place in Heenan's was taken by the American eagle, under the legend 'May the best man win'.

The Sayers colours were available from Harry Brunton's George and Dragon at the Barbican, from Owen Swift's Horse Shoe in Haymarket, and from George Bryer's Black Horse nearby. Those of his opponent were on sale at Nat Langham's Cambrian Stores off Leicester Square, with Jack Macdonald also authorised to supply them. In both cases, the price was one guinea, refundable in case of defeat.

On March 10th the *Clipper* carried Bill Bryant's account of his visit to the Benicia Boy at Salisbury, including a suspiciously deftly-phrased comment on these colours: 'Sayers has for his emblem the King Beast of the forest, while mine is the King Bird of the air, and if he does not clip my wings, I will cut his tail.' It seems that Heenan's – or more likely, Bryant's – knowledge of lions was not all it might have been.

Demand was high, and, predictably, the pirates got to work. It was not long before *Bell's Life* was warning its readers that both sets of colours were registered, and any unauthorised copying would be punished.

Meanwhile, the debate over the qualities of the British and the Americans went on. On March 18th, *Bell's Life* printed a letter from B.P.W. retailing the oft-repeated assertion that the American climate was not conducive to healthy growth and development:

> He [Young America] has no taste for the athletic games of 'Young England;' he seldom rides on horseback, or enters into the fagging exercise of the sports of the field, and usually grows up a tall, narrow-chested man, without muscular development, and weak, both constitutionally and bodily... Let but two generations pass without any mixture of imported blood from the old country, and then let us see the effect that the climate has on the Anglo-Saxon race.

The same issue of *Bell's Life*, however, gave a pessimistic opinion on the chances of putting B.P.W.'s opinions to the test. With the authorities now so vigilant, said the paper, it was hard to see how the fight could come off at all. There seemed to be little chance of arranging a special train, and the Fancy were tired of 'aquatic excursions'. Even if the mill did take place, it was certain that only a small number of spectators could be present.

In truth, it seems hard to believe that Frank Dowling seriously doubted that the fight would come off. It may be that he was merely hoping to discourage large numbers of would-be spectators whose inevitable disappointment could turn to anger, which might in turn lead to scenes that would bring obloquy on the rejuvenated prize ring.

Certainly *The Sporting Life* saw no serious danger that the fight might be prevented. Going straight to the heart of the matter, the paper pointed out that it was almost inconceivable that anything should go wrong with an event on which a huge amount of money had already been staked. As for transport, a special train might well be arranged – though if so, the fare would be set high enough to exclude 'roughs'.

Over in America, no one was even considering the possibility that the fight might be prevented. For one thing, newspapers would not have gone to the trouble and expense of sending special correspondents across the ocean to cover an event which might not even happen. On March 21st, *The Sporting Life* reported that cartoonist Thomas Nast of the *New York Illustrated News* was in Newmarket, sketching the preparations of Tom Sayers. He had already done as much for Heenan.

Such was the level of interest in the States that Frank Queen chose to bring out the March 24th issue of the *Clipper* a day early: 'We this week go to press one day in advance of our usual time... so that our readers may have the earliest intelligence regarding the progress of the "Great International Match."' The truth seems to have been that the first dispatch from Bill Bryant, describing his arrival in Liverpool and his movements in London, missed the March 17th issue in which Queen had expected to print it, and he was anxious to waste no more time.

In the same issue, Queen told his readers that 'From the orders already pouring in upon us for our INTERNATIONAL CLIPPER, it is evident that the circulation of that sheet will be greater than that of any newspaper ever issued.' Frank Queen did not go in for understatement.

As the month wore on, excitement mounted on both sides of the Atlantic, and American fight fans began arriving in London. Most prominent among them was John Morrissey, who, in company with Paddy Hughes and Dad Cunningham, had sailed on Wednesday, March 14th on the *Africa*, sister ship of the *Asia* which had taken Jack Heenan to England two months before. Also on board were Albert Berghaus and Dr Augustus Rawlings of *Frank Leslie's Illustrated Newspaper*. Just before they sailed, Morrissey had received a telegram. It gave him the news which was to appear in more detailed form in the *Albany Evening Journal* the following day.

> Drowned.—Joanna Morrissey, mother of John Morrissey, the pugilist, was yesterday morning found drowned in the Poestenkill creek, Rensselaer county. She was of intemperate habits, and has repeatedly served out terms of imprisonment in our penitentiary for intoxication. In attempting to cross the bridge she probably lost her way, and walked into the creek in a state of intoxication.

Morrissey might have been forgiven for wishing that the news had been kept from him till his return. There was not, after all, much that he could have done about it.

After a stormy crossing, the *Africa* arrived in Liverpool on the afternoon of Monday, March 26th. Two days later – the very day that Mr Godfrey wrote to Sir Fitzroy Kelly – Morrissey was in London, paying his respects at the offices of *Bell's Life*. 'His mug is all over that of a pugilist,' wrote Dowling, 'and there is a look about him that convinces one at once that he is a tough customer.' Morrissey said that, if reputation could be trusted, Sayers should win easily, but might have trouble if he was below his best. He had already staked £600 on the English champion, whom he would visit later that day.

The London correspondent of *The New York Times* was not impressed: 'I do not think it very creditable of Morrissey to interest himself so ardently in behalf of Sayers. Has he any spite against his former antagonist? Was he not satisfied with beating him?'

Morrissey would not have cared. Whatever the effect on him of his mother's untimely death, he was on holiday, and was lionised at Owen Swift's, Nat Langham's, Alec Keene's, and other sporting houses around town. He was also anticipating a big pay-day when Tom Sayers won the fight.

By the end of March, excitement on both sides of the ocean was intense. The *Clipper* spoke for all the United States on the last day of the month: '"Whate'er we do, where'er we be," fight, fight, fight is the topic that engrosses all attention; throwing for the time being the coming Presidential Conventions altogether in the shade.'

This was a reference to the presidential election due later in the year, for which the parties had yet to choose their candidates. Slavery – there were now nearly four million slaves – was a bitterly contentious issue, and some even feared that the Union might break apart if an anti-slavery candidate was victorious. Would the Southern states be prepared to accept, for example, the election of Abraham Lincoln of Illinois, one of the front runners for the Republicans? Just three months previously, a headline in *The New York Herald* had read 'THE BLOODY FRATRICIDAL WAR BETWEEN THE NORTH AND THE SOUTH FORESHADOWED'. For the time being, however, as the *Clipper* said, the big fight was all that most people cared about.

On the other side of the Atlantic, arrangements for the great day – still supposedly Monday, April 16th – were well advanced. By the beginning of the month it was known that, in spite of the expressed doubts of *Bell's Life*, a special train had indeed been organised. On April 1st, Dowling, mindful no doubt of the Home Secretary's anxiety to ensure that the fight did not come off in the Metropolitan district, warned his readers that 'The extraordinary distance which the vigilance of the authorities has rendered necessary involves a start long before daybreak.' *Bell's Life*, he said, was being swamped with letters requesting information, but none would be given without a remittance of two shillings and sixpence. 'It does not pay', said Dowling, 'to keep clerks for other people's amusement.'

Three days later, Henry Feist, Dowling's counterpart at *The Sporting Life*, reacted with fury to the news that warrants were now out for the arrests of both Heenan and Sayers. 'It is perfectly outrageous,' he thundered, 'that a few provincial Dogberries should be permitted to interfere with a contest of such international importance, and set themselves up as arbiters of taste throughout an entire kingdom.'

In truth, what was outrageous was that a supposedly respectable newspaper could fulminate openly against duly appointed magistrates for attempting to do what was no more than their duty. But by this time, nobody cared about properly constituted authority. All that interested most people was the fight, and anyone trying to prevent it might expect to be vilified.

The police were in a most unenviable position. There was really no question of stopping the contest, but the chief constable on whose patch it took place would probably have to carry the can for what was sure to be considered a major breach of the peace. From the start of the month, *Bell's Life* claimed on April 8th, Kent police officers had been posted on all bridges over the main London to Dover line, equipped with red flags and a signalling system which would ensure that developments were swiftly relayed to headquarters. Dowling thought that the chief constable should have found something better to do with his time and resources.

Certainly, the efforts of any one police force would be quite ineffectual in preventing the fight, and everybody knew it. The day before Dowling gave his opinion of the actions of the Kent police, *The Sporting Life* announced that over two hundred thousand orders had already been taken for the issue which would carry the report of the fight. That it would take place was apparent to all.

The same issue of the same paper reported something which bore out the eternal truth that where speculation is intense, rumour will be rife and gullibility high. In the previous few days, there had been great excitement at a report that the fight had already come off, and 'that Sayers had polished Benicia's child off in a few seconds, and broken his most important limbs.' A variation of this story appeared in *The Morning Star*, which claimed to know its provenance:

> A rumour prevailed in Liverpool yesterday that the fight between Tom Sayers and the 'Benicia Boy' came off in the morning. Sayers was reported to have thoroughly beaten his antagonist, and to have broken his own collar-bone.

Three and a half thousand miles away on the other side of the Atlantic, the *New York Clipper* claimed to be better informed. On April 14th, its subscribers read that the fight had indeed come off early, but not as early as *The Morning Star* had heard: 'we may state authoritatively, that the fight will take place on Friday, the 13th instant, instead of the 16th...' As for when *Clipper* readers might expect to hear the news, the *Africa* was to leave England on the fourteenth, but would not necessarily reach New York before the faster *Vanderbilt*, due to sail four days later.

Whichever vessel arrived first, the *Clipper* had a warning for its readers: 'No doubt there will be reports of the fight put in circulation the moment the steamer arrives. Be careful of all such. Bogus reports are now printed ready to be imposed on the public as genuine.'

As the day grew near, excitement turned almost to frenzy. On April 5th, New York's *Harper's Weekly* told its readers of the futility of preaching against the great event:

> ...moralists must be writing and clergymen must be preaching to very little purpose, since the bulk of the people in England and America are heart and soul engrossed in a fight compared to which a Spanish bull-bait is a mild and diverting pastime.

The Manchester Guardian on April 16th – the officially appointed day of battle – noted that interest extended even beyond England and America: 'certainly no pugilistic contest ever decided has excited so great an interest, both in this and other countries, as the forthcoming conflict between Sayers and Heenan.'

Even when it was all done, the press still struggled for words to express the extraordinary fascination which the fight had exerted over just about everyone. On April 19th, the *Daily News* said that, on the day of the fight, 'if a tame eagle had landed on Dover cliffs from the opposite shores with a manifesto of "liberation" under his left wing, the expectation and excitement could hardly have been more universal or more intense.' It could hardly have been otherwise when 'from duke to costermonger, men of all sorts, sizes, and degrees amongst us were thinking and talking and reading nothing but the Fight.'

Three days later, *The News of the World* looked back with wonder on the frenzied excitement which had swept through a nation which, a few short months previously, would barely have recognised its cause:

> The general public, perhaps, scarcely knew that there
> was such a pastime in England as 'prize fighting'... until
> the 'Benicia Boy' had arrived from the United States of
> America... when forthwith a wondrous excitement ran
> through all classes of society...

It was no different across the ocean: 'If Queen Victoria had eloped with Napoleon III, [or] his Holiness Pope Pius Ninth had committed suicide' said *The New York Herald* after the news of the outcome of the fight had reached America, 'the news could not have created more excitement than that which thrilled through our country on Saturday last.'

Two and a half thousand miles away in San Francisco, the *Daily Evening Bulletin* told its readers what they most certainly already knew: 'The fight swallows up all other topics.'

The New York Times, as befitted such a prestigious publication, was a little more reflective, looking forward to a time when the names of Sayers and Heenan, then more familiar even than those of the British prime minister and the American president, might be forgotten: 'The leading English and American journals of March and April, 1860, will be a curious study for the historian in the year 2000. He will find the names of Heenan and Sayers jostling those of Palmerston and Buchanan...'

CHAPTER 13

LONDON BRIDGE

BECAUSE PUGILISM was illegal, arrangements for a fight had to be clandestine. What this implied before the coming of the railway – which, for most parts of the country, meant the 1840s – was that, with the exception of the rich and leisured, only local people could attend a fight.

The railway simplified matters for fight organisers. Secrecy was now more easily achieved, since so few people needed advance information as to where the fight would come off. Indeed, with the exception of the organisers, only the train driver had to know, and even he could be left in ignorance until the train left the station – or even longer, as for the Sayers–Grant fight in 1852, when the driver had sealed orders to be opened en route.

For would-be spectators, it was necessary only to reveal, the night before the fight, the name of the station from which the excursion would depart, and the time. The result was that police and magistrates – unless, as sometimes happened, they had found means of getting the information in advance – had no idea that a breach of the peace was about to take place in their area until it was actually happening.

At that point they might, and often did, take steps to put a stop to it, but the Pugilistic Benevolent Association, under whose auspices prize fights took place in mid-century, were well versed in ways of making things difficult for the authorities. In addition to the maximum secrecy in organising a fight, they always looked for a location on the border of two counties – or more, if possible. This enabled them, in the event of interruption, to resume proceedings quickly nearby, since a magistrate's authority did not extend beyond his own county.

The other two important criteria were that the chosen site should be far from any major town which might have a sufficient number of police to be able to stop proceedings, and of course – unless a river journey was involved – that it should be near a railway. In the weeks preceding the big fight of 1860 there was endless speculation as to where it might come off. What everyone knew was that it would take place on or around April 16th, and that, in accordance with normal procedure, tickets would be available only the night before. The vital information would be printed in *Bell's Life in London*, and would certainly be ascertainable at any sporting tavern in the metropolis as soon as it was known.

It was on the morning of Sunday, April 15th that readers of *Bell's Life* learned that those wishing to attend the big fight should present themselves at certain of London's sporting houses the following evening. No one was in any doubt as to what this meant: the fight would come off on Tuesday morning. Despite the earlier information that it would be on the Monday, no one would have been surprised.

This information ensured, amongst other things, a very profitable Monday night for the taverns named. As it happened, they had been doing pretty well anyway, for so anxious were the Fancy not to miss the fight that, even as early as Saturday evening, most of the city's sporting houses were, as *The Sporting Life* put it, 'crowded almost to suffocation by anxious inquirers wishing to know the whereabouts, &c. of the forthcoming fight for the Championship.'

Sporting houses were a well-established phenomenon. Virtually every prize fighter of any note aspired to have his own pub, and Tom Sayers was not an exception. The only reason that he was not a publican was that his one foray into the business in 1853 had ended in the failure of the Bricklayer's Arms. Continuing success in the ring had rendered that failure less damaging than it might have been, but for many fighters, only a flourishing inn stood between them and destitution once their fighting days were over.

In *The Night Side of London*, J. Ewing Ritchie gave his view of such hostelries around 1858. One of their regular patrons had recommended them to him for 'fun, civility, mirth, good-humour... over a cheerful glass.' Ritchie decided to try one for himself. He identified Ben Caunt's Coach and Horses in St Martin's Lane just up from Trafalgar Square as 'perhaps the principal one', and it seems likely that this, the scene of the fire of 1851 which had taken the lives of two of Caunt's children, was the one on which he based his description.

Inviting his reader to come with him in spirit, he made his own opinion clear at the outset. 'In spite of the assurance of civility and good humour, I don't think you will stay long, but will feel on a small scale what Daniel must have felt in the lions' den.'

> We enter, we will say, Bang Up's hostelry, about ten of a Thursday evening; there is Bang Up at the bar, with his ton of flesh and broken nose. Many people think it worth while to go and spend one or two shillings at Bang Up's bar, merely that they may have the pleasure of seeing him, and consider him cheap at the money. I don't admire their taste.

The bar was downstairs, but the action took place upstairs. For a price, you entered a room in which a few gentlemen were drinking gin and smoking cigars, but the bulk of the company were not gentlemen at all: "Twenty or thirty mean-looking men are seated along the side; they are mostly dirty, and have broken noses; they are not very conversational... Gloves are produced, and some sparring takes place."

The room was decorated with portraits of Bang Up...

> looking grosser and more animal than ever. Secondly Mrs Bang Up, the exact counterpart of her bosom's lord; then a tribe of Bang Ups junior... Then – for the room is a complete Walhalla [*sic*] – we have portraits of sporting heroes innumerable, with villainous foreheads, all 'vacant of our glorious gains,' heavy eyes, thick bull necks, and very short croppy hair.

If it was Ben Caunt's which Ritchie visited, it is likely that two of the portraits which he saw in the upper room were of the children lost in the fire of January 15th, 1851. There could be tragedies even in lives as gross and animal as that of Ben Caunt.

The world had moved on since 1851, but Caunt had stayed put. The Coach and Horses was a successful business, and he and his family were prepared to live with their terrible memories. And on a good night when the place was bustling, life no doubt still held some meaning.

Sadly for Ben Caunt, his business was not bustling at the time of the big fight in April 1860, for, as a consequence of permitting gambling on the premises, he had just lost his spirits licence. Trouble was common at the Coach and Horses, and the magistrates' decision should not have surprised him. Still, coming on top of the death of his wife the previous year, the relegation of his establishment to the status of alehouse must have been a heavy blow.

The nearby Round Table, headquarters of the Heenan contingent, was itself relatively quiet on the Saturday before the fight, but just along the way at Oxenden Street, George Bryer's Black Horse was very busy, while in Soho, Alec Keene's Three Tuns was crowded with those anxious to have the landlord's informed opinion of the champion's condition. He was, said Keene, at his very best.

The following night the Round Table was livelier, the Americans in high spirits after receiving a heartening report of their man's progress. The Black Horse was packed, and in Tichborne Street off Haymarket, hundreds were locked out of Owen Swift's Horse Shoe. Swift was one of the fight organisers, and was thus considered an excellent source of information. Betting, without which prize fighting could not survive, was lively, one well-known patron of the ring laying £100 to £55 on Sayers.

A mile and a half away at Barbican, Harry Brunton was doing equally well at the George and Dragon. As the champion's trainer, Harry's opinion was sought by all, and his large hall, which seated upwards of two hundred, was full to overflowing.

———————

But if the sporting houses were lively on Sunday, it was nothing to the excitement of Monday. Owen Swift, Nat Langham, George Bryer and

Harry Brunton were all guaranteed a big night, *Bell's Life* having named them as ticket sellers. The Americans were out in force, and the home-bred Fancy had flooded into London by road and rail, determined to witness the greatest sporting event of the age. Writing in *The Illustrated Police Budget* some forty years later, a participant recalled the crush at Owen Swift's, where he was obliged to spend all evening, since 'having once got in I was utterly unable to get out.'

> … never have I seen anything to compare with that never-to-be-forgotten night preceding the great battle between Sayers and Heenan. The people were literally packed as tight as sardines in a box, or herrings in a barrel. The noise was awful. There was one continuous roar of voices shouting for tickets. It was impossible for half or even quarter of the throng to get near enough to the receipt of custom… to obtain what they wanted. And the language of the disappointed ones was of the strongest…

Harry Brunton's was just as bad.

The large crowd at the Black Horse included Tom's father, also his three brothers. Also present for at least part of the evening were John Morrissey and his former trainer, Jack Hamilton. Perhaps the most discriminating of Bryer's guests, however, was Harry Hill, an English exile whose New York bar had become famous. The betting was generally at two to one, with one well-heeled Sayers supporter prepared to offer two hundred to eighty.

At the Three Tuns, Alec Keene's clientele included Bob Brettle, who had so recently aspired to Tom's throne, and who had brought with him the massive silver belt which stood witness to his prowess. Also present was Sam Hurst, known as The Stalybridge Infant. Hurst was as yet a novice, but already his ambition flew as high as had Brettle's. And if the Birmingham man's failure had had anything to do with his small stature, this was not a problem for Hurst, who stood two inches above six feet, and weighed around two hundred and twenty pounds. Certainly, *The Sporting Life* was impressed:

> ... if he does not belie his cognomen, no one ever did; he is
> almost one of the most powerful-looking young men that
> we have ever encountered... he has a fine, keen piercing eye,
> a swarthy-looking mug, with the left eye slightly puffed,
> and very much discoloured; his smeller is of a size large
> enough for one to hit...

Owen Swift, as the correspondent of *The Illustrated Police Budget*
said, had more business than he could handle. From early afternoon the
Horse Shoe was host to a large crowd, all anxious to have the latest news,
and to get a glimpse of some of the noted pugilists who were certain to
put in an appearance. Outside, the pavement was blocked by those who,
unable to gain admittance, stood peering in. Hansoms arrived in quick
succession as the evening progressed, with, so *The Sporting Life* tells us
'cigar-smoking young "swells", who at once threaded their way into the
close atmosphere, and long narrow coffee-room.'

John Morrissey, having moved on from the Black Horse, was leaning
on a partition in front of the bar, smoking silently. The Horse Shoe was
not short of former champions, for Bill Perry and Ben Caunt – who must
have left someone else in charge at the Coach and Horses – were also
present. Bob Brettle, having quit the Three Tuns, took a seat briefly in
the middle of the crowded coffee room, before going on to visit other
houses.

It was just after nine o'clock when John Gideon put in an appearance.
He was, as *The Sporting Life* put it, 'all bustle and anxiety,' and 'at once
commenced diving in his capacious pockets for Tom's colours, which he
passed around with a mild enquiry of "Won't you take one of our little
man?"' A short time later, a number from the enemy camp appeared,
including Fred Falkland and Jack Macdonald, who rivalled Gideon in
the business he did with Jack Heenan's colours. The Americans readily
accepted two to one on Sayers, Falkland saying that in the previous few
days hundreds of bets had been made at those odds.

The only place which rivalled Owen Swift's for business on the night
was Harry Brunton's. At the George and Dragon, everyone wanted to
talk to Tom's trainer. One of his customers was Jerry Noon, who wished
to make an eccentric bet at ten to one that once the men were stripped,

the American would be favourite. He also claimed that during training, Heenan had sparred with Nat Langham and had come off second best.

Anyone wishing to establish the truth of that story would have had to go west to Leicester Square, where Nat's Cambrian Stores was busy all day, the odds in general being two to one on Sayers. Coincidentally, Nat was in the same plight as to his near neighbour and former mentor Ben Caunt: as a consequence of frequent disorder in the street outside his tavern, his spirits licence had been suspended. He was, however, still permitted to sell beer, and kept his house open on that basis. Many Americans were present, since Ould Nat's was the only place where there was any possibility that the Boy himself might show. They were to be disappointed.

Still, it was quite a night for all the sporting houses. As for its cause, those lucky enough to get tickets had to pay three pounds for them. The purchasers had no idea where they might go, but they could be quite sure that the railway, with well over a thousand tickets to sell, would make a healthy profit from the excursion.

As *Bell's Life* had warned, the departure time was very early. In fact, the expensive tickets required holders to present themselves at London Bridge Station at quarter to four in the morning. This told everyone that South-Eastern would be their carrier, and thus defined the area within which the battle would be staged. It was not the first time that South-Eastern's secretary Samuel Smiles – who knew exactly where they were going, and knew they were paying six times the normal fare – had done a deal with fight organisers. The archetypal Victorian, Smiles was a perfect exemplar of everything opposed to pugilism, but he was also a man of business. There were times when morality had to take second place.

Great was the speculation as to where exactly the fight would come off, but it didn't really matter. All that signified was that arrangements were well in hand, and nothing was now going to stop the big event.

The brutally early start, however, posed problems. If they had to be up by three o'clock, ticket-holders had to choose between going to bed very early, and not going to bed at all. With lax licensing hours, many of those who wanted to make a night of it simply stayed in the pub all evening. The sporting houses at least were unlikely to throw them out on such a night – always assuming they had been able to get in in the first place.

There were other hostelries, too, which might be expected to remain open well into the early hours. Richard Henry Dana, author of *Two Years Before the Mast*, wrote of one which he visited one night in July 1856:

> It being about midnight, I stroll through the purlieus of Covent Garden, all alive with Gin Shops, gas lights, flaunting women, and rattling carriages, and into Evans' famous Cyder Cellar. Here is a hall as large as the largest concert halls in America, open to all, with good music, vocal and instrumental, and supported solely by what the people who enter it buy to eat or drink. It was crowded, almost to suffocation. Only men are admitted, and the conduct of all was decent and orderly, and the constant passing in and out, showed the great number of people who visit it in the course of the night. The walls are lined with portraits, copies, chiefly of actors and poets, and each guest has given him a pamphlet of the ballads and songs sung here… After midnight, as it was, little ragged boys were running along the sidewalks about Covent Garden, turning somersets and standing on their hands, begging pennies from 'kind gentlemen' for 'poor boy and poor parents at home.'

The Cyder Cellar was packed the night before the big fight.

But there was another side entirely to London's nightlife, and it is a safe bet that a number of ticket-holders for the big fight took advantage of it. The police at the time claimed that London had ten thousand whores; the press multiplied that figure by ten. As *The Times* put it, on October 8th, 1858 (three days after Bill Benjamin's first encounter with Tom Sayers), in no other European capital was there 'daily and nightly such a shameless display of prostitution as in London.'

Different places were favoured depending on the time of day, but prostitutes were particularly noticeable in Fleet Street, the Strand and

Haymarket. In an attempt to raise the tone of their neighbourhood, Regent Street shopkeepers had, in 1848, succeeded in forcing the demolition of John Nash's Quadrant arcade, a notorious pick-up point.

For the vast majority of the city's prostitutes, there was barely a living to be made. As one magistrate expressed it in 1849:

> About this time, within our present district of Westminster, or halfway down the Strand towards Temple Bar, there would every night be found above five hundred or one thousand of that description of wretches; how they can gain any profit from their prostitution one can hardly conceive.

There was, however, a higher class of prostitute altogether, available to those who – like most of the ticket-holders for the big fight – had money in their pockets. Fronting on Haymarket, Kate Hamilton's was easily London's most famous brothel – though its proprietor would have thrown you out for daring so to describe it. Kate was fussy about who she admitted in the first place. Men needed money, women needed youth and beauty. It was a mix both combustible, and, for Mrs Hamilton, lucrative.

Looking back from the early years of the twentieth century, Donald Shaw, in *London in the Sixties*, painted a vivid picture of Kate Hamilton's in the sixties:

> 'Don't go yet, dear,' appealed a sweet siren as Bobby, looking at his watch, swore that when duty called one must obey, but eventually succumbed to a voice like a foghorn shouting, 'John, a bottle of champagne,' and the beautiful Kate bowed approvingly from her throne. Kate Hamilton at this period must have weighed at least twenty stone, and had as hideous a physiognomy as any weather-beaten Deal pilot. Seated on a raised platform, with a bodice cut very low, this freak of nature sipped champagne steadily from midnight until daylight, and shook like a blancmange every time she laughed.

Approached by a long tunnel from the street – where two janitors kept watch – a pressure of the bell gave instant admittance to a likely visitor, whilst an alarm gave immediate notice of the approach of the police.

Finding oneself within the 'salon' during one of these periodical raids was not without interest. Carpets were turned up in the twinkling of an eye, boards were raised, and glasses and bottles – empty or full – were thrust promiscuously in; every one assumed a sweet and virtuous air and talked in subdued tones, whilst a bevy of police, headed by an inspector, marched solemnly in, and having completed the farce, marched solemnly out.

One of those who preferred not to make a night of it, at Kate Hamilton's or anywhere else, was John Hollingshead, who had been deputed by Charles Dickens to report on the fight for his weekly *All the Year Round*, the successor to *Household Words*. It struck Hollingshead as he left his house that the policeman who saw him knew exactly what he was about, and his driver was 'bursting with intelligence of the great prize-fight.' From two o'clock, similar scenes were being enacted in many places around town.

Hooves clattered, harness jingled, metal-rimmed wheels rasped as the fight-goers made their way through the dark deserted streets. There had been other early-morning fight excursions from London Bridge Station, but they were as nothing to that of Tuesday, April 17th, 1860. The bridge itself, with nearly everyone coming from north of the river, was almost as much of a bottleneck as during the day.

At the centre of each span, balustrades either side supported a gas light, which illuminated the most animated scene the bridge had witnessed at such an hour. Workmen's carts, gigs, hansoms, broughams, for all the world as if it were the middle of the working day. And the clatter of hooves was accompanied by the tramp of feet as heavily-clad walkers, faces wrapped up to the eyes against the chill, made their more energetic way to the station. Below on the black water, barges and ferries crossed from the north bank.

As the crowds converged on their goal, windows were opened by curious householders, few of whom would have been in any doubt as to what was going on. And far from attempting to prevent an impending breach of the peace, the crushers patrolling the dark streets would even call to the cabs to bring back good news.

Bill Bryant described for readers of the *New York Clipper* how the Benicia Boy's inner circle spent the night. After the Round Table was closed to outside customers, they chatted about the only topic which interested them – and agreed that, barring accident or foul play, victory was certain. No one risked going to bed, and at one in the morning the Boy himself appeared in company with Jack Macdonald. They took breakfast at three o'clock, then boarded their cabs to join the crowds making for London Bridge.

At the station the noise was deafening as cabs forced their way through the throng, drivers all trying to outshout each other. 'Long before four o'clock this morning,' reported *The Globe* later in the day, 'the London-bridge station was literally besieged with spectators anxious to witness the fight.' For the *Clipper*, Bryant estimated that at least ten thousand people were there, and while this sounds seriously exaggerated, it is certain that there were far more people than tickets. Many were in possession of neat wicker baskets, *Bell's Life* having warned prospective fight-goers that refreshments would not be supplied. In the station yard, said Bryant, were at least three hundred cabs. *The Sporting Life*'s reporter did not mention his American counterpart, but noticed the arrival of Fred Falkland, carrying a large stone bottle and whispering confidentially to Jack Macdonald.

———————

London Bridge Station, the city's busiest terminus, was universally considered an eyesore. Constructed by South-Eastern ten years previously to replace an earlier building, not the least of its affronts was that it virtually blocked the view of the adjoining Brighton Railway terminus, an altogether superior edifice.

But such aesthetic considerations were not of concern to the besieging crowds in the early hours of April 17th, 1860. Anticipating that many would turn up without tickets, South-Eastern had retained a number for sale on the spot, and shortly before four o'clock a window opened. There followed an unseemly rush, leading to a press which made things difficult for everybody, and facilitated the theft of a number of tickets. One purchaser, seeing the danger, put his ticket safely inside his mouth the moment he got it.

As the throng waited for the station gates to open, numerous ruses were employed by those whose moral scruples were overcome by their determination to see the fight: one unfortunate person, producing his ticket in response to a call of 'Get your tickets ready, gentlemen!' dropped his precious pass when his hand was grabbed and his fingers bitten. He did not see it again.

At last the gates were opened. John Hollingshead found it a strange business altogether. For a start, they were opened by the police, who should theoretically have been determined to keep them locked. And then there was the behaviour of everyone involved:

> ...there was an affectation of caution on the part of the railway company in dividing the passengers, and admitting them simultaneously at different entrances. These passengers moved silently along the passages, and across the platforms, as if they were trespassers upon the company's property, who had stolen in while the directors were asleep, and were about to run away with the rolling stock, with the connivance of a small number of the railway officers.

Hollingshead was being facetious, but any of the directors of South-Eastern who read his report in *All the Year Round* might have been forgiven for failing to see the joke. Less than five years had passed since the sensational robbery in which £12,000 in gold had been stolen from the night mail to Paris, the bullion being replaced by lead of equal weight. Train robbery was no laughing matter at London Bridge.

But despite the failure of the blues to prevent that crime, many of those present on April 17th, 1860 feared that they might yet stop the big fight, and every unfamiliar figure in the crowd, Hollingshead wrote, was suspected of being a policeman. He thought that in truth any apparent indication that the police were intent on preventing the fight was sheer affectation. 'The nation', he wrote, 'has no logical complaint against the law for standing still on this occasion, but only for its ridiculous pretence of being constantly on the alert.'

A train of thirty-three carriages, with an engine front and back, filled up quickly, and then a thirty-carriage train, likewise with two engines, was called up. There was a weird assortment of rolling stock, much of it superannuated. Of the carriages, mostly some twenty feet in length, some resembled wheeled cottages, others were more like cattle trucks. The windows, according to one commentator, included Gothic, Norman and Early English. It was unimportant. The fight was the thing.

As for the nature of the crowd, Hollingshead thought that 'The two or three hundred Americans, and the small sprinkling of aristocracy and visitors, were not sufficient to modify in any perceptible degree the thoroughly animal character of the train.'[16] *The Sporting Life*, on the other hand, spoke enthusiastically of 'such a fashionable and aristocratic party as never on any previous occasion congregated round a prize ring', while *The Daily Telegraph* understood that 'authors, poets, painters, soldiers, and even clergymen, were present.' Hollingshead would have been appalled to have found himself in the midst of a more typical gathering of the Fancy.

At about four fifteen, a thrill ran through the trains, and heads appeared at all windows. Wearing a fur cap, and with an Inverness cape covering his smart suit, Tom Sayers was walking down the platform accompanied by his father, by his seconds Harry Brunton and Jemmy Welsh, also by Farmer Bennett and John Gideon. And just five minutes later, the American champion made his appearance, in the company of Fred Falkland, Jim Cusick and Jack Macdonald. Sayers had made no effort to disguise his appearance, but Heenan was hard to recognise behind a dark bushy beard and whiskers.

At Tom's carriage door, the two men met for the first time, Jack Macdonald making the introductions. The American party was last to board the first train, and at half past four a bell rang. Steam hissed as the engines snorted louder and louder, faster and faster. Smoke belched from funnels, couplings snapped taut, the carriages lurched forward. They were on their way.

CHAPTER 14

CRESCENDO

RAILWAYS, UNKNOWN thirty years before, still embryonic ten years on from that, were now a fact of life. London had had to accommodate their termini almost in its very heart, and the shining rails were the arteries of the nation. You could now travel the five hundred miles from the capital to Aberdeen by train. It took sixteen hours in dimly lit and unheated carriages, and there were no toilets, restaurant cars or sleeping cars; but it could be done.

Nothing so arduous, however, was in store for the passengers on the two trains at London Bridge Station that morning and when they pulled out, the luminous streaks brightening the eastern sky seemed to promise a fine day. With most of the passengers still half asleep, talk in the carriages, so Hollingshead tells us, was fitful for several miles.

But as they left the town behind, a serious topic of conversation arose: in the broadening daylight ominous figures were visible at frequent intervals along the line. Clad in knee-length navy blue coats and stovepipe hats, police officers armed with cutlasses watched their progress with grim impassivity. And here and there could be seen mounted officers who would gallop off as soon as the trains came into view, their task being, presumably, to report the news to higher authority.

There was some nervousness among the passengers lest the expedition might be stopped, but this was the last thing that Metropolitan Police Commissioner Sir Richard Mayne had in mind. His only concern, in fact, was that it should *not* stop in any area under his jurisdiction. The truth was that neither Sir Richard nor any chief constable much cared what happened between Sayers and Heenan provided only that it did not happen on his patch. John Hollingshead was not alone in his belief that the authorities knew exactly where the fight would come off, and that any indication that they were intent on stopping it was pretence.

The atmosphere on the trains lightened as it became increasingly apparent that they were not to be halted, and the Fancy relaxed sufficiently to hurl cheerful insults at the crushers as they sped past. But the less cynical still wondered what would happen if the police were guarding the line at their destination.

Such a problem did not arise. London Bridge being the station for Brighton and the south coast, the police, whatever their motivation, were on full alert all along the London to Brighton line. At the last possible moment, however, the pointsman at Reigate Junction diverted the trains westward, and the Fancy were not to see the blues again for some considerable time. More officers were waiting redundantly further down the Brighton line, but none on the westbound track along which the trains were now travelling.

After a halt at Guildford for the four locomotives to take on water, they came at length to the desolate heathland around Farnborough in Hampshire, and there they stopped. 'Of course,' John Gideon told *The Illustrated Police Budget* many years later, 'there were no police visible here; they were manfully doing their duty elsewhere, with a pretence of zeal which was very creditable to their talents as actors.'

The platform was not long enough to accommodate the monster trains, and many of the passengers alighted directly onto the grassy bank. But they had arrived, and that was all that mattered. It was approaching six forty-five and the early morning sun was painting the landscape in the brilliant colours of spring.

———————

The location for the fight had been selected by John Gideon as excursion manager, and Tom Oliver in his capacity as commissary general of the prize ring. Isolated, though not too far from London, served by the railway and on the border between two counties, Farnborough was an ideal choice. Winchester, the headquarters of Hampshire constabulary, was far away, while magistrates in Farnham, the nearest town of any size, had no authority outside Surrey.

In their search for a suitable location, Gideon and Oliver had travelled to Farnborough by South-Western and returned by South-Eastern, each of which had its own station. That the village should be served by two lines seems remarkable, considering that its population in 1851 was under five hundred. The census of 1861, however, showed a population of five and a half thousand, for in the middle of the decade the Army had moved in and set up large permanent military camps between Farnborough and Aldershot.

As a result, the centre of gravity of the village had moved south, and the old village of Farnborough Street was soon overshadowed by South Farnborough, closer to the camps. The fight was to take place near South-Eastern's station, which had opened in 1849 at the north end of Farnborough Street.

The old village had two pubs, the Ship and the Prince of Wales, and one substantial shop, which occupied part of a long, low half-timbered building on the street which ran between the two stations. There was a leaded window with small, diamond-shaped panes, and a sign above the door, which read 'Susanna Smith, licensed to sell Tea, Coffee, Tobacco, Snuff, Vinegar and Soap'. The shop was kept scrupulously clean, and was fondly remembered sixty years later by Jessie Challacombe in *Jottings from a Farnborough Note Book*:

> Think of the appetising air of Susan's shop! Tallow candles, tobacco, lard and butter, tea, coffee, snuff, vinegar and soap, cheese, carraway seeds, bacon, bread and maybe, bloaters. Then there were Susan's lollipops, pear drops, acid drops and peppermints, balls of string, and drawers containing other mysteries. Together they produced that mysterious smell which is to be found nowhere but in a village shop.

But not everything in Farnborough was so clean and well-ordered. On either side of the roadway was an open ditch, often stagnant with sewage, while the pigs kept by many villagers were allowed to roam freely, and ducks and geese waddled where their fancy took them. Farnborough was an unassuming location for one of the greatest sporting events the country would ever know.

Crescendo

Frederick Locker-Lampson, poet and man of letters, recalled in the final years of his life the sheer joy of being there:

> For several months I had been confined to London pavement and the dead timber of the official desk. How well I remember the strange delightfulness of the green trees, the fresh grass, cool beneath my feet, and the gracious April air as it played upon my face!

But Farnborough was less delighted with the Fancy than the Fancy were with Farnborough. The villagers were well aware of what was coming – Gideon and Oliver's negotiations could not be kept secret from the local people – and they knew from previous experience what to expect. Doors were locked, guard dogs snarled, Susanna Smith's shop was secured. Fortress Farnborough was ready to defend itself.

The fight-goers, however, had nothing in mind other than to get to the scene of the action as quickly as possible, and the village was to get off lightly. But Locker-Lampson and his companions, much as they might have enjoyed being out in the country at last, were not to have an easy time of it. Old Tom Oliver, said to have witnessed every championship fight for fifty years, led the way. Carrying the brand-new ropes and stakes – the latter painted bright blue and mauve, and all bearing the letters PBA (Pugilistic Benevolent Association) in brilliant yellow – were his son Fred, and assistant Puggy Ryan. It was to be a most awkward cross-country hike. *The New York Herald* gives some idea of the scene:

> First went the ring maker, who cleared a wide ditch and a hedge; and after him followed the crowd. Such mishaps we never remember to have witnessed; not one half of the crowd who attempted to leap the hedge and ditch succeeded, but either slipped backwards when they reached the opposite bank, or else fell headlong in the stream. In one place, there were two frail spars or rails across, and

here several adventurous individuals attempted to effect a crossing in safety; several succeeded, but a young sprig of the aristocracy, who was accompanied by his groom, broke the bridge in the middle, and dropped himself comfortably into the stagnant waters.

Clothes were soaked and torn, feet got stuck in bogs. And beds of stinging nettles lay in wait for the unwary, the Americans apparently faring worst through lack of familiarity with the dangerous plants. The sheer incompetence of these city-dwellers in negotiating the minor hazards of a short country walk must have made them seem much less threatening to the villagers cowering behind their closed windows, and, curiosity getting the better of them, many now ventured out to swell the numbers. Some of the sturdier ones even made money by hiring themselves out as bearers to those fight-goers who preferred not to risk getting their feet wet.

The Sporting Life told the tale:

> ... the crowd dashed through the hedges and leaped the various ditches with the utmost enjoyment. Some of the brooks were, however, too formidable to render a jump secure and those unwilling to ford them in true campaigning fashion paid eager rustics to carry them pigaback to the opposite embankment.

After covering nearly half a mile in this boisterous manner, the fight-goers came to a meadow some three hundred yards long and transected by the railway by which they had arrived. It would in fact have been easier and quicker simply to have followed the track and cut across the field. The chosen spot was circled sparsely by trees, which afforded the more agile and enterprising spectators the best possible view of the coming action. The choice of location was generally approved by those who understood such things, and it was noted with satisfaction that the ground was soft, lessening the possibility that a chance injury from a fall might spoil the contest.

As the Olivers and Puggy Ryan set about establishing the fighting area – which had to be twenty-four feet square and surrounded by ropes at two levels – a brisk trade was done in tickets for the inner ring. At ten shillings, these were unusually expensive, but many were sold to the likes of Locker-Lampson and Lord Beaufort – one of an improbable-sounding eighty-seven noblemen who, according to Bill Bryant, had acquired from Fred Falkland advance information as to the time and place of the fight. Nor was there any shortage of buyers for camp stools for the inner ring at a sovereign apiece.

As it turned out, however, this was something of a swindle, for the second enclosure was never established, and those who parted with their money derived no particular benefit. The only spectators who enjoyed genuinely privileged positions were newspaper reporters such as Bill Bryant, Ned Smith of *Bell's Life in London*, and Nicholas Woods of *The Times*.

Under inspector Billy Duncan there were twenty-two ring keepers, among them several of Tom's former victims: as well as Dan Collins, Jack Grant and Bob Brettle, there was Tom Paddock, his face still mangled from the brawl at Nat Langham's six weeks before. (A fortnight had passed since Paddock's assailant had been sentenced at the Old Bailey to nine months' hard labour.) To assist them in keeping the crowd in order, they had whips and clubs with which they would unmercifully belabour any spectator who came nearer to the ring than they thought proper. They were to have a busy day of it.

In the early stages, however, the spectators were tractable enough, and did not venture so close to the ring as to raise the ire of these formidable stewards. The nearest finally settled down some six feet from the ropes while others further back jostled for the best vantage point. And while a few resourceful entrepreneurs moved among the crowd selling oranges and ginger beer, the ring-makers put the finishing touches to the fighting area. The spaces for the seconds were defined, the scratch was scored in the middle.

When all was ready, a plush cap skimmed through the air into the ring, to be followed more sedately by its owner, Tom Sayers. In token of acceptance of the challenge, a very similar cap was then thrown in, and the Benicia Boy came through the ropes after it. The two principals approached each other, and Harry Hill, English proprietor of New York's most celebrated sporting house, reported the brief conversation which followed a warm handshake.

'How are you, my boy?' asked Tom, 'A fine morning this.'

'Yes,' replied Jack, 'we've got a beautiful morning for it.'

'If a man can't fight such a day as this,' said Tom, 'he can't fight at all.'

The pleasantries continued between the seconds – Brunton and Welsh for Sayers, Macdonald and Cusick for Heenan – each pair having a large square wicker basket containing water bottles and sponges. Heenan then tossed a penny and, Sayers calling wrongly, chose the marginally higher ground with the sun behind him. This conferred some small advantage, since boxers might face each other without moving for some time at the start of a round, and were permitted to go to their seconds for treatment during it. The man in the corner facing the sun would have to contend with the glare markedly more often than his opponent.

Almost all of the Americans moved immediately over to Heenan's corner. They meant, of course, to give moral support, but they may also have been anxious to ensure the safety of their man in the midst of a largely hostile crowd. George Wilkes, notebook in hand, was among them, but John Morrissey, along with Jack Hamilton and a few others, moved to the English side of the ring.

Having retired to their respective corners the boxers, aided by their seconds, now stripped for action. Sayers's plaid suit came off to reveal white knee breeches, stockings and high quartered shoes. It was noted with interest that Heenan, similarly clad beneath his overcoat, wore ultra-modern slip-on shoes with elastic sides. As ever, two sets of the colours would be on display – one worn belt-fashion by each man, a second twined round one of the neutral stakes.

It was not until the heroes were stripped that the contrast in physiques became fully apparent, a contrast which would not be seen in the ring after the introduction of formal weight divisions at the end of the century. Little over five feet eight inches tall and of average build, Tom Sayers was conceding five inches and nearly forty pounds to a challenger who was also some eight years younger. And Jack Macdonald had done a fine job on the American, who was clearly in superb condition. Locker-Lampson heard the apprehensive comment of Bob Brettle: 'Well,' he said, 'Tom may beat him, but may I be damned if he can eat him!'

In reality, of course, he was suggesting that the champion might even lose. And Brettle was far from being alone in this opinion, many of the backers of the champion, whose faith in their man had hitherto been absolute, beginning to feel twinges of nervousness. The match was, as one put it, 'a horse to a hen'. But their man had also trained hard, and the greater size of an opponent had never troubled him before.

And there was one thing in the appearance of the two fighters which seemed to be in his favour: apart from the difference in stature, the greatest contrast between them was in complexion, for Sayers was almost copper-coloured while Heenan's characteristic pallor had already earned him the nickname 'the Magnesia boy'.

It was generally believed, at a time when sun-tans were not at all fashionable, that the American champion had been too vain to allow his skin to go through the toughening process which had darkened that of his opponent. This was a potentially significant matter, for a fair skin might damage easily, and the pickled fists of Tom Sayers were ideally suited to the task.

But before the issue could be put to the test, the officials had to be appointed: an umpire for each man and a referee to arbitrate between them. Heenan nominated Fred Falkland as his umpire, while Sayers chose John Gideon. As was fully to be expected – the matter had presumably been settled in advance – Frank Dowling was appointed referee.

All was now ready, the crowd, in Ned Smith's words, being 'disposed in tolerable order by the exertions of those of the ring keepers who chose to do their duty.' The laxity of a number of these gentlemen – not entirely surprising when one of them, Ned Adams, could be openly described in *The Sporting Life* as 'drunk as usual' – was to be a matter of some controversy before the day was over.

The two principals now advanced to the scratch in the middle of the ring and took up the conventional fighting stance, turned half-on to each other, with the left foot advanced, the left arm extended and the right held diagonally across the chest. There was a moment of utter silence, recalled by Locker-Lampson as a 'tremor', before John Gideon called 'Time!'

The next few minutes were to be something of an anticlimax, but this was no surprise to experienced fight fans: where two men felt mutual respect, a highly tentative first round was always likely. For some minutes they scarcely moved, doing little more than to tap the advanced foot and dab out the left fist from time to time as if feeling their way. At length, both dropped their hands and laughed, perhaps genuinely showing how relaxed they were, perhaps protesting a little too much.

Then they took guard again, and the phoney war was resumed. The less knowledgeable spectators found it all quite tedious, but it gave Thomas Nast and the other illustrators an excellent opportunity to make a preliminary sketch of the scene. Eventually, Sayers got home on the American's nose, and the announcement of first blood was greeted with cheers from his supporters, many of whom made money out of this small success.

Heenan's fists had not found their target even once in this opening round, but he was to do much better in the second. After Tom had, in the words of Bill Bryant, 'got a stinger on the gob, which opened his lip and brought the claret', the challenger concluded the round by throwing his smaller opponent. Skill and experience could not altogether offset size and strength when the two men came to grips, and Harry Brunton was vociferous in his advice to Sayers not to attempt to wrestle.

Round three brought the first knock-down blow, thus described in the pages of *The New York Herald*: 'Heenan let out with his left, and gave [Sayers] a terrible blow on the forehead, which sounded like a clap of thunder, and knocked Sayers on the ground.' With odds being shouted throughout the fight – though with very few takers, so much money having been staked in advance – the jubilant Americans were now offering as much as five to one on their man.

The next couple of rounds were similarly one-sided, and some of the champion's partisans began to despair. Every time Sayers was down, he would kick up his legs and come up laughing, but the funny side of it was not apparent to his supporters. Even Jerry Noon, one of the ring keepers, said that it was 'all over with Tom'. His fists were ineffective, and he had no chance in a clinch. It began to look as if he was, for the first time in his illustrious career, truly overmatched.

In reality, however, the punishment which the champion had taken thus far was nothing to one of his formidable powers of endurance; it had merely helped him to gauge his task. Far from being finished, he was only now about to begin. It was in the sixth round, just when it seemed he was a beaten man, that he began to make a fight of it. Nicholas Woods of *The Times* described graphically his first really telling punch:

> ...a terrific smash full in the eye, splitting up the cheek and sending his antagonist reeling like a drunken man back into his corner. The effect of this blow was so tremendous that even before half a minute had elapsed Heenan could scarcely be recognised as the same man, so swollen, disfigured and blood-stained were his features. There were loud cheers for Sayers, who went up to Heenan's corner and peered into his face with a curious, half-puzzled expression as if he too was astounded by the effects of his own handiwork.

A strange feature of the middle part of the contest, in fact, was to be Sayers's habit of approaching Heenan's corner to inspect the damage which he had inflicted.

The sixth-round exchanges, though not all in favour of Sayers, made it apparent to everyone that he was far from finished, and the betting even began to swing in his favour. But the way Heenan fought back in the long and desperate seventh showed that he too could absorb punishment. *The Sporting Life* told the tale in the argot so familiar to the Fancy: 'Heenan opened the ball readily with his left, and made Tom's ivories rattle again, and coloured them with the Chateau Margaux.' As Ned Smith reported, however, the American did not have things all his own way: 'Heenan napped another slashing crack on the right cheek, which had the effect of at once closing his dexter goggle.'

This was no small matter. Nat Langham had beaten Sayers by closing both his eyes, and it now began to seem as if the champion might do as much for Heenan, whose right eye was now, Bill Bryant tells us, 'closed as tight as a miser's heart'. But Smith's practised eye had noticed something still more ominous for Sayers than the damaged eye was for Heenan:

his right arm was beginning to swell, and he was keeping it close to his body as if to support it. What chance would Tom Sayers have without the 'auctioneer'?

After thirteen minutes of incongruously blended skill and savagery Heenan brought round seven to a bloody conclusion. 'Striking Sayers on the nose with a blow that was heard all over the meadow,' wrote Woods, 'he felled him like an ox.' But the American too was unsteady on his legs, and both men had to be carried back to their corners. The Fancy were getting their money's worth.

A quieter round might have been expected to follow such ferocity, but in the event round eight would be little less brutal, and would last considerably longer. It would also be witnessed by a couple of police officers and by a number of country people, including women and children – their presence ignored as ever by reporters and illustrators. The handicaps of the two men were now plain to all the spectators, and the champion was loudly and frequently encouraged to close Heenan's other eye. He needed no telling.

'Sayers stepped up to the van and planted his left on the knowledge-box,' said *The Sporting Life.* 'The blow was an awful stab and it resounded all over the ring.' But Heenan was giving as good as he was getting, and Smith described 'a severe counter exchange… in which Tom got a hot'un on the whistler, which shook his ivories, and turned on a fresh tap.' The spirit of the Benicia Boy was undiminished, and he ended the round with another knock-down.

So it went on, virtually every round ending with Sayers down, yet his supporters now happy to stake money on him. Much was made of the knock-downs by the Americans, but the champion was simply putting to use the tactic he had learned from Nat Langham. And like Antaeus, he seemed only to gather strength from frequent contact with the earth, coming up laughing every time. Heenan too tried to laugh, but suspicions as to the toughness of his hide had been justified, and his face was now so disfigured that its expressions were becoming hard to read. As Harry Hill put it:

> He took every blow in first rate humour, and as long as
> his mug could show a smile, it had a smile upon it. He

tried to laugh two or three times after Sayers had cut him bad, but, 'pon my soul, his face was so out of shape you couldn't tell whether he was laughing or crying.

The same observer, much as he admired the English champion, was unimpressed by his supporters who, he said, behaved:

> ... damned shamefully. Good many of the Englishmen seemed to doubt Heenan's pluck, and every time that Sayers got a little the upper hand, they'd sing out "ere's another sure thing, ain't it, ho, ho, ho, take him away,' and such like expressions, blackguarding Heenan and his friends in the worst style.

In fact, it seems that English discourtesy towards Heenan was well matched by American mockery of Sayers, who was laughed at when he spat blood, and several times asked if he meant to fight another round. But the Boy's supporters were still more demonstrative in encouraging their own man than they were in jeering his adversary, and one of the reports carried by *The New York Herald* gave Americans the chance to see themselves through English eyes:

> We will here state that the Americans have a most unusual manner of exhibiting their satisfaction and delight. At the conclusion of each round they would clap [Heenan] on the back as if they were desirous of testing the thickness of his skin; then, when he hit Sayers well, they would jump up in the air like so many antelopes, waving their hats and shouting as though mad.

Their man was giving them plenty to shout about, seeming to put Sayers down almost at will. Bryant described a typical moment from round fourteen: 'Benish now feinted with the left, and then let go his right, planting a staggerer on Tom's bread basket'. With his right arm now useless for any purpose other than painful defence, the champion was clearly suffering. By round fifteen, he was, according to Bryant, 'very weak on his pins.' Two to one on Heenan.

Yet Sayers it seemed might still prevail if he could only close Heenan's left eye. All his energy, all his strength, all his skill were now brought to bear on that one object. Jack Macdonald frequently counselled Heenan against rashness, but many thought that the longer the fight went on, the better would be the Englishman's chances. For all his great natural physical advantage, Heenan might yet find himself at the last blind and helpless before the champion's slashing left fist.

Accordingly, Sayers set about prolonging the contest, at times even turning tail and running round the ring, a maddened Heenan pursuing him hotly and striking him on the back. And every chance that Sayers got, he went for the left eye. No one could say how the desperate struggle might end.

By the end of the seventeenth round, according to the *Herald*, there was a swelling above Heenan's right eye as big as a hen's egg. And to make matters worse, his left hand was badly swollen from the number of times it had made violent contact with the tough hide of Tom Sayers.

Still, fighting one-handed, and showing clear signs of weariness, the older man himself must have wondered if he could stay on his feet long enough to finish his task. Some of the spectators, with large sums of money wagered on the outcome of the contest, turned away and walked up and down the meadow in an agony of apprehension, unable to watch.

By round twenty-three and in defiance of the rules, Heenan was resting on a stool between rounds. A complaint from the champion's corner led to its removal, and the Boy was obliged to return to the knee of Jim Cusick. And several rounds later the American risked disqualification by striking his opponent when he was down. Dowling, however, judging that he was now almost blind, ruled the blow accidental.

Sayers was weakening all the time – 'tottering', according to Bryant – and Heenan could scarcely see, but the savagery, as Smith relates, was relentless: 'Exchanges; Heenan on the tater trap and Tom on the nose, a smasher, each drawing the cork.' So it went on. Whistlers were hit, ivories were rattled, corks were drawn, taps turned on; ruby and carmine flowed in profusion.

Bryant conceded that Heenan could by now scarcely see, but insisted that he was increasingly dominant. By the end of round thirty-three, he said, the Boy's supporters were offering five to one on their man, while those of Sayers were in despair. He claimed that many of the latter were now crowding round their man's corner, threatening the integrity of the ring by pushing against the ropes and stakes, the ring keepers being 'unwilling or unable to keep order.' They were also, according to Bryant, drawing loud attention to the growing presence of the police, who, since they had made no attempt to interfere with proceedings, had hitherto been largely ignored.

Nor had much notice been taken of a quite different group of newcomers. Thirty thousand soldiers were stationed in the military camps nearby, and when the news came that Sayers and Heenan were fighting at Farnborough, many hastened to the scene, arriving in time to witness the conclusion of the battle. Among them was W.H. Russell, former war correspondent of *The Times*, the man whose dispatches from the Crimea just a few years previously had done so much to reveal the sheer incompetence of British military organisation.

More familiar with chaos than most (though Nicholas Woods, then with the *Morning Chronicle*, had also been in the Crimea), Russell may not have been as shocked as some to see the men fight on in the absence of a referee. Bill Bryant was in no doubt as to whose fault this was, describing a scene of utter confusion, during which 'Referee Dowling, the unmanly and cowardly scrub, left his position without the slightest cause...'

Russell was present for round thirty-seven[17], by which time both men were in a desperate condition – though, as his *Times* colleague Woods put it, 'Sayers showed not half the awful marks of punishment visible all over Heenan, who was now a disgusting object.' The American was by now so nearly blind in his left eye as well as his right that it was clear that he would have to win soon if he was to win at all. It seemed, however, that he might well do so – his supporters considered it a certainty – for Sayers appeared close to collapse. Something would have to give.

Whenever the two men came to grips, the size and strength of Heenan gave him an insuperable advantage, and Sayers accordingly did all he could to keep his man at a distance. But he could not hope to succeed every time, and things went badly wrong for him in the thirty-seventh round. Nicholas Woods describes what happened:

> Heenan got Sayers's head under his left arm, and supporting himself by the stake with his right held his opponent bent down, as if he meant to strangle him. Sayers could no more free himself than if a mountain was on him. At last he got his left arm free, and gave Heenan two dreadful blows on the face, covering them both with the blood, but Heenan, without relaxing his hold, turned himself so as to get his antagonist's neck over the rope, and then leant on it with all his force. Sayers rapidly turned black in the face, and would have been strangled on the spot, but that the rules of the ring provide for what would otherwise be fatal contingencies, and both umpires called simultaneously to cut the ropes. This was done at once, and both men fell heavily to the ground, Sayers nearly half strangled.

Now this account is broadly in agreement with other sources until Woods claims that the cutting of the ropes was in accordance with the rules. This is simply not true, and it is certain that Falkland, as Heenan's umpire, would not have sanctioned such action just when his man seemed to be on the verge of victory. What is not to be doubted, however, is that the ring was broken in, and it is virtually certain that the Englishman was thereby saved from immediate defeat if not worse.

The upshot, in any case, was utter confusion, with spectators encroaching on the fighting area and Frank Dowling no longer relevant. It seems that he may have tried to end the contest at this point, but if so his instructions did not get through to the combatants, and the battle went on for some time in an increasingly confined space before he finally managed to reassert his authority and call a halt. Sources differ widely on the number of rounds fought after the cutting of the ropes, but it is clear that, before Dowling's return, Sayers was refusing to fight on.

An enraged Heenan, believing that he was being cheated, went over to the opposing corner, sent Jemmy Welsh flying, and attempted to claim victory. W.H. Russell, now at the ringside, and of all those present the one most used to describing carnage, gives us some idea of the extraordinary atmosphere:

> In two hours the youthful giant is a fearful object, blinded, bloody, infuriated as a wild beast, bellowing with rage, striking right and left, friends and foes – his fair hide covered with blackened weals, his hands puffed with dealing heavy blows, hideous gashes on his face – the centre of a yelling maddened crowd...

Dowling, however, finally managed to get back into position and order a halt. By this time he probably had no option. Not only had the fighting area been reduced to a space described by Woods as 'not much larger than an ordinary dining table', but the crushers were now present in numbers and were forcing their way through the crowd in order to break up what had become a riot. It was around nine forty, and the men had been fighting for well over two hours.

English and American sources are hopelessly at odds over what happened. 'The end of the fight is not correctly reported in London, and perhaps will not be,' said *The New York Times*. Broadly speaking, Sayers supporters claimed that the ropes were cut in order to save the champion's life, and that this was an entirely reasonable thing to do. The American camp, by contrast, claimed that Heenan would ultimately have thrown his opponent, who would then have been unable to respond to the call of time for the next round. The cutting of the ropes, they said, was the work of the champion's supporters, and was done purely to protect the investment they had made in wagers.

As for the police, no one denied that they were present in numbers by the end of the fight, but the Americans claimed that they were making no serious effort to interfere until they were encouraged to step in by the supporters of Sayers. According to *The New York Times*, 'the police were not obeyed, nor the ring broken down, till it was evident that Sayers was a whipped man.'

One interesting theory which was to gain some currency on the western side of the Atlantic was that the destruction of the ring was the result of a criminal conspiracy only indirectly linked to the fight. *The New York Herald*'s 'Southampton correspondence' reported that 'The breaking in of the ring was a concocted plan of the pickpockets to rob the Americans. The plan succeeded admirably, nearly every American losing his watch or pocketbook.'

It seems, in fact, that some of the unfortunate visitors had been robbed already. As *The Illustrated Police Budget* explained it, this was because they, unlike the home spectators, 'with a touching confidence in British honesty, had brought their watches and purses with them...'

But whatever the truth of the accusations and counter-accusations that were to embitter relations between the two camps in the days and weeks following the fight, the chaos which caused all the controversy would never have come about had the ring keepers only done their duty. Smith, however, says that only eight of the twenty-three really justified their fee: 'All the others were either indifferent or too much interested in the fight.' Two were suspended from such duties for twelve months, and pay was withheld from these and another two, including the drunken Ned Adams. The American claim that ring keepers colluded with Sayers supporters in cheating Heenan of victory cannot easily be dismissed.

But everyone had to accept that the fight was over, and the Olivers and Puggy Ryan now set about gathering up the ropes and stakes. The spectators began to make their way back to the trains, cutting across the meadow to the railway, which they then followed a couple of hundred yards to the station. It was a shorter and easier route than the one by which they had come.

Heenan, however, furious at having been, as he saw it, cheated of victory, had a point to make: to show his reserves of strength and energy he ran for some thirty yards at top speed, leaping two small hedges. According to English sources (but not to American), he was then forced to stop, quite unable to see his way ahead, and was led the rest of the way to the train with a blanket wrapped round him. Some American commentators claimed that Sayers actually had to be carried to the station, but this seems unlikely.

As for the spectators, they had been royally entertained for their three pounds, and would have quite a tale to tell when they got back to London. Some ninety minutes elapsed between the end of the fight and the departure of the trains, which pulled in to the Bricklayer's Arms Station (quite unrelated to Tom's old alehouse), the better part of a mile south of their starting point, shortly after one o'clock. A crowd of two or three thousand awaited the news with breathless anticipation, and the story was soon echoing round the capital and on its way across the Atlantic.

CHAPTER 15

ENGLISH ECHOES

THE NEWSPAPERS were full of it. *Bell's Life in London* brought out a special edition the same day, giving the most detailed report ever seen of a prize fight. And the story was exactly what the Fancy wanted to hear: 'this was decidedly the very best Championship fight we ever witnessed. It was... fought out with a manliness, a fairness, and a determination on both sides worthy of the highest commendation.'

In the midst of all the excitement, it would have been easy to forget that opposition to the prize ring remained powerful. If anything, in fact, the hullabaloo over the great fight had made it the more determined. The following day, the *Daily News* reiterated its implacable opposition to pugilism. Normally, the *News* told its readers, it would not stoop to report such an ignominious event, but:

> There are times, however, when the sensitiveness of quiet, easy-going people ought not to be spared, and we think that English society which, forewarned for weeks, promoted the exhibition at Ash [near Farnborough] yesterday, has no right to complain at being confronted with its hideous details. If there are any of our readers who can peruse it without regret we confess we cannot print it without shame.

The Saturday Review was more of the opinion of *Bell's Life*, but its report betrayed a hint of unease:

If the British spectators did not witness exactly what they had expected, they saw an even finer sight. Never in the annals of pugilism were skill, coolness, judgement, variety of resource, pluck and bottom displayed in such wonderful degree.

But whatever the conflicting opinions, the fact remained that the event had been a breach of the law, and the two people who had to answer for it were the chief constables of Hampshire and Surrey, on whose borders the fight had taken place. The day after the event, the Home Office wrote to both, requesting a report on what had happened.

Surrey's man, Hastings, said he had done everything possible, but that the crowd had held his men back. (Though Hampshire had been the scene of the action, it seems that Surrey officers had been present, the police needing no magistrate's authority to step in once a breach of the peace was in progress.) Chief Constable Forrest of Hampshire replied at considerably greater length, attributing his failure to prevent the fight to a lack of cooperation from Hastings and from Sir Richard Mayne of the Metropolitan Police. He enclosed copies of the favourable replies he had received to letters written in early April requesting the assistance of neighbouring chief constables should the anticipated breach of the peace come off in Hampshire.

Whether Forrest would in fact have done himself any favours by preventing the fight is at the least doubtful. The power in the land was Prime Minister Palmerston, whose domination of his cabinet was unquestioned, and everyone knew Palmerston's position. In a written reply to an MP who, after the event, complained of the government's manifest lack of will to take preventive action, the Prime Minister said that he couldn't see that there had been any very serious breach of the peace. Palmerston really would not have been happy with Forrest, Hastings or anyone else who had been so unwise as to stop the fun.

The public in general were not interested anyway. The fight had been tremendous, and they wanted to read about it. The special edition of *Bell's Life* sold in huge numbers, and John Hollingshead's report ensured Charles Dickens of a big payday with the next issue of *All the Year Round*. For *The Times*, no report of Nicholas Woods had ever been so avidly read.

For all the difference in language – *The Times* and *All the Year Round* had little to say of peepers, smellers, claret and knowledge boxes – the stories tallied. There had been a terrific fight, and the issue had been in doubt up to the moment that the excited crowd and the interfering police had brought it to a premature conclusion.

But there was another story, told by George Wilkes and Bill Bryant. It was the American story, and it differed profoundly from the English account, especially as to the later stages of the fight. Frank Dowling published part of Wilkes's account on April 22nd.

By round thirty-three, said Wilkes, although England's champion was still on his feet and still fighting, he was a beaten man: 'It was plain that the fight was nearly out of him, and his friends saw clearly that his chance was gone.' It was at this point, according to both Wilkes and Bryant, that cries of 'Police! Police!' were heard. The police in fact were looking on quietly, and the warning was an attempt by supporters of Sayers to distract the inexperienced American, in order that Sayers might have the chance to get in the decisive blow on his left eye.

The ruse failed, but was repeated many times by those now desperately afraid of losing substantial amounts of money which they had wagered at two to one on the home fighter. It was, Wilkes said, a common trick used in England with novices, and the only reason that it did not affect Heenan was that Cusick and Macdonald had warned him about it.

In the thirty-seventh round, when the English champion was helpless on the ropes, Wilkes reported that 'the adherents of the Champion actually took hold of Heenan's arm, and while they kicked and struck at him, dragged the beaten Champion from his hold.' In the following round, 'the ring being broken in by the friends of Sayers, the referee very improperly got up and retired.' (The fact that Bill Bryant has Dowling leaving his post three rounds earlier tells us a lot about the sheer confusion in the later stages of the fight.)

Frank Dowling was having none of it. The notion that the cry of 'Police!' was a ruse to distract Heenan he called 'utterly absurd', while to suggest that he had voluntarily quit his post was 'a plain misstatement of fact': he was forced aside by the pressure of the crowd. He also claimed that even Heenan's corner had called for the fight to be stopped – an assertion denied by Wilkes.

There was more, but all to the same general effect. The American position was that, as soon as it became clear that Heenan was likely to win, his opponent's supporters resorted to every dirty trick in the book to ensure that he did not. The British position was that Sayers had held the advantage up to round thirty-seven, and that the absence of a referee amidst the subsequent chaos rendered irrelevant anything that happened thereafter. And in any case, *The Sporting Life* pointed out, had the referee been in his place, he would certainly have had to award the fight to Sayers if, as was widely reported, Heenan had hit him while he was on his second's knee.

The argument that Sayers had been on top up to round thirty-seven depended on one factor – the state of Heenan's eyesight. No one disputed that his right eye was closed, but Sayers supporters claimed that the left was also closing fast, and that by the end of the fight he could scarcely see at all. Heenan had an answer. Shortly after arriving back in London, he had been examined by a doctor, who testified that 'The right eye was closed, but the left, though swollen, the sight was clear and distinct.'

Here was a nasty one for the champion's supporters, but they had an answer. *The Sporting Life* was not alone in pointing out that the medical authority in question was Dr Rawlings, who had come to England as correspondent for *Frank Leslie's Illustrated Newspaper*. How much weight could be attached to the opinion of an American reporter?

A war of words between journalists was never going to solve anything. Only the two principals could do that, and only in the ring itself. With this in mind, Heenan – though he was not the author of letters which bore his name any more than Sayers was the author of those bearing his – wrote to *Bell's Life* on April 20th, asserting that he had been cheated of a victory fairly won, and demanding that battle be renewed. If his opponent was unwilling or unable to fight again – a reference to the fact that Tom's arm was now in a sling – the belt should be his.

There was considerable annoyance in the American camp when this letter – which was published elsewhere – did not appear in the next issue of *Bell's Life*. Dowling explained the following week that they had gone to press three hours before it arrived, and reasserted his belief that, had the fight been allowed to continue, Sayers would have emerged the victor. In particular, had he seen Heenan lift Sayers off his knees in round thirty-seven as many alleged, he would have had no option but to award the fight to Sayers. As things now stood, there should be no question of renewing the battle until Tom's injured arm had recovered.

Just in case anyone should fail to understand that relations between the English and American camps were now ice-cold, Dowling also complained that Heenan had not attended the meeting called at *Bell's Life* for the Friday after the fight, sending Falkland and Macdonald instead. Had the gloves ever been on, they were certainly off now.

All of this kept the pot boiling nicely. In the words of *The Sporting Life*, 'The excitement in the public mind relative to the recent magnificent mill for the Championship has rather increased than diminished.' As everyone now knew, Heenan had demanded that, in accordance with normal (though not universal) practice when a fight was interrupted, battle should be renewed within a week. And if either man was unwilling or unable to fight again in that time, victory should be awarded to his opponent. Heenan emphasised his opinion in a letter to *The Times*:

> ... instead of being called a 'boy,' I ought to be termed a baby, if after having come so far, and not having got a settlement, I should be willing to relinquish my purpose for a few good-natured pats on the back, and being told I am a fine fellow.

The Sporting Life and *Bell's Life* were inundated with letters from those who had seen the fight, or who felt they had the right to an opinion regardless. With America still in ignorance of the outcome, the letters were almost exclusively from Englishmen, and the general opinion was that Sayers had been on top, and Heenan's tactics in round thirty-seven had been unethical at best.

Unfortunately for patriotic English sentiment, however, there were dissenting voices. On April 28th, for example, *The Sporting Life* carried a letter from 'Lex', whose opinion was that 'Sayers is a brave fellow, and deserves the highest approbation; but that is no reason why we should not deal honourably with a foreigner.' Then the following week there was 'Fairplay', who styled himself a mechanic (i.e. skilled working man) employed near Westminster Bridge, and who stated bluntly that *The Sporting Life* was biased, and the American had been cheated of victory. And in the same issue, 'Nemo' said that the ropes should not have been cut, pointing out that no one had ever died of strangulation in a prize fight.

But a much more guarded opinion may, paradoxically, have been the most damaging of all to Tom Sayers. The esteem enjoyed by *The Saturday Review* ensured that no one could take lightly its statement that 'We are not without our suspicions that the ring would have been better kept, if the English Champion had been fighting a manifestly winning battle.'

A point of which surprisingly little was made by Sayers supporters was that the moment at which Heenan unquestionably gained the upper hand was, at least arguably, the moment at which Sayers might have been given the decision. The issue of *The Sporting Life* which carried the contributions of Fairplay and Nemo, also published a letter from 'A Friend to the PR', who drew attention to Rule 28 of the London Prize Ring:

> That where a man shall have his antagonist across the ropes in such a position as to be helpless, and to endanger his life by strangulation or apoplexy, it shall be in the power of the referee to direct the seconds to take their man away, and thus conclude the round, and that the man or his seconds refusing to obey the direction of the referee, shall be deemed the loser.

In appearing to allow the referee to decide whether or not to save a man's life, this rule seems odd, and it is scarcely surprising that it was later revised to read that 'if a man in any way makes use of the ropes or stakes to aid him in squeezing his adversary, he shall be deemed the loser of the battle.'

If we accept, as seems likely, that the clumsily-phrased original was really intended to give the referee discretion in determining whether or not a man's life was in danger rather than discretion in determining whether or not to save him if it was, it seems strange that Dowling did not call Heenan off. It is hard to resist the conclusion that, amidst the chaos (and despite Wilkes's assertion that the referee was still in place at the time), Dowling was no longer in control.

Equally hard to resist is the conclusion that the general silence of the champion's supporters on this point – 'A Friend to the PR' was the exception – is evidence that they were wary of looking for excuses, lest this be seen as an implied admission that their man had been losing. It was all most unsatisfactory.

Whatever his condition at the end of the fight, the champion did not take long to recover. The morning after the battle, police had to hold back a cheering crowd as he boarded the cab which took him from his base at the Gordon Hotel, Covent Garden to the office of *Bell's Life*, and his driver had a hard time getting through the press. In the evening, he visited Owen Swift's and George Bryer's. His almost unmarked face persuaded *Bell's Life* that 'either Heenan is not the hard hitter he appears, or Tom's nob must be of such a consistency as almost to defy the visitations of a sledge-hammer.'

But however well he seemed in other respects, the fact that he had been in a fight was witnessed by the black leather sling supporting his right arm. And this effectively settled the issue of whether or not battle should be resumed.

Four days after the fight, the arm was examined by Messrs Sydney Jones and Edward Clapton of St Thomas's Hospital, and they were 'of opinion from the contused state of the muscles, tendons, and inner bone of the right forearm that he would be unable to use that arm for at least a couple of months, or probably more.' Theoretically, then, Sayers might, at the outside, have been ready to fight again sometime in late June. But June 16th was the date on which the belt should become his, and beyond which its ownership could not be disputed. It was an impasse.

Almost from the moment they arrived back in London from Farnborough, Heenan and Wilkes were asking for battle to be renewed, but the decision was in the hands of the referee, and Dowling was not having it. As late as May 4th, they visited *Bell's Life* to demand a date, but by that time they were really doing so only in order to make a point. And two days later, the matter was settled when Dowling announced that the Home Secretary had served notice that no second fight would be permitted.

Little was made of it at the time, but it was on the face of it an extraordinary line for Lewis to take. He was clearly implying that the first fight had taken place with the permission of the Home Office. But of course, everyone knew this anyway, and the Home Secretary was not even going to bother pretending.

Heenan was still not giving up – or at the very least, was still determined to make entirely certain that everyone knew how he felt. A few days later, he wrote to *The Times*, repeating his determination not to return home empty-handed. In accordance with one public suggestion, he said he was prepared to accept a replica belt for each man, the original to remain with Frank Dowling. He would even take half of the real belt, but what he really wanted was all of it, to which end he proclaimed his willingness to run, swim, wrestle, fight four men at thirty-day intervals, or jump off the top of a house.

It was all to no avail, and when American reactions reached England, the opposing positions only became further entrenched. In the words of *The Sporting Life* of May 16th, 'The New York papers received yesterday are full of the fight for the Championship, and as usual a wild spirit of boasting is indulged in, characteristic of the Yankee character.'

During all this exchange of fire, life went on, and Tom Sayers at least seems to have taken little interest. Things might not have been entirely as he would have wished, but he retained the championship, and he had no intention of fighting for it again. Four days after the battle, arm still in its sling, he visited Epsom races, where he was rapturously received.

Any disappointment he might have felt over his inability to defeat his formidable adversary must have been mollified by knowledge of the subscriptions pouring in, often spontaneously, to a fund which was clearly going to make him, by the standards of the day, a wealthy man. Just two days after the fight, a group of Liverpool merchants subscribed an unsolicited £70, while one anonymous admirer left £100 at *Bell's Life*. And so it went on.

The Stock Exchange took contributions, as did the Houses of Parliament, where Lord Palmerston's wish to donate five guineas was frustrated by the ruling of a maximum one guinea per member. The Guards' Club in Pall Mall contributed £250, while the members of Pratt's Club subscribed £40. The most august bodies in the land were falling over themselves to reward an illiterate member of the working class for his indulgence in an illegal activity which many viewed with utter disgust.

What began as a spontaneous outburst of generosity from groups and individuals was soon organised into a common fund. So widespread was the desire to contribute that individuals were nominated around the country to accept donations. In Birmingham, for example, the duty fell to Bob Brettle. And when unease was expressed in some quarters over the lack of a fund for the gallant American, one was started for him too, although it was thought likely that he would be rewarded in his own land. Tom Sayers could hardly have done better had he emerged the uncontested victor.

On the last day of April, together with Bennett, Gideon and one Jack Coney, he left London for the first time since the fight. Their destination was Liverpool, and when they pulled in to a cheering Lime Street Station, the press was such that it was some minutes before they could alight. With the throng outside the station growing all the time, Tom was smuggled out by a side exit. It made no difference. He was spotted, and the adoring crowd swiftly unharnessed the horse from his cab and pulled him to the Talbot Hotel in Great Charlotte Street, where flags were already flying in expectation of the arrival of their famous guest.

Later he visited Liverpool's Stock Exchange, and received a gift of £150 and other testimonials. One gentleman meanwhile entrusted a large sum to Mr Stent, host of the Talbot. Tom Sayers was having a profitable trip.

And as the champion basked in Liverpool's limelight, his opponent was only a few miles away, for Jack Heenan was visiting Chester Racecourse. The reception he received was ample evidence that, however heated the post-match controversy might have become, the Benicia Boy remained very popular with the English people.

Arm still in its sling two weeks after the fight, Tom Sayers himself arrived in Chester the following day, to another rapturous reception. He and his companions put up at Blossom's Hotel, which was soon surrounded by crowds whose cheering was audible all over the city. And when the champion's colours were hung outside his window, their enthusiasm was boundless. To gratify them, Tom was obliged to go to the window and bow over and over.

The next day, Wednesday, he visited the Racecourse, taking his place in the grandstand to a predictable ovation. And in the evening, in the company of *Sporting Life* editor Henry Feist, who had decided to follow him to the north-west, he went to the Music Hall, where Campbell's Minstrels were performing. The audience rose en masse when he entered, cheering and waving hats and handkerchiefs. At one point during the performance, one of the minstrels kicked a hat which by chance landed on Tom's head. Joining in the spirit of hilarity, he pulled it down over his eyes. When he left the hall, he found a huge crowd waiting for him: such was the press that Henry Feist thought it safer to leave and catch up with him later.

Whether the two fighters met in Chester, history does not relate, but it seems more likely that, with the controversy over the battle at its height, they would have stayed clear of each other in order to avoid embarrassment.

Anyway, they were in Chester together for just one full day, for Jack Heenan returned to London via Liverpool on the Thursday. The following afternoon, Henry Feist, now himself back in London, met him at the photographic studio of John Watkins in Parliament Street. The Boy was still complaining bitterly of having been let down by the referee, but – a couple of days before the Home Secretary finally put the lid on all talk of a second fight – spoke more of his hopes of a rematch with John Morrissey than of his chances of fighting Tom Sayers again. There was also talk of a possible match with Sam Hurst, the Stalybridge Infant, but the American champion dismissed this notion with contempt.

In the midst of all the ballyhoo, the Benicia Boy remained the same open-hearted, quick-tempered, expansive personality he had always been. One of the charms of Tom Sayers, by contrast, was that he was so manifestly ill-equipped to stand in the limelight. When called upon to say a few words at presentations of money or other tokens of admiration, he was hopelessly tongue-tied, but his manifest unease seemed only to emphasise his heroic stature. He seemed to embody ancient, manly virtues, and to be out of place in the effete world of nineteenth-century England.

Jack Heenan was quite different. On Monday evening, he presided over Fred Hogg's Harmonic Meeting at the Angel Inn, Stratford, and from an early hour the vicinity was, as *The Sporting Life* put it, 'crowded beyond description', for there was a large Irish presence in the east end of London. But in the same issue, the paper carried a letter from Jack Hamilton, complaining that the Boy had used 'the most violent language' against him at Lime Street Station just days previously. Was it, Hamilton asked, because he was a friend of Tom Sayers, or because he had trained John Morrissey for the fight at Long Point? He received no public response.

The month of May wore on, all talk of a second fight ceased, and it became increasingly clear that some sort of compromise between the two pugilists would have to be reached, if only to save the face of the prize ring. Thus it was that, on Friday, May 18th, Jack Heenan and Tom Sayers met at the offices of *Bell's Life*, and an agreement was finally reached: a new replica belt would be made for each man, the original staying with Frank Dowling. Tom and Jack shook hands, and then, with the friends who had accompanied them to *Bell's Life*, adjourned to Jem Parish's tavern on the corner of Newcastle Street and Strand, where they sealed their friendship over some bottles of wine.

Five days later, their new-found amity was made fully public when they attended the Epsom Derby together. They received a tremendous ovation.

But others would not so easily forget the recent bitterness. The Derby provided another chance to measure the new country against the old, for the American horse *Umpire* was among the favourites. When *Umpire* failed, *The Sporting Life*, haughtily disclaiming any patriotic pride in the result, informed its readers that 'the excitable population of the United States, who are never content unless everything be made to minister to their vulgar vanity or egotism, insisted that the reputations of the old and new countries were at stake.'

Jack Heenan, however, in the wake of the reconciliation, became almost an honorary Englishman. He and his former adversary, now that they could be a double act, attracted the interest of the entertainment industry, and the day after the Derby they went to Somerset House to sign contracts to appear together at various public venues around the country over the following five weeks. According to *The Sporting Life*, each was to earn the extraordinary sum of £250 per week – as much as many working men might expect to earn in five years.

Their first engagement was at London's Alhambra Palace at nine o'clock on the evening of Wednesday, May 30th. A programme of light entertainment preceded the presentation of the replica belts – made, like the original, by Mr Hancock of New Bond Street. George Caldwell spoke first, identifying himself as Censor of *Wilkes' Spirit of the Times*. Then Frank Dowling presented Heenan with his belt, and George Wilkes did the same for Sayers.

It was all quite splendid, but for one thing: the auditorium contained empty spaces. *Bell's Life* was not impressed, saying that the presentation had not been properly advertised, and that the prices – one guinea, ten shillings and sixpence, and half a crown (two shillings and sixpence) – had been too high. It would also, thought *Bell's Life*, have been far better had the two men appeared in fighting gear rather than in evening dress, and had they sparred a little. The two heroes were beginning to look very expensive at a five-week total (if *The Sporting Life* was to be trusted) of £2,500.

Still, the contracts were signed, and the show, with sparring added, went on. Six days later, they began their provincial tour in Manchester. The Free Trade Hall put on one show at three in the afternoon, and another at eight in the evening. Tickets had sold so slowly that prices had been halved some days before, but there was still only a small audience at the afternoon performance. Attendance was considerably better in the evening, but *The Sporting Life* thought that prices might profitably have been cut still further.

That there was still great interest in the gladiators was evidenced by the large crowds outside the theatre afternoon and evening. Many people, it was clear, still wanted to see and cheer their heroes, but they were not necessarily prepared to pay for the privilege.

The tour was to continue at Liverpool, Leeds, Sheffield, Nottingham (or perhaps Leicester) and Bradford, but was it worth it? It didn't take long to decide. On June 16th, *The Sporting Life* told its readers that 'it is well known that the Sayers and Heenan benefit scheme has been a signal failure, and will not be continued longer than this Saturday evening.'

There was little now to keep Jack Heenan in England, especially when he had, as *The Sporting Life* said, many potentially profitable invitations to return to America. In fact, with the always unlikely Heenan–Hurst match now definitely off, he was making plans to return to New York in three weeks' time, in the company of Jack Macdonald.

There was, however, one last chance for those who saw Sayers and Heenan as a potentially profitable double act on the eastern side of the Atlantic: there was Ireland. The success of the meeting at Stratford's Angel Inn pointed the way: British rule had been bitterly resented in Ireland for centuries, and with memories of the famine still raw, Irish Catholics would certainly turn out in numbers to welcome anyone of Irish blood who was seen to have put John Bull in his place.

As was only to be expected, there was opposition from the enemies of the prize ring: the *Irish Times* of June 23rd published a letter from one Robert Nelson to the Lord Mayor of Dublin asking for the forthcoming exhibition to be banned.

He might as well have saved his ink. Dublin's Rotunda Gardens was not the Alhambra, nor was it the Free Trade Hall. On Monday, June 25th, in the words of the *Irish Times*:

> This extraordinary exhibition, which has engrossed the thoughts and occupied the hours of every bully, sot, *roué*, and 'fast man' in the metropolis for several days past, came off yesterday, in the Rotunda Gardens. The so-called champions arrived lately in this city, and put up at the Prince of Wales Hotel, Sackville-street, which ever since has been besieged by the class above alluded to.

As in Manchester, there was an afternoon performance at three o'clock, and an evening performance at eight. With tickets priced at one shilling and half a crown, both drew huge crowds, who witnessed the presentation and buckling on of the belts, followed by an exhibition of sparring.

Attendance was all the organisers could have wished. There was a refreshment tent where strong drink was sold at inflated prices, and there was also, again in the words of the *Irish Times*, 'one of the very worst of those German bands which make the loudest noise in our streets, and are noted for murdering our finest and most familiar airs.'

Reporting the afternoon performance, the *Irish Times* had nothing good to say of pugilism, its practitioners or its supporters, expressing satisfaction that at least 'very few women were present – probably not more than a dozen altogether, and they obviously of the lowest class, who frequent every place of public resort, and who are respected nowhere.' Sayers, smoking a cigar and apparently drunk, was physically unimpressive, while Heenan was 'undoubtedly, a good specimen of a man, in the ordinary sense of the word, but he has, at a glance, the fault of nearly all Americans – he is not sufficiently developed.' Better physical specimens than Heenan and Sayers could easily be found – and with training, they could easily beat both.

As for the sparring exhibition, 'one of the exhibitors resembled most a battered bull-dog set upon two legs, with lowering brows and forbidding countenance' and the mass of the spectators were 'the very dregs of society.'

The afternoon performance had at least gone off without serious trouble, but the evening was different. The vast crowd – over ten thousand – rioted, breaking the platform in pieces and tearing the carpet to shreds. First Sayers called for order, then Heenan, but to no avail. The *Dublin Evening Post* described 'a scene of tumult and disorder perhaps never equalled in Dublin.' The refreshment tent collapsed and all the drink was taken. Order was restored only by the intervention of large numbers of police.

In its leader the following day, the *Irish Times* explained in passing why interest in Dublin was so much greater than in Manchester:

Last night there were drunken men parrying and buffeting the air, led home to practise upon their wives the lesson they had received, while our streets rang with execrations upon Sayers, who, as an Englishman, was an object of dislike to the *canaille* which claims Heenan and MacMahon [a noted French general of Irish descent] as their own. The disgraceful riot which ensued last night was a practical illustration of the mischief caused by such exhibitions.

Leaving Dublin to clean up behind them, the two fighters took the train to Belfast the following day. Crowds swarmed round them at every stop. At Drogheda, in the words of the *Dublin Evening Post*, 'each of the doors and windows of the carriages were [*sic*] besieged, and the panes literally covered with flattened noses.'

Arriving in Belfast to find a crowd of several hundred waiting to greet them, they put up at the Commercial Hotel, which was soon beset by fans. Again they put on one show in the afternoon and one in the evening, when the house was packed. This time, however, there was no trouble, even though, according to *The Northern Whig*, 'Their presence has caused an amount of popular commotion which that of Majesty alone could rival.'

———————

The next day, the two fighters left for Glasgow on board the *Leopard*, and *The Northern Whig*, still with royalty in mind, said that they boarded 'amid the cheers of the greatest monster meeting that has been seen on the quays of Belfast since the Queen's visit eleven years ago.'

It was on June 28th that Sayers and Heenan gave their final exhibitions, this time in Edinburgh's Zoological Gardens. Prices were the same as in Dublin, and attendance, if not quite what it had been there, was still much more satisfactory than in England. Some fifteen hundred people turned up in the afternoon, and perhaps four or five times that number in the evening. Scotland and Ireland had saved the Sayers–Heenan tour from disaster.

The time was approaching when Jack Heenan would leave again for his homeland, but he had one more major engagement to fulfil in London. On the evening of Sunday, July 1st, he was invited to Mr J. Cavanagh's White Bear at Ratcliff Cross in Limehouse. It was another Irish occasion, and a crowd of seven or eight thousand made progress difficult when he arrived with Jack Macdonald at eight o'clock. But the trip was worth the Boy's while: after dinner, he was presented with an emerald-studded gold ring, bearing an Irish harp surmounted by a shamrock.

Shortly before he was due to depart, he invited Henry Feist to visit him at the New York Hotel, Leicester Square. Feist found him in high spirits, determined, he said, to take on first John Morrissey and then Sam Hurst, who, in spite of all discouragement, was not giving up his quest for the title. On a more altruistic level, one of the Benicia Boy's last acts in England had been to give £80 to raise a stone over the grave of Charles Freeman.

Nicknamed the American Giant, Freeman had been brought to England by Ben Caunt in 1842 on his return from a spell in the United States. He had defeated Bill Perry, but neither man had been national champion at the time, and the excitement which their meeting had admittedly generated was nothing to what was to come eighteen years later. With Perry dwarfed by Freeman much as Sayers would later be dwarfed by Perry, the fight, which took two meetings to decide, was generally considered to have been something of a farce. Freeman had died young without ever quite capturing the public imagination, and without ever again seeing his homeland.

Raising a stone over his grave was a gesture typical of Jack Heenan's generous nature, but the Boy gave out more largesse than he received: embarrassingly, as Feist discovered, he would be returning home without the replica belt, which was not yet paid for. As *The Sporting Life* put it, 'as things stand at present the presentation at the Alhambra was a mere farce.'

Henry Feist was with the Benicia Boy when he left for America on Wednesday, July 4th. The patience of well-wishers who thronged the entrances to Waterloo Station from an early hour was rewarded just after ten o'clock. The hero's substantial entourage included Jack Macdonald, Owen Swift and Jerry Noon, but most prominent among them was

Tom Sayers, in company with his son. There was, said *The Sporting Life*, 'such cheering as had never been heard before between the walls of that station.'

Tom was very lame, having hurt his leg in a fall from his gig, and Jack would not hear of him coming all the way to Southampton, since it would only cause him pain to no good purpose. When the whistle sounded, Feist told the readers of *The Sporting Life*, 'one of the most affectionate adieus was taken by the two Champions that we ever witnessed, each almost shedding tears at the prospect of separating.'

As the train started for Southampton, the Benicia Boy put his head out of the window to shout, 'Damn me if Tom Sayers is not the best fellow in the whole world, and I would not go almost to the end of the earth to serve him!'

The party lunched at Davis's Railway Family Hotel in Southampton, then made their way through enthusiastic crowds to the dockside. At twenty past three, to the cheers of a throng which included a number of ladies, they boarded the tug which would take them to the paddle-steamer *Vanderbilt*, standing off Cowes on the Isle of Wight twelve miles away.

There was some embarrassment when the absence of the ship's owner forced Heenan and Macdonald to pay for their crossing: the promise of free passage would have to be redeemed in New York. But it was a small matter. For the most part, the Benicia Boy had been a resounding success in England, and was taking home some impressive souvenirs. He had acquired a bulldog, a Newfoundland, a black retriever and a brace of pointers – all, thought Henry Feist, very fine.

The only thing he lacked was the belt.

CHAPTER 16

AMERICAN ECHOES

ALL AMERICA waited tensely for the news from England. Had the fight taken place just twenty months previously, they would have known the result almost immediately, but the 1858 attempt to lay an Atlantic cable had enjoyed only brief success.

In 1860, news from across the Atlantic again had to wait on steamships which generally took at least ten days to reach New York, but whose arrival time could never be known with precision. Together with uncertainty as to the date of the fight, this meant that the evening of Wednesday, April 25th was about the earliest that news might be anticipated. And sure enough, at six p.m. that day, as people were on their way home from work, it was announced on the newspaper bulletin boards around town that the *Vanderbilt* from Southampton had been intercepted off Cape Race by the news yacht of the Associated Press, and her intelligence telegraphed to the city. A full account of the fight would be published in an hour's time.

And so it was. At seven o'clock, *Wilkes' Spirit of the Times* brought out an extra – a single sheet, fourteen inches by twenty, divided into three columns. It bore the news that everyone wanted to hear:

THE BENICIA BOY VICTORIOUS

The fight was reported to have taken place at Mildenhall in Suffolk on Monday, April 16th, when youth and size had triumphed over experience and agility. It had been a tremendous battle lasting an hour and twenty minutes, and Queen Victoria herself had received the victor at Buckingham Palace the following day. So favourable was the impression he made that she had even asked him if he would act as bodyguard to her son the Prince of Wales on his forthcoming visit to the United States.

No newspaper had ever sold so fast. 'The least skillful of the vendors,' said *The New York Times* the following day, 'realized from 4 to 6 cents per copy: the most daring – the incipient Astors of the sidewalk – swept dimes by the dozen into their ragged pouches.'

All New York, it seemed, was desperate for the news. The excitement of the Fancy, of course, could be taken for granted, but even those whose social standing would normally have precluded an interest in the prize ring were gripped by the drama. At the Academy of Music on the north-east corner of Fourteenth Street and Irving Place, seventeen-year-old Adelina Patti was left singing Flotow's *Martha* to an empty house when the entire audience, hearing the cries of the newsboys outside, quit their seats and rushed out to learn how the battle had gone.

Not until much later, by which time some thirty thousand copies of the extra had been sold, did it become clear that the whole thing was just the hoax against which the *Clipper* had warned on April 14th. The newsboys had done well out of it, and someone – whose identity was never established – had done considerably better.

Had there ever been any doubt as to the scale and intensity of interest in the fight, it existed no longer. All America was lining up to hear that the lion's tail had been tweaked, and New York was at the head of the line. It was not to be wondered at, for the city had issues with England. They went back at least as far as the Revolution, when the fire which had devastated a quarter of the town in 1776 had triggered a terrifying rampage by occupying British troops, who blamed it on the citizens. Having seen their own quarters destroyed in the blaze, the soldiers took over as many homes as they required, leaving their former occupants to live in squalid misery for the rest of the conflict.

But that was history. Much more significant by 1860 was that New York was more than a quarter Irish. The Irish had been streaming across the Atlantic for decades, and the desperate famine of the late forties had greatly accelerated the influx. More than a million had died of hunger and disease, and still greater numbers had left the island for good, hundreds of thousands fleeing to the other side of the Atlantic, where their hearts still beat for Erin. Their former masters, always fiercely resented, were guilty in their eyes of callous indifference in the face of unimaginable suffering, and their bitterness was reflected in an intense desire to see England humiliated.

This urge had already manifested itself in 1849, when William Charles Macready, leading light of the London stage and close friend of Charles Dickens, had performed in New York. Dickens had preferred not to see Macready off from England, fearing that this might cause ill-feeling among Americans, who, still smarting from the barbs of *American Notes* and *Martin Chuzzlewit*, might hold the actor guilty by association. In the event, his tact went for nothing, for American actor Edwin Forrest, who blamed Macready for the failure of his *Macbeth* in London four years previously, fomented trouble which came to a head outside the Astor Place Opera House on May 10th.

The violence was generally thought to have been instigated by Isaiah Rynders, at whose Empire club the teenage John Morrissey had nearly been killed just months before. Ned Buntline, a weird combination of writer, publisher and gangster, joined such notorious thugs as Yankee Sullivan and Dirty Face Jack in inciting a mob estimated at fifteen thousand to attack the theatre. With police unable to control the escalating violence, the army was called in, and before the night was out, more than twenty people lay dead in the street.

Macready's early removal to a place of safety had gone unnoticed, since few of the rioters much cared about him anyway. They were mostly Irish, and Rynders and his henchmen had had little difficulty in persuading them to give violent expression to their long-standing grudge against Great Britain.

What this meant for the big fight a decade later was clear. With thousands prepared to risk their lives to take sides in a tiff between two actors, it was never likely that New Yorkers would take the Sayers–Heenan contest lightly. The city was full of people who could readily identify with any Irish American who lived among them, and fuller still of people happy to see any American get the better of any Brit.

By the morning of Saturday, April 28th, when the *Vanderbilt*, a wooden vessel a hundred metres long with paddle wheels, two funnels and two masts, arrived for real, New York was aquiver with anticipation. The voyage, despite strong westerly winds part of the way, had been notable in itself: nine days, twelve hours and thirty minutes was a record for the westbound crossing. But this did not concern the crowds who swarmed around her wharf on the Hudson River. All that interested them was the fight.

The city into which the *Vanderbilt* steamed that day – or at least the southernmost part of it where the ship docked – would not have looked out of place in Western Europe. In residential areas, ramshackle houses clustered in tangles of narrow, dingy streets, and even the grandest buildings – in all cases commercial or business premises – hardly ever rose above five stories.

But New York was poised already to become unique, for it was now six years since Elisha Graves Otis had given a successful demonstration of his safety elevator. Its contribution to the Manhattan skyline was still impossible to foresee, but together with a bold vision of nearly fifty years earlier, Otis's invention would determine the direction which the expanding city would take, horizontally and vertically. Finalised in 1811, the Commissioners' Plan had envisaged vastly extended north–south avenues crossed by scores of east–west streets all the way up to one hundred and fifty-fifth – ghosts from a future as unimaginable as it was inevitable.

By 1830 Manhattan was well developed as far north as Canal Street, and within a few years Washington Square – under which, from its days as a potter's field, lay twenty thousand unremembered dead – was a building site. A little to the north, Union Square had been out in the country in 1830. By 1845, some of New York's most fashionable residences surrounded its elegant park. Madison Square opened to the public in 1847.

Throughout the forties and fifties, the city was creeping north at a rate of three streets a year, and the pattern was clear. As the residential streets of the old city were taken over by trade, the well-to-do moved north, ahead of the warehouses, offices and stores. Money was made in the south, but it lived in the north. Only the poor continued to live where once everyone had lived. And they congregated, as Edward Winslow Martin tells us in *The Secrets of the Great City*, in ethnic ghettoes.

> The population is made up from every nation under Heaven. The natives are in the minority. The foreign element predominates. Irishmen, Germans, Jews, Turks, Greeks, Russians, Italians, Spaniards, Mexicans, Portuguese, Scotch, French, Chinese – in short, representatives of every nationality – abound. These frequently herd together, each class by itself, in distinct parts of the city, which they seem to regard as their own.

Only in Walt Whitman's 'hurrying feverish electric crowds' travelling through the expanding city, would rich and poor rub shoulders. On Broadway, to quote Martin again, 'Fine gentlemen in broad cloth, ladies in silks and jewels, and beggars in squalidness and rags, are mingled... in true Republican confusion.'

The city's eight hundred thousand people certainly knew the meaning of traffic, all horse-drawn, and much of it composed of all-purpose two-wheeled delivery carts driven by white-smocked carmen. These were the terror of all, and were responsible for most of the road accidents, many fatal, which were common throughout the city.

As in London, fine carriages ensured that the rich were as far as possible insulated from the poor, but most people used public transport. This meant either the omnibus (also known as the stage) or the streetcar. By 1860, the cheaper (and dirtier and more crowded) streetcar had largely displaced the omnibus above Fourteenth Street. Below Fourteenth, however, the total absence of rails left the omnibus unchallenged. There were many different lines, all privately owned. Walt Whitman, in *Specimen Days*, recalled from the 1850s 'The Yellow-birds, the Red-birds, the original Broadway, the Fifth Avenue, the Knickerbocker, and a dozen others...'

———————

It was early morning when the *Vanderbilt* arrived in this vibrant and chaotic city. As soon as it was known that she was coming up the bay, crowds began to gather at her berth on the Hudson. In typically American fashion, class distinctions were ignored as ragged paupers from the Bowery eagerly demanded news of the well-heeled passengers. As *The New York Herald* put it:

> Passengers were unceremoniously tackled by the enthusiastic roughs; carriages on their way up town were brought to a stand still, while a crowd would seem to spring out of the earth, and, levelling whole batteries of questions through every aperture where sound could penetrate, detain the occupant as long as he would stay, and when he drove off he would be sure to find one or two sitting on behind talking confidentially in his ear.

The newspapermen who had crossed the Atlantic to cover the fight were desperate to get through the crowds. The *Clipper* office on the corner of Ann and Nassau was virtually under siege by seven thirty when Bill Bryant arrived. With an unprecedented number of orders, the *Clipper* posted a notice announcing that no papers would be delivered until five p.m. The presses ran all day and through the night, went on running day and night on Sunday, and did not satisfy demand until Monday morning, by which time a quarter of a million copies had been printed.

'The excitement regarding the news eclipsed anything we ever saw in the newspaper world', said the *Clipper*, whose headlines left no doubt as to Bryant's opinion of the fight:

Disgraceful conduct of the Mob
COWARDLY FLIGHT OF THE REFEREE

Just along the road, at the corner of Broadway and Ann, stood the white marble headquarters of *The New York Herald*, which the following day told how the news of the *Vanderbilt*'s coming was received:

> A simple notice on the bulletin board of the *Herald* announced the arrival of the steamer with the news of the fight, and hardly was the paste dry before we were thronged

with the multitude. The inside of the office was a jam, and buzzed like a hive of bees… Fulton street became almost impassable.

Soon a rumbling from below told the crowd that the three huge presses were in motion, throwing off twenty thousand sheets an hour. And then the first copies were ready. The ragged newsboys – many numbered among the city's tens of thousands of homeless children –

stop a second to read the heading and see that it's all right – for your newsboy is a connoisseur in these matters – and on they rush, screaming as they run, with a mixture of patriotic pride and enterprise, "Ere's the extra '*Erald*…'

Extra *Heralds*, said the paper, 'abounded like snow flakes'. Between the *Spirit of the Times* hoax and the reality of three days later, the newsboys did well out of Heenan and Sayers.

And it was a newspaper-vendor, who, with the exception only of the mastermind behind the great hoax, did best of all. August Brentano, a poor Austrian immigrant who had begun selling newspapers on the streets in 1853, earned so much by offering batches of *Heralds*, *Clippers* and others at a dollar apiece, that he was able to buy his own emporium just months later. His bookstore was to be a byword among booklovers for generations to come.

Never had there been so many newspapers on the streets of any American city. In addition to the huge numbers of New York journals, the consignment of papers which had left England for America with news of the fight was the largest that had been seen. And the reports were discussed as avidly as they were read. By the Saturday evening, everyone knew the story, and everyone had an opinion. From the finest restaurants to the lowest Bowery dives (where glassless drinking was on offer: for three cents you could suck on a thin tube fed from a beer barrel behind the bar until your breath failed) it was the only thing to talk about.

The colours of Heenan and Sayers, together with representations of the two men and of the fight, hung in hundreds of windows, and were nowhere more prominently displayed than in the sporting houses. And it was here that interest was most intense.

Most famous of all was Harry Hill's, readily identifiable by the huge red-and-blue globular lantern which hung outside. Its location – like those of most sporting bars – was not the most salubrious: it stood on the corner of Broadway and Houston, from where, even twenty years later, it was said that you could fire a shotgun in any direction without hitting an honest man.

Like many other saloons, Harry Hill's had a bar downstairs and a large hall upstairs. To enter the latter, men had to pay but women got in free, by their own door at street level. The hall, which was largely responsible for Harry's increasing wealth, consisted of several rooms with the partitions removed. There was a bar at one end, at the other a stage. Here farces might be seen, or Punch and Judy shows, or even prize fights. Most evenings, though, a small orchestra played dance music. The walls featured such poetic homilies as 'If you wish to here remain / Do not talk loudly or profane.' The proprietor was a better businessman than he was a poet.

Like all of those who had crossed the Atlantic to see the fight, Harry was much in demand for his first-hand information. At the time he left England on the *Vanderbilt*, there was no still no official result, but he was sure, he told his customers, that a draw would finally be declared. Another ten minutes would have settled it one way or the other, but he preferred not to say which. Nor would he be persuaded to make any criticism of the referee.

At the Malta saloon on the corner of Broadway and Thirteenth – which had been Jack's headquarters before he sailed – the Boy's colours were prominently displayed above the bar. Many other engravings and prints il-lustrating the great event hung on the opposite wall, among them a picture of Tom Sayers, with the results of his fights given below. To this list, some-one had added in pencil: 'Beaten by John C. Heenan, April 17, 1860.'

A copy of one fight report was read aloud in the Malta, and when the story reached the thirty-seventh round, one over-excited individual climbed onto a chair and offered to bet 'a hundred against anything upon Heenan.' There were no takers.

Feeling against John Morrissey was strong. This was inevitable anyway, for he was considered a traitor, but wide credence was also given to a groundless rumour that he it was who, fearing the loss of a rumoured $10,000 stake, had cut the ropes in order to save Sayers. One angry patron approached his engraving on the wall and, cursing as he worked, hacked at the features with a knife until they were unrecognisable.

Fred Falkland's Dexter House in Broome Street, perhaps the most upmarket of the sporting houses, adjoined the establishment of one T. Prendergast, and, as the *Herald* tells us:

> ...between the two places, which are regarded as the headquarters of Benicia's partisans, there was a constant ebb and flow of the tide from morning until night. The enthusiasm was intense and every now and then some half intoxicated individual would boil over, and mounting chair or table, get off a roaring whoop te-doodendoo speech, which would almost make a man's hair stand on end.

But New York was not devoid of Sayers partisans, even in the haunts of the Fancy. There was, for example, the saloon kept by Jemmy Massey, otherwise known as 'the little man', at 282½ The Bowery near Houston. Formerly landlord of the King's Arms in Soho, Jem had followed Harry Hill across the Atlantic, and in a prominent place behind his bar was the broom with which he had promised to sweep a crossing on Broadway in the event of a Heenan victory. Most of his clientele, convinced that the American had been cheated, thought he should use it. Their opinion was widely shared. Outside Jake Roome's on Mercer Street the colours of Tom Sayers, which were displayed below those of the Benicia Boy, were draped in black.

At the Falstaff in Chatham Street (later Park Row), where the two sons of proprietor Izzy Lazarus gave lessons in self-defence, the *Herald*'s man found 'several pugilistic Israelites congregated' under the lithographs of boxers and scenes of the Farnborough battle which adorned the walls. The fight was all they wanted to talk about.

It was the same at the whorehouse saloon kept by John Allen, who, two years earlier, had been stakeholder in the first attempt to arrange a Heenan–Morrissey match. It was the same at Kit Burns's Sportsmen's Hall, commonly known as the Rat Pit on account of its notoriety as a centre of the sport of ratting, in which spectators would bet on how many rats a dog might kill in a given period. It was no different in the numerous basement saloons which specialised in oysters, the fast food of the day.

Higher in the social scale, the audience roared their approval when a man burst in during a performance in one of the Bowery theatres to announce: 'Ladies and gentlemen, I feel it to be my duty to inform you that John C. Heenan has won this fight!'

Even the Germans, the most numerous national group in New York next to the Irish, took great interest in what was for them a quite alien topic. The *Herald*'s reporter visited one of their lager saloons – lager having been introduced to the United States by a German immigrant twenty years earlier – and found one of the company translating an account of the fight for the benefit of those whose English did not suffice:

> ... seated in the midst of a gaping crowd it was amusing to watch the varying emotions on the countenances of each, or the puzzled expression of the translator when he came to such words as 'mug,' 'smeller,' 'claret,' 'peeper,' and like technical terms of the P.R. vocabulary, which he rendered as best he could, or omitted with some learned remarks as to their probable meaning.

The fight was an obsession, and not only in New York. On Friday, April 27th, *The Press and Tribune* of Chicago published a spoof article, claiming that such was the demand for news that they had secured the services of a medium, who had tried to obtain the information from the spirit world. Sadly, the ethereal beings, upset by the ridicule attracted by spiritualism (an invention of the clever Fox sisters in upstate New York twelve years previously), refused to tell what they presumably knew.

The *Boston Evening Transcript*, on April 30th, brought together the two big news stories of the day – for the fight had not entirely eclipsed interest in the Democratic Convention at Charleston – and, referring to the North–South split on the issue of slavery, wrote that 'The South were fairly knocked off their pins at every blow... and were only saved from utter discomfiture by a general rush into the ring, and a sudden suspension of the conflict.'

Two days later, another Boston paper, the *Herald*, adopted the line taken by the respectable American press in general (the *Herald*'s New York namesake being of the most dubious repute): left to ourselves, we would rather not report this disgraceful happening at all, but feel we have a duty to satisfy the curiosity of our readers (and by the way, our Boy was terrific):

> We yield to the demand and present this morning such authentic particulars as have come to hand, expressing our gratification that the snatching of the coveted prize from Heenan, which he had fought for and won, by a trick to which none but ruffians would resort, has exploded the notion upon which the English devotees of the prize ring have insisted – the notion that honor, manliness and fair dealing are the inevitable accompaniments of the fistic art.

News of the unsatisfactory outcome of the fight led to some violence both in New York and elsewhere. In New Orleans at about seven thirty on the evening of Saturday, April 28th, James Weyman, a Heenan supporter, shot dead one Daniel Cunningham, who had been so unwise as to speak out in support of the hated John Morrissey. And one week later, in Albany, New York, Thomas Halloran, a Sayers man, was stabbed to death by John McCotter, who was not prepared to tolerate any argument as to the Boy's superiority.

Nowhere, not even New York, had awaited the news more anxiously than California, for it was there that the Benicia Boy had made his name. The Pony Express had made its first delivery exactly two weeks before the mill at Farnborough, and it was only the sixth westward trip which brought news of the fight. On the morning of Monday, May 7th, there was great excitement in San Francisco when it was heard that the Express had reached the point from which intelligence could be telegraphed to the city.

At half past ten, a red-faced man rushed out of the telegraph office, shouting 'He's got it!' Inarticulate with excitement, he was, so the *Daily Evening Bulletin* tells us, 'dragged off to where, with strychnined whisky they wash the secrets out of over-excited persons.' It may be that the dangerous-sounding whisky was the motivation for his exuberance, for just half an hour later it was announced that there was still no communication from the Pony Express after all.

Interestingly, when the news did arrive the following day, the *Bulletin*, anxious that San Francisco should not be duped as New York had been, was inclined to doubt its authenticity. How likely was it, the paper asked, that almost every round should end with Sayers being knocked down, Heenan suffering that indignity only once? Was it possible that a hoax report had been telegraphed to St Joseph, Missouri, the Express's jumping-off point, so late as to leave no time for the deception to be exposed before the rider left? But the news was genuine, and in the town which had given Jack Heenan his nickname, it was readily believed, and was celebrated with a 100-gun salute. Benicia was proud of its Boy.

———————

One man of whom very few Americans were proud was John Morrissey. Despite convincing denials, not only by Morrissey but by others present, that he had in no way interfered in the fight, it was still believed by many that he had personally cut the ropes in order to prevent a Heenan victory. There was even a rumour, taken seriously in some quarters, that he had tripped his old adversary.

So strongly ran the feeling against him that the authorities in Boston resorted to deception in order to ensure that there would be no trouble on his homecoming. Bostonians were given to believe that the *Canada*, on which he returned in the company of Paddy Hughes and Dad Cunningham, had not left Halifax, Nova Scotia, until midnight on Wednesday, May 2nd. In fact, it had left three hours earlier, the result of the subterfuge being that its arrival in Boston at six on the Friday morning was quite unexpected except by the police, who were at the wharf in numbers just in case.

And the deception did not end there. When the news of Morrissey's arrival got out, it was claimed that he had already left the city, on the morning train to Albany. It was true that he had wasted little time in Boston, true also that he had left by railroad, but he had in fact gone to New York, and it was the fear of trouble there that prompted this second piece of disinformation. In the event, Morrissey's presence in the metropolis excited surprisingly little interest, and there was no trouble in the sporting houses which he visited that evening.

But whatever New York's attitude to Morrissey, interest in the Benicia Boy remained high throughout May and June, and there was great excitement when it became known that he was finally to return to America in mid-July. Anticipating his arrival – coincidentally on the *Vanderbilt* – on Friday, July 13th, Messrs Campbell and McCabe of the Malta saloon organised a party of some seventy-five of the Boy's friends to intercept the ship in the bay. They set out in the morning aboard the steam-tug *John A. Lockwood*, carrying quantities of food and drink as well as a small brass cannon on the forward deck to fire a salute.

An added bonus for the high-spirited party was the execution for piracy of the notorious Albert W. Hicks, scheduled that very morning to hang on Bedloe's Island – which, twenty-five years on, would become home to the most famous statue in the world, the name of which it would later adopt. Hicks was in the charge of Isaiah Rynders, who had moved on in the decade since he had instigated the Astor Place Riot. In mid-nineteenth-century New York, Rynders was ideally qualified for the post he now held as US marshal: as well as being an urban gangster, he had in his day been a Mississippi riverboat gambler and knife-fighter, chased from Vicksburg by vigilantes in 1835.

His prisoner that day was in reality more small-time waterfront thug than pirate. His life had taken a fatal turn four months earlier in Cherry Street, where John Morrissey had once lived, and where the young butcher had defeated the champion of Hickory Street in 1823. While drinking in the Sink or Swim saloon, Hicks had been drugged by proprietor Phil 'Plug Ugly' Boston, and handed over to Captain Burr of the sloop *E.A. Johnson*. When he awoke, he was not best pleased to find himself on the way to Virginia to pick up a cargo of oysters.

Five days later, the *Johnson* was found drifting off New Jersey, bearing marks of bloodshed, but unmanned: there was no sign of Captain Burr, of Hicks, or of the two young Watts brothers who completed the crew. Having in the meantime been seen in Manhattan with a great deal of money, Hicks was the obvious suspect. He was soon arrested in Providence, Rhode Island, where he was found still to be in possession of some of the crew's effects. At first, he denied that he had ever been on the *Johnson*, but, with so much evidence against him, he finally admitted to having slaughtered Captain Burr and the Watts brothers with an axe.

As Campbell and McCabe were organising their excursion that morning, Hicks, in the charge of Marshal Rynders, was on his way to Bedloe's Island aboard the steamship *Red Jacket*. Some fifteen hundred prominent citizens accompanied him, including Tom Hyer and Awful Gardner, who, as Morrissey's bottle-holder, had joined in the fight with Yankee Sullivan at Boston Corners in 1853. A notorious thug, Gardner had, to general amazement, kept his vow of three years earlier that he would henceforth be a model citizen.

At the request of several of the guests – supported, apparently, by Hicks himself – the *Red Jacket* made a detour in order to see the *Great Eastern*, presently docked on the Hudson.

By the time the condemned man was finally on the scaffold, which had been erected almost on the water's edge, land and sea were covered with sightseers. Small boats made an almost solid mass for some thirty metres from the shore, while larger vessels, most of them specially chartered excursion boats, stood a little further off. Decks, masts and rigging were black with onlookers, and it was estimated that more than ten thousand were present when, at exactly eleven fifteen, a ghastly hush marked the fatal moment.

The event was, however, something of a disappointment for the Heenan welcoming committee, because they were not on the scene early enough. By the time the *Lockwood* was fairly in position, Hicks's body was already swaying in the wind.

Even so, a dangling corpse was better than nothing, and anyway, witnessing the hanging had not been the object of the excursion. Still in high spirits, they moved on to spend the rest of the day off Sandy Hook, the spit of land from which they could best observe vessels coming up the bay. But they were to be disappointed, and that night they cast anchor off the Government Docks on the Jersey shore. After a barbecue, much singing and still more drinking, they were kept awake most of the night by the crass antics of the more dedicated practical jokers among them.

Unrefreshed, they returned to Sandy Hook in the morning to resume their vigil, but again they were disappointed. By Saturday afternoon, running short of food, drink and coal, they admitted defeat and the *John A. Lockwood* returned to New York. After a brief stop at Coney Island, she arrived at her berth around nine o'clock.

Just two hours later, the *Vanderbilt* steamed into the bay, and the Benicia Boy, in the company of Jack Macdonald, disembarked on Staten Island and put up for the night at Tom Burns's hotel. As soon as they heard the news, Campbell, McCabe and others, still recovering from their unsuccessful trip on the *Lockwood*, took a rowing boat to the island.

It was a joyful reunion. As their hero gave his account of the fight, there were roars of laughter from the welcoming committee at the English accent which the impressionable Boy had acquired in his six months on the other side of the Atlantic. They were particularly fascinated to hear of the tremendous welcome which he had received in Dublin.

In the morning he went for a drive and, after breakfast, came to Manhattan on the ten o'clock ferry, thus avoiding almost all of the crowds who had crossed over to see him.

Nor, for many hours, did most of them manage to see him even in the city. As his admirers waited anxiously in the Malta, easily the likeliest place, Jack preferred to take a drive during the day, on the Bloomingdale Road and through the new Central Park. Until evening, the crowds at the Malta had to be satisfied with admiring the two gifts which the Boy had presented to Frank McCabe on Staten Island. In addition to a set of his colours, there was a large handkerchief on which, surrounded by a border in the form of the championship belt, a laurel wreath and a circle of thirteen stars (representing the original states of the Union) floated over the hero's portrait, with the legend 'John C. Heenan, the fourteenth star of America'.

The Boy, still in the company of Jack Macdonald, finally turned up in the evening and, much as he hated to be the object of such curiosity, was persuaded to put in an appearance in the bar before retreating to a private supper room. The confirmation of his whereabouts brought still more people to the scene, and made it hard for the young fighter to put into effect his decision that it would be best to pass the night elsewhere.

By the time he was ready to leave, the crowd had overflowed into the street, and it was only with great difficulty that he was able to force his way out to the waiting coach. And even when he was safely aboard, his admirers came close to achieving their aim of unharnessing the horses so that they could pull him themselves. The Benicia Boy was learning that fame has its price.

When the initial excitement over his return had subsided, giving him chance to think about the immediate future, Heenan made plans to give exhibitions in all the principal cities of the land. He also began to prepare himself for a 'reception festival' in New York, scheduled for Tuesday, August 14th at Jones Wood on the East River to the north of the city blocks. Somewhat incongruously, it was organised by members of the new Muscular Christian movement, to whose blandishments the Boy had succumbed. It was to be quite an occasion.

On the other side of the world, twenty thousand British and French troops were on their way to Beijing to conclude the Second Opium War and make China safe for European trade and missionaries, but in New York all roads led to Jones Wood. From midday to three o'clock, all the city railways on the east side were crowded, and the avenues leading to the arena were thick with vehicles of all kinds, from aristocratic carriages to tradesmen's wagons. Spectators paid twenty-five cents each to enter an amphitheatre looking down on a ring fronted by an arch bearing the motto 'May the Best Man Win' – a reference to the fact that the main entertainment of the day was to be a sparring exhibition, culminating in an appearance by the Boy himself.

By two o'clock, some twenty thousand were present, with more arriving all the time. Then the show began, with Jack Macdonald sparring with Jim Cusick. More boxing followed, all of it much tamer than the Fancy were used to, before the moment came for which all had been waiting.

The New York Herald described the scene:

> The conquering hero rides in an open barouche, surrounded with a large amount of American flags and policemen... The champion is urbane. He bows on either side as the crowd shout loud hosannas and cheer him most lustily.

The *Herald*'s reporter, noting that Heenan's features were – despite the battering they had taken at Farnborough – singularly free of the marks of punishment characteristic of the prize fighter, thought that 'if he had lived in the age of Phidias, Heenan would have been chosen as a model for a statue of Olympian Jove.'

Certainly there was no danger that his looks would be spoiled in the exhibition he now gave. After four opponents had come and gone without greatly exciting the spectators, the Boy retired to get cleaned up and to put on more formal attire. He then returned for the presentation of a cheque for $10,000, and a gold ring to represent the belt which all true Americans thought he should have been awarded.

The spectators generally found this considerably more interesting than the boxing, and police were obliged to make use of their clubs to hold back the more eager of them. Jack Macdonald also received a ring, but when he found that there was none for Jim Cusick, the Boy immediately gave him his own, saying that he would easily get another one.

It was a spontaneous gesture typical of Jack Heenan's easy-going open-handedness. The Benicia Boy made a highly satisfactory hero. Like Tom Sayers three and a half thousand miles away in London, he could do no wrong.

CHAPTER 17

DIMINUENDO

JOHN L. SULLIVAN was one of the roughest toughest men ever to walk the planet. He boasted, famously, 'I'm John L. Sullivan, and I can lick any man in the house.' Whichever house he was in, the boast was never idle.

He was a drunk and he was a wife-beater. He specialised in the extreme abuse of his own body and those of others, and he was spectacularly successful at both activities. His massive alcohol intake ensured that, however big and tough he was, he was in pretty poor physical shape most of the time. Unfortunately for those who fell foul of him outside the ring, he could batter them senseless anyway. And sadly for those who met him inside it, he always managed to get himself into condition when it really mattered.

Like so many American fighters, he was essentially Irish, having been born in Boston to immigrant parents on October 12th, 1858, some two years after the death of Yankee Sullivan, and just a week before Morrissey's victory over Heenan at Long Point. He had taken no notice of the Sayers–Heenan fight, having been only eighteen months old at the time, but his mean and aggressive streak – very mean and very aggressive – showed early in life.

He was only twenty-three when, to no one's great surprise, he won the American heavyweight championship with victory over Paddy Ryan, another Irish American, on February 7th, 1882 – the thirty-third anniversary of the day on which Tom Hyer became America's first champion by overpowering John L's namesake Yankee Sullivan at Still Pond Heights.

Nobody could touch him, and he became a superstar – a hero to those who idolised raw power and aggression. Like the great figures of the prize ring who went before him, John L. Sullivan became a true working-class hero. But even for a prize fighter, he was marked by his self-destructive tendency – in particular, his fondness for the bottle.

Still, his crown sat securely on his head for seven years, until a challenge was thrown down by the one man who, it seemed, just might have a chance against him. Jake Kilrain, born John Joseph Killion, had in common with John L. Sullivan that he was of Irish blood and that he was a prize fighter. Otherwise, Kilrain was everything that Sullivan was not, and nothing that Sullivan was. He was essentially a quiet family man, for whom fighting was a career rather than a compulsion. But he was good at it, and with Sullivan notoriously careless of his health, there were many who thought that Jake Kilrain might be too much for him.

On the morning of Sunday, July 7th, 1889 – two months after the opening of the Eiffel Tower in Paris – a special train from New Orleans crossed the border into Mississippi. The prize ring was no less illegal there, but the organisers of the Sullivan–Kilrain fight had given their word that the event would not come off in Louisiana.

The train finally came to a halt some one hundred miles north-east of New Orleans at a little place called Richburg. It was not much more than a lumber camp. The two fighters, both of whom had arrived the day before, entered the ring at three o'clock on a blazingly hot afternoon. Any notion that the champion would be out of condition was exploded by the sight of him. Having been trained by William Muldoon, probably the only man who could have held him to a strict and alcohol-free régime, he looked as mean and as tough as ever. It was not what Jake Kilrain and his supporters had expected.

Amongst the officials appointed for the fight were two timekeepers, one for each man. Kilrain's was Bat Masterson, one-time sheriff of Dodge City, friend of Wyatt Earp, and now a boxing writer for the press.

He and the two thousand or so paying spectators saw quite a fight. The heat alone made it a gruelling ordeal for the two men, and the sun raised blisters on Kilrain's back. By round forty-four, Sullivan was vomiting, but refused his exhausted adversary's offer of a draw, and after seventy-five rounds, Kilrain's corner threw up the sponge. John L. Sullivan had retained his title.

The fight had attracted huge interest, but its chief significance became clear only in retrospect. Never again would a major heavyweight championship be contested with bare fists under the rules of the London Prize Ring. It was truly the end of an era.

When the fearsome John L, in need of another big payday to sponsor his hell-raising three years later, issued a challenge to all comers, he specified that he would fight only under the Queensberry Rules. Gentleman Jim Corbett of California stepped forward, and in New Orleans on September 7th, 1892, proved with his gloved fists that John L. Sullivan could no longer lick any man in the house.

The end of the bare-knuckle era had been coming for a long time. In the years following the Sayers–Heenan fight, the English prize ring had virtually died, and boxing's centre of gravity had crossed the Atlantic. But even in America public disapproval had driven it deep underground, and it was clear as the last decade of the century approached, that it would have to adapt to survive.

Fortunately for fight fans, a new format was already available. Just five years after the Sayers–Heenan fight, a versatile young sportsman by the name of John Graham Chambers had drawn up a new set of rules for boxing. Two years later, they were published under the patronage of the eighth Marquess of Queensberry, under whose name they became generally known.[18]

They differed very significantly from those of the London Prize Ring. For one thing, they defined boxing more clearly by forbidding wrestling. But their most controversial provision was that fighters should wear gloves. It had taken more than a century, but the mufflers of the father of boxing, Jack Broughton, had come of age.

At first, the Queensberry Rules were considered suitable only for amateurs – as anyone might have expected, bearing in mind that, apart from their use by professionals in sparring practice, gloves had previously been used only by gentlemen who enjoyed boxing as a recreation. But the social acceptability of amateur boxing was to prove their trump card. If gentlemen might box with gloves, why should everyone not do so?

The notion, propounded by Broughton, Gentleman Jackson and others, that gloves would enable Lord Byron and his peers to avoid unsightly injuries was never entirely accurate, but their use certainly cut down the quantity of blood that was spilled in a fight. And in doing so, it undermined one of the main arguments of the anti-fight lobby – that boxing reduced the human face, God's handiwork, to a bloody mess.

In an increasingly squeamish age, this was a significant matter. After the flogging to death of Private John Frederick White in 1846, agitation against the use of the lash had led to its outlawing by the services. The Army had ended peacetime flogging in 1868, and given the cat up altogether thirteen years later; the Navy had taken the same two steps in the 1870s. And in the year that the Army had begun the process, public executions had been discontinued. The direction society was taking was clear, and if pugilism could not be stamped out completely, anything that might make it a little less gruesome was always going to be a plus.

But there was far more to the Queensberry Rules than just the use of gloves. Equally important was the introduction of the count of ten. Under the LPR Rules, a fighter had more than half a minute to recover from a knock-down, which led to the unedifying spectacle of half-dead, blood-spattered men staggering to their feet for round after futile round. Now a man who could not get back on his feet after ten seconds was deemed beaten.

Then there was the fixed-length round. With boxers fighting for three minutes, then resting for one, tactical falling, long a bane of the prize ring, was ended at a stroke. And while they were no part of the original Queensberry Rules, fixed-length bouts were a natural development from fixed-length rounds, which meant that spectators would no longer turn up at a fight with no idea of how long it might last. Fights with a time limit were much more in keeping with an age in which time was more regulated than ever before. The Queensberry Rules were what boxing needed if it was to survive.

Like all social evolution, it took time. A generation passed before the new code, expanded and improved by London's National Sporting Club in 1891, finally supplanted that of the LPR, and even then boxing remained a contentious and sometimes chaotic activity. In 1896, for example, the police captain in charge of public order had to disarm a man who entered the ring in San Francisco wearing a revolver. It was the referee, Wyatt Earp, who had followed Bat Masterson's path from the Wild West to the boxing ring.

And the controversy extended to the fight itself, for there was outrage when Earp declared the outclassed Jack Sharkey the winner over Englishman Bob Fitzsimmons, the man who had taken Jim Corbett's title. Sharkey was on the deck at the time, and Earp, unlike just about everyone else present, deemed that the solar plexus punch which had put him there was a low blow. Suspicions that the fight was a fix have never gone away.

But such things were increasingly rare after the death of the bare-knuckle prize ring. Boxing by the Queensberry Rules, while never exactly respectable, was well set to continue in rude health throughout the coming century.

Without the Queensberry Rules, it is hard to see how it could have survived at all, except as a genuinely underground activity. Trouble at fights was so common by the time Sayers met Heenan that it took something pretty bad to shock the Fancy. But the mayhem of the third Caunt–Bendigo fight, as well as the chaotic ending of the mill at Farnborough, were perfect examples of the sort of scene that society as a whole was no longer prepared to tolerate.

America had been no better. In fact, it seems likely that, in percentage terms, there was still more trouble at fights in America than at fights in England. Deaf Burke was lucky to escape with his life when he fought Sam O'Rourke in 1837, the whole career of Yankee Sullivan in the 1840s had been a disgrace, George Thompson had valued his life too much to beat John Morrissey in 1852... The list was endless. And yet boxing had survived in America after it had died in England.

The explanation seems to be that the United States was still a young country, its ethos not yet fully formed. And perhaps more significantly, magistrates and police were far more thinly spread over such a vast land.

In England, things were never the same after the Sayers–Heenan fight. Outside the ranks of the Fancy, few people took any interest in the next title bout, when Sam Hurst, having failed to tempt Jack Heenan back into the ring, defeated an ageing and ailing Tom Paddock. For all his physical attributes, Hurst was not an impressive fighter, and a man little bigger than Tom Sayers took the title from him with ease in June 1861. It was Jem Mace, who had beaten Bob Travers just weeks before the Farnborough mill.

He won the crown in the sort of truly bloody fight which was no longer even marginally acceptable. *The Times*, less shy of reporting the prize ring since the mill at Farnborough, told its readers the day after the battle, that 'Hurst was literally deluged with blood, which poured over his huge figure in such streams that Mace himself was covered with it, and the clothes of Hurst's seconds almost saturated.' Even the noise of the fight was affected: the sound of Mace's punches, said *The Times*, 'gradually deadened down to a splashing sound like striking raw meat, that was sickening to hear.'

Jem Mace, who had Nat Langham to thank for his start in pugilism, was one of the pivotal figures in boxing history. If John L. Sullivan was the man mainly responsible for the slow transition from bare fists to gloves in America, Mace was his transatlantic counterpart. Known as the Swaffham Gypsy, though he almost certainly had no Romany blood, Mace was at one time close to Adah Menken. His preference was to use his hands in playing the fiddle, but there was more money in boxing.

During his extraordinary career, which went on until he was nearly sixty, he once inexplicably failed to show at a fight with Mike Madden (a couple of years after the latter's fatal contest with John Jones), and his three-minute knockout by Bob Brettle six months later was widely thought suspicious. *Bell's Life in London* went so far as to call him 'the most unmitigated coward and impostor that ever laid claim to the title of a fighting man'. But he could fight well when he chose, and he was regarded by many as the most scientific boxer the world had seen. His influence over the sport worldwide – he lived for extended periods in America and Australia, and toured New Zealand – was considerable.

The English prize ring received its death-blow in 1868 – the year that the Army ended peacetime flogging, and public executions were banned – when legislation effectively prevented the railways from running fight specials. The result was that English pugilism, with Jem Mace to the fore, upped sticks and crossed the Atlantic. Even *Bell's Life* ceased to cover prize fights except on very rare occasions, and boxing in England survived only in sparring exhibitions at sporting houses and at circuses. Without going through the list of farcical fights of the 1860s, it would be fair to say that those who attended them were in general lucky to do no worse than waste their money.

By the time John L. Sullivan and Jake Kilrain fought out the last big bare-knuckle battle, the remnants of English prize fighting had taken to the Continent. On a tennis court in Bruges on December 23rd, 1889, English slugger Jem Smith, a victim of Kilrain's in an earlier fight, took on Australia's Frank Slavin, known as the Sydney Cornstalk. Smith was outclassed, but before he could be quite beaten, he was saved by the sort of intervention that had done as much as anything to destroy the prize ring.

Squire George Alexander Baird, who preferred to style himself Squire Abingdon, was himself a first-class amateur jockey and a noted patron of blood sports: in addition to pugilism, he took a great interest in dog fighting and ratting. And human beings were no safer than animals when Squire Baird was around. Lily Langtry, the most celebrated actress of her day, paid with at least one nasty beating for allowing the squire to share her bed.

Baird had bet a substantial amount that Smith would not lose to Slavin, and, just in case things did not go his way, he turned up at the fight in company with a crowd of thugs armed with coshes and knuckle-dusters. When it became clear that Slavin was going to win, Baird let his dogs off the leash. The referee responded by calling a draw, explaining afterwards that it was clearly impossible for the Australian to have fair play, and any other decision would have endangered his life.

As the twentieth century approached, such scenes were no longer tolerable.

As for the heroes of Farnborough, neither would rise so high again. They were to meet once more in the ring, however, on December 10th, 1863, when Tom seconded the Benicia Boy, now returned from

America, against England's Tom King at Wadhurst in Sussex. It was the sixth anniversary of Heenan's exhibition match with Joe Coburn in New York, and it was to be his last fight. King had been beaten by the smaller but more talented Jem Mace two years before, but had become champion in November 1862 when, on the very verge of defeat in his second encounter with Mace, he had effectively ended the fight with one tremendous blow.

Jack Heenan was tempted back to the ring by the prospect of gaining at last the title of which he felt he had been robbed at Farnborough. At first, it was all very similar to April 1860, with the fight train leaving London Bridge Station early in the morning. Just before the fight began, as *The Times* reported the following day,

> men with foreheads villainously low came trampling past with bundles of notes in their hands, shouting again that they were ready with £20 to £7 on Heenan, but they found few takers, for the American was already considered the winner beyond all chance of accident.

The same report described the clumsy opening round: 'Another minute and they were struggling upright for the fall with their great powerful forms interlocked, and swaying to and fro like a huge, uncouth machine, stamping heavily from side to side.'

It was typical of the early part of the fight, in which there was much more wrestling than boxing. Heenan was on top, but was not altogether well served by his seconds. Again he had Jack Macdonald in his corner, and to assist him there was Tom Sayers. *The Times* made much of the contrast in their contributions:

> Macdonald is fortunately one of Heenan's seconds, and Sayers is unfortunately the other, for the champion pugilist is at sea in this mild office, and is about the worst second that ever crossed the ropes, lifting his man by the hair, or ear, or nose, or wherever he first catches hold of him.

Poor Tom, conspicuously attired in fur cap, yellow jacket and jackboots, was not up to it. He was clearly in poor health, and showed little aptitude for the work required of him.

Even so, his man was well on top in the early stages, and claims were even made after the fight that King was given more than the allotted thirty seconds to recover from one knock-down. The odds against Heenan shortened still further as, in the words of *The Times*, 'sundry flat-nosed men, whom no one would think of trusting out of handcuffs, swagger about, and loudly offer 100 to 5 on the American.'

The fight developed into a struggle between a wrestler (Heenan) and a boxer (King), with the latter coming gradually back into contention as it wore on. After about half an hour, King it was who had the upper hand, and before forty minutes was up, victory was his. His beaten opponent, *The Times* tells us, was in a dreadful state: 'One man was trying to heave up his immense inanimate form, while another stripped the wet drawers, stained deep with his own blood, from the limbs of the stunned athlete.'

Heenan was taken ill after the fight, and ever afterwards claimed, not implausibly, that he had been doped. The truth has never been established. Outwith the ranks of the Fancy the fight failed entirely to recreate the excitement of the Sayers–Heenan battle of 1860, and did little more than deal another blow to the embattled prize ring.

By this time, Tom Sayers had already suffered a wounding experience when he had taken over Howes and Cushing's Circus, an American outfit touring in England. Travelling circuses were very popular at the time, and sparring was one of the attractions. The former champion, however, had already shown his lack of business acumen when the Bricklayer's Arms had failed, and it was no better this time. His personal appearances as an excruciatingly unfunny clown did not help, and it was fortunate that the £3,000 which had been collected for him in testimonials after the big fight was safely invested.

To make things worse, his home life was more chaotic than ever. His last public appearance before his unfortunate showing at Wadhurst had been ten months earlier in February 1863. *The Times* reported proceedings at Clerkenwell Police Court:

> Charlotte Sayers, aged 30, residing at 10, Bellevue-cottages, Camden-street, Camden-town, described as of no occupation, was charged before Mr. D'Eyncourt with wilfully breaking 20 panes of glass, value 10s., the property of Thomas Sayers, ex-champion of England and circus proprietor.
>
> The defendant, who has been living with the complainant, said she had been badly used by him. She was covered with bruises where he had knocked her about, and her arms were black and blue from his ill-usage. He had repeatedly knocked her about.
>
> The complainant said that the defendant had been from home for two nights, and on her return had illused him. On Thursday, at about 12 o'clock, she went to his house and made a great disturbance. She then went outside and threw stones through the windows. She broke 20 panes, and the damage amounted to about 10s. He wanted the defendant to keep away and not molest him any more, as he was tired of it. She caused a large mob of persons to assemble round his house.

Charlotte said that after her husband left her eight years before, Tom and his children had come to live with her. On the Wednesday night he had come home drunk, broken her furniture, thrown it out onto the street, and her after it. He had said she could return the next day and take the remainder of her possessions, but when she tried, he refused to give her them. Tom denied having any of the items she listed, but said she could have anything that was hers, since he wanted nothing more to do with her. Mr D'Eyncourt made clear that he was unimpressed by either party, but bound Charlotte over for £10 to keep the peace for six months.

It was an unedifying case, and Tom did not come out of it well. Charlotte claimed a history of physical abuse at his hands, saying that on one occasion 'he nearly killed her, and, although he was then taken to the police-station, she would not attend and press the charge. She now had bruises on her arms and body from his violence.'

The case raises the question of the identity of Charlotte 'Sayers'. Since Tom and Sarah were certainly never divorced – it was virtually impossible at the time they separated, and prohibitively expensive thereafter – she could not have been legally married to him. So who was she, and how long had she and Tom been living together?

The 1861 census shows Thomas Sayers, thirty-five ('PUGILIST: Champion of England!!!') living at 10 Belle Vue Cottages with Charlotte Sayers, twenty-four, 'Wife', and Peter Sayers, twelve, 'Son'. This would make it unlikely, to say the least, that Peter was Charlotte's son, and it makes more sense to believe the court report of 1863 which gives her age as thirty.[19] If so, Peter may well have been Charlotte's son, but probably not Tom's, since he would have been born while Tom was still living with Sarah, and before the births of their own children.

As for the latter, Sarah Sayers, eleven, and Thomas Sayers, ten, appear on the 1861 census as 'Scholars' at what seems to have been a dame school in Finchley. These are surely the children of Tom Sayers, though it is hard to explain why the 'Where Born' column reads 'Not Known' in both cases. It may be that the children were not available when the census enumerator called, and the person interviewed was unable to supply the information. This could also explain why Thomas's age is given as ten when he was in fact only nine.

Charlotte's claim that Tom had moved in with her after her husband left her eight years previously is intriguing. The wording seems to indicate that she did not live alone for long, if at all. If this is the case, it would mean that when Tom and Sarah parted in 1855, he and his children moved in with Charlotte straight away. He, however, had let it be known that he was living with his sister and brother-in-law, Eliza and Robert King. If he was in fact with Charlotte all the time, this would explain the difficulty that Henry Downes Miles and others had in finding him at home.

But however long he had been living with Charlotte, they certainly broke up in 1863, and Tom's life does not seem to have improved thereafter. In June 1865, just five months before his death, he was back in Clerkenwell Police Court, this time accusing seventeen-year-old George Powell of stealing a coat and a telescope from his house. Under cross-examination, Tom denied cohabiting with George's mother, and denied that he and George were related – though he later said, in blatant contradiction, that he was related to his mother. He claimed to have kept the young man for the previous twelve years out of pure charity.

The former champion came across very badly. Defence counsel argued that he had brought the case out of spite, and should be held to account for his lies. In the event, no action was taken, but the judge discharged the accused with his character intact. Tom was booed and hissed as he left court.

Looking at the detail of the case, it seems unlikely that he could have kept George Powell for twelve years as he claimed, since this would take us back to 1853, the year that Tom and Sarah were married, and when they were certainly living together with their two children. While it was very common for members of different families to live under the same roof – Tom and Sarah with the Bales in Bayham Street, for example – it is scarcely credible that he would have been prepared at that time to keep another child out of simple altruism.

Assuming nonetheless that he and George Powell had been under the same roof for ten years, we know that Tom was during this time cohabiting with Charlotte. She, however, would only have been fifteen years old at the time of George's birth, so is it likely that she was George's mother? And why is he not on the 1861 census? Could he and 'Peter Sayers' be one and the same, with Peter's age, like Charlotte's, being wrongly recorded?

About the only thing to emerge with any clarity is that the life of Tom Sayers did not go well after 1860. His foray into the circus business was a disaster, and his marital affairs became ever more tangled and miserable. Add to this his declining health, and the picture is dark indeed. By the time his life was ended by a combination of diabetes, tuberculosis and alcohol, he had probably had enough anyway.

And things were to become still worse after his death. On Tuesday, April 21st, 1868, *The Times* reported a case from the Court of Chancery. Sarah challenged Tom's will, in which he had left to their two children the annuity fund put together from the subscriptions he received after the big fight. She argued that the three children she had subsequently had while living with James Aldridge – James, Alfred and Charles, all of whom were given the middle name Aldridge and the surname Sayers –

were in fact Tom's. And since she and Tom were by then legally married, it was the Aldridge Sayers children who should inherit, and not the illegitimate Tom and Sarah.

The Times summed up the finding of the Master of the Rolls:

> The evidence adduced, which was principally that of women, was too low and nasty to set forth in detail... His Lordship, having listened with every attention to the evidence adduced before him, held that it was insufficient to satisfy the Court that the separation between Tom Sayers and Sarah his wife had been so complete as to preclude his being held the father of the three Aldridge Sayers – James, Alfred, and Charles – and that these three children must be held entitled to take the fund in question under the trust and provisions of the deed of June, 1861, in favour of the children of Tom Sayers.

Had it not been for the goodwill of those who had stood Tom's friends during his difficult life, young Sarah and Tom would have been left penniless. Whatever her husband had done to earn her hatred, Sarah Henderson must have been a hard woman to wish to disinherit her own children by him.

———

The personalities of the heroes of Farnborough could scarcely have been more different, and Jack Heenan's later life contrasted strongly with that of his old adversary.

It goes without saying that Adah Menken was not present in July 1860 at his great triumph at Jones Wood. He had at the time taken up with one Harriet Martin, of whom little is known other than that Adah named her in her divorce petition. (Why she needed to be divorced from a man to whom she was probably never legally married is difficult to comprehend, but there it is.)

America, for all its excitement over the mill at Farnborough, never accorded Jack Heenan quite the status that England gave his opponent. When the Prince of Wales crossed the Atlantic later in 1860, everyone forgot the Benicia Boy. There had been endless talk of a rematch with John Morrissey, but it had never really looked like happening, and attempts in 1861 to arrange a match with Jem Mace likewise came to nothing.

In March 1862, he returned to England, where he remained highly popular in spite of all the controversy over the big fight. The Civil War was almost a year old, and he did not return to America until the end of 1865, when the fighting was over. Like Tom, he made circus appearances – though unlike him, he never invested in the business. He also worked as a bookmaker, and followed what remained of the prize ring.

Then in December 1863, he fought Tom King. Whether or not he was fairly beaten, his defeat sickened him, and, though still in his twenties, he never fought again. He had never had the single-mindedness of Tom Sayers, and was never a career fighter as England's champion had been.

The train crash at Egham the following year seems to have had lasting effects, and his failure to show at the Sayers funeral in 1865 may suggest some disenchantment with England in general. He claimed to have visited his old adversary during his last illness, and to have found it a distressing experience, but to stay away from the funeral was hardly the behaviour of one who valued greatly his standing with the British public.

It was little more than a month later that he left England, and returned to a homeland transformed by war. The South was defeated, slavery was outlawed, the Union was saved. The last-ditch resistance of the defeated Confederacy, an underground organisation calling itself the Ku Klux Klan, was just beginning.

Jack Heenan, however, was one of many Yankees who had shown no interest in any of it. He never settled to any career. Still known as a prize fighter, he did some exhibitions, and returned for a time to his old job as hired muscle for corrupt politicians. Hoping to make money from an activity which genuinely interested him, he made a number of attempts to run gambling houses, but with little success.

In 1870, he made his last appearance in the ring. He had become friendly with Jem Mace and agreed to act as second when Mace, having crossed the Atlantic, fought America's Tom Allen. As so often in his long and brilliant career, Mace won well. His second, by contrast, had fought only three times, and had not recorded a single victory.

Jack's first opponent, John Morrissey, remained his bitter enemy throughout life, and did not attend his funeral. Morrissey had all the application which the Benicia Boy lacked, and his success in running gambling houses – and most famously, in founding Saratoga Racetrack – must have been galling to his old enemy. At a time when politics was an immensely lucrative free-for-all, he even became a congressman, and when he died in 1878, aged forty-seven, tens of thousands lined the streets to watch his cortège pass.

The name of John Camel Heenan had, by contrast, lost much of its resonance by the time of his death five years earlier. Still, and for all his faults, there were many who sincerely liked him. Christopher O'Connor, one of his backers against Sayers, said of him that 'He wore his heart outside his overcoat. Why he never was any more than a twelve year old boy. Anybody could impose on him by an appeal to his feelings.'

Certainly he was vulnerable to the charms of the other sex. By 1873 he had been married for some time to American actress Sarah Stevens. Many thought she was a positive influence on his life, but she was performing in England when news reached her that her husband was seriously ill, and he was dead and buried before she could get back.

———————

Whatever the truth about his relationships with the Josephine who had claimed to be his wife back in 1860, with Harriet Martin, whom Adah Menken had cited in her divorce petition, or with Sarah Stevens, to whom he was certainly married, Jack Heenan's name would forever be linked with that of Adah Isaacs Menken. She was not blessed with remarkable talent as actress, as poet or as anything else. But she was a star. She married five times, and made friends with all the right people. There was Walt Whitman, Mark Twain, Charles Dickens, Algernon Swinburne, Alexandre Dumas and many others. Making an impact, particularly on men, came naturally to her.

It would be unjust to think of her as a one-trick pony, but she failed as a serious actress – her Lady Macbeth was, said one critic, 'devoid of

Shakespeare or, for that matter, any known playwright' – and her name will always be associated with one role above all others. She first performed *Mazeppa* in 1861, wearing for one scene the body stocking which would earn her the soubriquet of the Naked Lady. 'No pure youth,' said one newspaper, 'could witness her performance and come away untainted.' It was another two years before it became her principal role, but by 1865, Menken meant Mazeppa, and Mazeppa meant Menken.

Having conquered America, she conquered Europe, but her most famous role presented her with one of the trickiest problems for any actor: what to do for an encore. It was a problem she had not solved when she died suddenly in Paris in 1868, at the age of thirty-three. Contrary to popular perception, her greatest role had not been Mazeppa: it had been Adah Isaacs Menken.

Charles Dickens, one of several former friends who did not respond to a request from the *Clipper*'s Ed James to contribute to the cost of a tombstone, himself found a permanent home in Westminster Abbey just two years later. Had he followed up his original intention to go to Farnborough in April 1860, he would have been the most famous person present. And had he given us an account of the day, Heenan and Sayers would never have been forgotten.

By contrast, Samuel Smiles was, as regards the fight, the most enigmatic and the most self-effacing of those who made it happen. *Self-Help* has given him immortality, even if, as an expression of the values of high Victorian England, it has long been unfashionable to the point of ridicule. Smiles was the archetypal Victorian. Born seven years before the Queen in 1812, he outlived her by three, dying in 1904. The mill at Farnborough was the negation of all he held dear, yet he was prepared to aid and abet even criminality if it would turn a profit. Samuel Smiles was a true Victorian.

He died on the forty-fourth anniversary of the day on which the Fancy had besieged London's sporting houses for tickets to the big fight. In those forty-four years, science and technology, harnessed by the ethos which Smiles represented, had transformed the world.

The *Great Eastern* (which took eighteen months to break up when she went for scrap in 1889) had in 1866 at last laid a successful Atlantic cable, and a brief message might now receive a reply from across the ocean in three minutes instead of three weeks. In 1901, Marconi had cut the time still further, bypassing the cable entirely to send a signal across the Atlantic by wireless telegraphy. The telephone was now well established, enabling people to hear each other's voices over extraordinary distances.

The Wright brothers had pioneered powered flight at Kitty Hawk, and on the ground the internal combustion engine was already beginning to put the horse out of business. Much more significantly for the time being, the bicycle, unknown in 1860, was now giving poorer people a freedom of movement they had never before known.

Then there was politics. In 1860 England had had a bare minimum of democracy. The opinions of the dispossessed had carried no political weight, except in so far as they were seen as a threat to public order. By the time Samuel Smiles quit the scene, most adult males had the vote, and real democracy, allowing even women to participate, was on the way.

The United States had always been more democratic than the old country, and Wyoming Territory, where the Benicia Boy died, had in 1869 been the first place on earth to give women the vote. Slavery had ended with the Union victory in the Civil War, but equality between black and white was still worlds away. A hundred years would pass before discrimination on the grounds of colour would be outlawed. As for the surviving American Indians, they had ceased to present any serious threat to the white invaders. And whatever the legends, it was neither Colt revolvers nor Winchester rifles that had won the West. It was the iron horse.

There were still transatlantic tensions, but they were not what they had been. What Ralph Waldo Emerson had predicted half a century before was now coming to pass. Although Britain still held a huge empire, it was already clear that a vast, rich and stable nation like the United States would soon become incomparably stronger than its island parent.

For the time being, however, Europe remained the world's centre of political gravity. Ten years after England and America had clashed at Farnborough, France and Germany clashed at Sedan, in the first of what was to be the three-round European superheavyweight championship. And the Prussian victory had led to the short-lived Paris Commune, the first practical demonstration of a political philosophy immensely threatening to the Continent's capitalist establishment.

England preferred to stand aloof from Europe's travails, and administer her empire as best she could. To this end, Disraeli had pulled off a coup in 1875 when he won control of the new Suez Canal, which slashed the time it took to get to India, the most prized imperial possession. Less comfortingly, England had had a salutary taste of African nationalism when the Zulus had massacred a substantial British force at Isandhlwana in 1879. And she had had her first serious encounter with Islamic fundamentalism in the 1880s, when the revolt of Sudan's Mahdi had torn a vast tract of land from the grasp of the island queen.

And still there was Ireland. There was always Ireland. Emigration had solved nothing, the famine had solved nothing. Still the Irish yearned for independence, and still they could not get it. By now, the real problem was Ulster, where no one doubted that the Protestant loyalists would fight to the death rather than become part of a united, Catholic Ireland. No one could see a solution.

The world moved on, as it always does. Historians who see turmoil and transformation as characteristic of that part of the human story which they have chosen to study, would do well to try another time and another place and see if it was any different.

Pimlico, where Tom Sayers was born, has long since disappeared under much more salubrious architecture; Jack Heenan's birthplace of West Troy has been transformed into Watervliet, and little of the old Benicia now stands. Manhattan island, its head in the clouds, is quite literally unrecognisable from the place he knew as home, while Tom's old slum of Agar Town disappeared in 1866 under the approaches to the new St Pancras Station. And now a still newer terminal links England and France via the Channel Tunnel first mooted a quarter of a century before Tom Sayers was born.

As for Farnborough, some of the village of 1860 still stands, but the expansion of the army camps established just a few years earlier has led to a population increase from fewer than five hundred in 1850 to nearly sixty thousand today. Farnborough, a military town like neighbouring

Aldershot, is, in the eyes of the world, the site of an international air show.

But for just one brief morning in the spring of 1860, it was the battleground on which England faced America for the championship of the world.

ENDNOTES

1 Costermongers were barrow boys, of whom there may have been more than thirty thousand in London at the time. John Camden Hotten, in his 1859 slang dictionary, defined them as 'street sellers of fish, fruit, vegetables, poultry, &c.', and said they were distinguished by their 'low habits, general improvidence, pugnacity, love of gambling, total want of education, disregard for lawful marriage ceremonies ...' Their most prized article of clothing was a brightly-coloured neckerchief known as a kingsman.

2 According to a story relating to Tom's time as a Jack in the Water, in July 1837 or possibly 1839 he gave some assistance to a Mr and Mrs Machin when they took a trip in a pleasure boat. The couple were next seen ten days later, when their bodies were washed up on the beach. Tom, the last person known to have seen them alive, gave evidence at the inquest. He felt a strong aversion to the sea ever after.
The tale sounds likely enough, but I have been unable to substantiate it, and cannot therefore present it as fact.

3 Generally speaking, an alehouse – which was simply a pub without a spirits licence – afforded the proprietor only a tenuous living. Consequently, all publicans obtained a spirits licence if they possibly could – and lived in constant dread of its suspension by magistrates.

4 It is frequently said that Stevenson died of injuries sustained in this fight, and that the tragedy prompted Broughton to draw up his famous rules. This, however, is false. Contemporary sources say nothing of Stevenson's death, and it was another two years before Broughton's Rules were published.
The misunderstanding may have something to do with the fact that Broughton had once fought an opponent known as the Barber, and a

barber was crushed to death at the Stevenson fight. Then there is *The Gymnasiad*. Whitehead does indeed pronounce Stevenson dead at the end of the fight, but a careful reading suggests that he is speaking figuratively. In his *Treatise upon the Useful Science of Defence*, Captain Godfrey has Stevenson still alive in 1747, and he seems to have acted as bodyguard to the future prime minister, the Earl of Bute, in 1761. A later source, William Hazlitt (who erroneously dates the bout to 1770), tells us in *The Fight* that Stevenson lived into old age.

5 The popular story that Cumberland put Broughton out of business as an act of spite is a little too pat. Broughton's amphitheatre was still open three years after the fight, so if the Duke was intent on revenge, he took his time about it.

As for his withdrawing patronage from Broughton, it is clear that the latter had no further need of it anyway. His amphitheatre was highly profitable, and he had come out of retirement to fight Slack in what was, for him, a grudge match rather than a payday. We rely for our knowledge of the bout largely on Pierce Egan, who, more than sixty years after the event, tells us in *Boxiana* what ensued for Broughton: 'His Royal Highness instantly turned his back upon him, and by the interference of the Legislature, his Amphitheatre was shut up!' It is an unjustified leap of the imagination to infer that Cumberland was responsible for the closure – or even that Egan believed he was.

Certainly, the oft-repeated tale that the Duke lost £10,000 on the fight is nonsense. *The Gentleman's Magazine* of April 1750 talks of 'a peer of the firſt rank, who betting 10 to 1 loſt £1000.' Not £10,000, and possibly not even Cumberland.

Even so, it does seem that the Duke's disillusion with boxing set in with Broughton's defeat, and that the withdrawal of what was effectively royal protection had disastrous results for the prize ring.

6 It is frequently asserted that the very first fight to be held under the LPR rules was the 1839 contest in which Thompson defeated Deaf Burke, but this is not the case. Six months earlier, in August 1838, John Hannan and Thomas Maley had fought under what were then called simply 'the new rules'.

7   The prohibition against going down without a blow, which would be included in the LPR rules framed four months later, had already become universal.

8   It is Nat Fleischer, in *Black Dynamite*, who claims that Zachary Molineaux was Tom's father. Fleischer, not always the most reliable authority, is somewhat vague about his sources, but very insistent on the accuracy of his findings.
    He claims that four of Zachary's brothers were also pugilists, and that Tom won his freedom fighting for his owner, Squire Molineaux. (Freed slaves frequently took their former owner's name.)
    It all sounds quite convincing, but Fleischer is clearly wrong in his claim that 'pugilism in this country was founded by the Negro race through Zachary Molineaux.' Even if Molineaux was the first – which would surely be impossible to prove – boxing as it came to be known in the United States developed in the North, not the South, and was for long an exclusively white activity.

9   It is not at all easy to establish the truth about Yankee Sullivan's career prior to his fight with Hammer Lane. According to *The Illustrated Police Budget*, his real name was Frank Amor, he was transported for fourteen years when still a boy, and given his ticket-of-leave after eleven. The account which I offer is more in line with majority opinion, but, on my part at least, is no more than a best guess.

10 Something should be said on the subject of the sponsors or backers of prize fighters. A fighter needed to find a stake of as much as £200, the sum depending on his standing and that of his opponent: the bigger the fight, the bigger the stake. He also had to cover his training expenses at a time when he would have no other income: there were trainers and sparring partners to be paid, there was food and accommodation to be arranged, and so on. It was very rare for a boxer to be able to afford to fight at all without backers. A boxer would generally have more than one sponsor for a fight, and we know that well over twenty were involved in backing Tom Sayers for his last eight battles. Where a single sponsor is named, it may be assumed that this was the

man who took it on himself to find the required money, but he was not necessarily the only one involved.

11 Henry Downes Miles was the pre-eminent ring reporter of the day, writing for *Bell's Life* and other London papers. His three-volume *Pugilistica* is, along with Pierce Egan's *Boxiana*, the principal contemporary source of information on the bare-knuckle prize ring.
Wherever I quote him, I am quoting from *Pugilistica*, but I should point out that not all of the ring reports which it contains are Miles's own work. Many are from before his time, and the later ones are simply taken from *Bell's Life*, whoever contributed them. Still, it was Miles who brought them all together, and it is certain that he was personally responsible for many of them.

12 I have been unable to establish when Tom's association with Jack Atcheler began. John Gideon, who would become his most significant patron, told *The Illustrated Police Budget* some fifty years later that, on coming to London, Tom 'threw away hod and mortar', and went straight into Atcheler's service. Gideon might be expected to have known, but his testimony cannot be taken at face value: he is (understandably, given the lapse of time) not entirely reliable on other matters, and anyway he did not become acquainted with Tom until 1856, ten years after the latter settled in London.
Other sources suggest that Tom worked as a bricklayer in the capital for years, and this seems inherently more likely: there was plenty of work available, and it would seem strange that he would so readily abandon a recently-acquired skill which could be relied on for a steady income at a time when anything less was extremely risky for anyone without private means. Then there is the fact that on his 1853 marriage certificate he gives his profession as bricklayer. This does not prove that he was still in the building trade, but had he been working at something else entirely for seven years, he might have preferred some other designation.

13 Census records of 1861 and 1871 identify James Aldridge as a cab driver, but it is worth mentioning that Tom Langley (*The Life of Tom*

Sayers) and Alan Lloyd (*The Great Prize Fight*) both call him Alfred Aldridge, and say that he worked as a croupier in his brother John's fashionable gaming house. Since he called his second son Alfred (the first was James), it is at least possible that Alfred was his middle name, and it is certain that any connection with a world of money and status would have appealed to Sarah. I have, however, been unable to verify the story told by Langley and Lloyd.

14 Many who have written about Adah Menken, including her most recent biographer, Renée M. Sentilles, have mistakenly identified the New York Clipper's Edwin (Ed) James, her staunchest ally, with a notorious English barrister and occasional thespian of the same name. Edwin James, said to have been the original for Dickens's overbearing lawyer Stryver in *A Tale of Two Cities*, crossed the Atlantic in 1861 in the hope of retrieving his fortunes in America after he was disbarred in England. Having been admitted to the New York bar, he remained in the United States until 1872. His namesake Ed James was a sporting journalist. The two are quite distinct.

15 Curiously, Wilkes would report the fight not for his own publication, but for *Frank Leslie's Illustrated Newspaper*. This was because the *Spirit* already had an English ring reporter in the shape of George Caldwell, who wrote as Censor. Under the name of Childers, Caldwell also contributed to *The Field*: he it was who had described Jack Heenan's headquarters in Salisbury.

16 Hollingshead hugely overestimates the number of Americans present: far from two or three hundred, there were probably only twenty or thirty. His error was almost certainly innocent, but exaggeration of crowd numbers (and of money staked on a fight) was frequent. Generally speaking, the lowest estimates are likely to be the most trustworthy.

17 There is a problem with the numbering of the rounds of a pre-Queensberry Rules prize fight. The number was never called, with the result that different reporters often counted them differently. Writing in

Bell's Life, Ned Smith gives the crucial round of the Sayers–Heenan contest as thirty-seven, but other witnesses count it variously between thirty-five and thirty-nine. I have taken thirty-seven as a compromise, but anyone wishing to see the original reports should be aware that George Wilkes, to give just one example, has it as thirty-eight.

18 John Sholto Douglas, infamous for hounding Oscar Wilde to disgrace and ruin, is sometimes called the eighth marquess, sometimes the ninth. The designation depends on whether his ancestor James Douglas (1697–1715) is accorded a place in the succession. James Douglas, a mentally retarded homicidal maniac, was disturbed in 1707 eating a kitchen boy whom he had killed and roasted. He inherited some of his father's titles, but not others.

19 Census data is in general far less reliable than most might think. In the mid-nineteenth century, there was a particular problem with the age of respondents. Because the civil registration of births (as of marriages and deaths) in England began only in 1837, many people did not know exactly how old they were.

BIBLIOGRAPHY

Intending to write a popular rather than an academic work, I have avoided footnoting my sources: numerous footnotes are inevitably distracting, and would not have been in keeping with my purpose. For those wishing to locate a source, a trawl through this bibliography will be necessary.

Books

Place of publication is London unless otherwise stated.

Sayers and Heenan

An authentic history of the prize ring and championships of England; together with a faithful record of the great... encounter between Tom Sayers and John Heenan, etc. 1860

Brooks, Chris. *Burying Tom Sayers.* 199?

Dowling, Francis L. *The Championship of England. Being a continuation of 'Fights for the Championship.' To which is added a Brief History of Tom Sayers and (J.C. Heenan) the Benicia Boy, and an account of their Chief Prize Battles.* 1860

Langley, Tom. *The Life of Tom Sayers.* Leicester, 1973

Lloyd, Alan. *The Great Prize Fight.* 1977

Miles, Henry Downes. *Tom Sayers, sometime Champion of England, his life and pugilistic career.* 1865

Noel, Baptist. *The Fight between Sayers and Heenan. A letter to the Noblemen and Gentlemen who attended the fight.* 1860

Wright, Alan. *Tom Sayers: the last great bare-knuckle champion.* Sussex, 1994

The Prize Ring in Britain

Allanson-Winn, R.G. *Boxing.* 1889

Anderson, Roger. *The Fighting Irish: inside the ring with boxing's Celtic warriors.* Edinburgh, 2004

Badcock, John. *Fancy-ana, or a history of pugilism.* 1824

—*The Fancy: or, true sportsman's guide: being authentic memoirs of the leading pugilists from the days of Figg and Broughton to the Championship of Ward. By an Operator.* [1821–]1826

Batchelor, Denzil. *Big Fight: the story of world championship boxing.* 1954

—*Gods with Gloves on [Biographies of boxers. With illustrations].* 1947

Birley, Derek. *Sport and the Making of Britain.* Manchester, 1993

Brailsford, Dennis. *Bareknuckles: a social history of prize-fighting.* Cambridge, 1988

—"Morals and Maulers: the ethics of early pugilism". *Journal of Sport History,* Summer 1985.

Bunce, Steve. *Boxing Greats: legendary boxers, fights and moments.* Godalming, 1998

Butler, Frank. *A History of Boxing in Britain: a survey of the noble art from its origins to the present-day.* 1972

Cleveland, Harry E. *Fisticuffs and Personalities of the Prize Ring.* 1923

Davis, Jim. *The Great Fight on Hungerford Common* [Neat v Hickman]. Hungerford, 1987

Deghy, Guy. *Noble and Manly: the history of the National Sporting Club, incorporating the posthumous papers of the Pelican Club.* 1956

Doherty, William J. *In the Days of the Giants: memories of a champion of the prize ring, etc.* 1931

Dowling, Francis. *Fistiana: or the oracle of the ring.* 1841

Egan, Pearce. *Boxiana: sketches of ancient and modern pugilism* (facsimile edition). Leicester, 1971

Elliott, William James. *Cameos from the Prize Ring.* 1939

—*Great Stars of the Prize Ring.* 1939

Farnol, Jeffery. *Epics of the Fancy.* 1928

Ford, John. *Prizefighting: the age of Regency boximania.* Newton Abbot 1971

Fox, Richard Kyle. *Prize Ring Champions of England from 1719 to 1889.* New York, 1889

Furniss, Harold (ed.). *Famous Fights, Past and Present: Police Budget Edition.* 1901–04.

Gee, Tony. *Up to Scratch: bareknuckle fighting and heroes of the prize ring.* Harpenden, 1998

Godfrey, John, Captain. *A treatise upon the useful science of defence: connecting the small and backsword and showing the affinity between them... also some observations upon boxing, and the characters of the most able boxers, etc.* 1747

Golding, Louis. *Bare-Knuckle Breed.* 1952

Hartley, R.A. *History and Bibliography of Boxing Books: collectors guide to the history of pugilism.* 1988

Hazlitt, William. *The Fight and other Writings / William Hazlitt: edited by Tom Paulin and David Chandler.* 2000

Henning, Fred. *Fights for the Championship: the men and their times.* 1900

Johnson, Dick. *Bare Fist Fighters of the 18th and 19th Century: 1704–1861.* Lewes, 1987

Lynch, John Gilbert Bohun. *Knuckles and Gloves.* 1922

—*The Prize Ring.* 1925

Macdonald, Alan. *Champions by Acclaim: prize-ring rulers of the lighter weight divisions.* 1994

Mace, Jem. *In Memoriam, Book 1: Fifty Years a Fighter: the life story of Jem Mace.* 1998

Mahon, G.R. "The S.E.R. and Prize Fights of 1859". *The Railway Magazine,* June 1959.

Maxted, Harry G. *The Story of the Prize Ring.* Windsor, 1949

Mee, Bob. *Bare Fists.* Snitterfield. 1998

Miles, Henry Downes. *Pugilistica: being 144 years of the history of British boxing* 1880

Myler, Patrick. *Regency Rogue: Dan Donnelly, his life and legends.* Dublin, 1976

Pancratia, or a history of pugilism. 1812

Pugnus. *History of the Prize Ring, parts 1 & 2.* 1876

Sargent, Harry R. *Thoughts upon Sport.* 1894

Sawyer, Tom. *Noble Art: an artistic & literary celebration of the old English prize-ring.* 1989

Sayers, Henry. *Fights Forgotten: a history of some of the chief English and American prize fights since the year 1788.* 1909

Sugar, Bert Randolph. *The Great Fights: a pictorial history of boxing's greatest bouts.* 1981

Swift, Owen. *The Hand-Book to Boxing; being a complete instructor in the art of self-defence.* 1840

Thormanby (pseudonym of W. Willmott Dixon). *Boxers and their*

Battles: anecdotal sketches and personal recollections of famous pugilists. 1900

Whitehead, Paul. *The Gymnasiad; a very short but very curious epic poem: with the prolegomena of Scriblerus Tertius, and notes variorum.* 1744

Wignall, Trevor C. *The Story of Boxing.* 1923

Wilson, Peter. *Boxing's Greatest Prize: memorable fights for the world heavyweight championship.* 1980

The Prize Ring in America

Allen, Frank. "When Boxing was a Martial Art: the sweet science of bare-knuckle pugilism." *Kung Fu Magazine*, July 2001.

Benedict, George H. *Manual of Boxing, Club Swinging, and Manly Sports, etc.* New York, 1886

The Black Champions of the Prize Ring from Molineaux to Jackson. New York, 1890

Dizikes, John. *Sportsmen and Gamesmen.* Boston, 1981

Fleischer, Nat. *Black Dynamite. The story of the negro in the prize ring from 1782 to 1938.* New York, 1938

—*The Heavyweight Championship: an informal history of heavyweight boxing from 1719 to the present day.* New York, 1949

—*A Pictorial History of Boxing.* New York, 1959

Gorn, Elliott J. *The Manly Art: bare-knuckle prize fighting in America.* Ithaca, New York, 1986

Grombach, John V. *The Saga of the Fist: the 9000 year story of boxing in text and pictures* (first published as *The Saga of Sock).* New York, 1949

Isenberg, Michael T. *John L. Sullivan and his times.* 1988

Johnston, Alexander. *Ten – and Out!: the complete story of the prize ring in America.* New York, 1927

Kofoed, Jack. *Brandy for Heroes. A biography of the Honorable John Morrissey, champion heavyweight of America and State Senator.* New York, 1938

Naughton, W.W. *The Fight of the Century: an album of 81 photographs of the World's Championship contest at Carson on March 17th, 1897... History of the famous match and ring records of Corbett and Fitzsimmons, etc. no. 1.* San Francisco, 1897

Sullivan, John L. *I Can Lick Any Sonofabitch in the House!* 1979

Nineteenth-Century England

Ackroyd, Peter. *Dickens*. 1990

—*London: the biography*. 2000

Adburgham, Alison. *A Punch History of Manners and Modes, 1841–1940*. 1961

Alpert, Michael. *London 1849: a Victorian murder story*. Harlow, 2004

Altick, Richard Daniel. *Victorian People and Ideas: a companion for the modern reader of Victorian literature*. New York, 1973

Archer, Thomas. *The Pauper, the Thief and the Convict: sketches of some of their homes, haunts and habits*. 1865

Barker, Felix. *Highgate Cemetery: Victorian Valhalla*. 1984

—*London: 2000 years of a city and its people*. 1974

Baron, Xavier (ed.). *London 1066-1914: literary sources and documents*. (Volume II). Robertsbridge, 1997

Bennett, Alfred Rosling. *London and Londoners in the Eighteen-Fifties and Sixties*. 1924

Bentley, Nicolas. *The Victorian Scene: a picture book of the period 1837–1901*. 1968

Betjeman, John. *London's Historic Railway Stations*. 1972

Blanchard, Edward Litt Leman. *The Stranger's and Visitor's Conductor through London: giving a… description of everything that can be seen, and how to see it, within the limits of the metropolis; corrected to the latest period, etc*. 1857

Bourne, George (pen name of George Sturt). *William Smith, Potter and Farmer: 1790–1858*. 1920

Briggs, Asa. *Victorian Cities*. 1963

—*Victorian People: some reassessments of people, institutions, ideas and events, 1850–1867*. 1954

—*Victorian Things*. 1988

Buck, Anne. *Victorian Costume and Costume Accessories*. 1961

Camden Town and Kentish Town Directory, 1867. 1867

Campbell, C.J. *Campbell's Visitors' Guide to the International Exhibition, and handy-book of London*. 1862

Canning, John (ed.). *The Illustrated Mayhew's London: the classic account of London street life and characters in the time of Charles Dickens and Queen Victoria*. 1986

Carder, Timothy. *The Encyclopaedia of Brighton*. Lewes, 1990

Carlyle, Jane Welsh. *Letters and Memorials*. 1883

Cassin-Scott, Jack. *Costume and Fashion in Colour, 1760–1920*. 1971

Challacombe, Jessie. *Jottings from a Farnborough Note Book*. Aldershot, 1922

Chapman, Harold. *Victorian Life in Photographs*. 1974

Chesney, Kellow. *The Victorian Underworld*. 1970

Cobbett, William. *Rural Rides*. 1830

Coke, Henry J. *Tracks of a Rolling Stone*. 1905

Coleman, Terry. *The Railway Navvies: a history of the men who made the railways*. 1965

Cranston, Robert. *The Waverley Guide to, through, & about London, & Exhibition*. 1862

Cruchley, George Frederick. *Cruchley's New Guide to London*. 1862

Cruikshank, Robert James. *Charles Dickens and Early Victorian England*. 1949

Dallas, George Mifflin. *A series of Letters from London*. Philadelphia, 1869

de Saussure, César. *A Foreign View of England in the Reigns of George I & George II. The letters of Monsieur César de Saussure to his family*. 1902

Denford, Steven L.J. *Agar Town: the life & death of a Victorian 'slum'*. 1995

—and Woodward, F. Peter (eds.). *Streets of Camden Town: a survey of streets, buildings and former residents in a part of Camden*. 2003

Dickens, Charles. *Dombey & Son*. 1846–48

—*Nicholas Nickleby*. 1838–39

—*Sketches by Boz*. 1836

—*Sketches of Young Gentlemen*. 1838

Diprose, John. *Diprose's London Guide*. 1856

Dyos, H.J. and Wolff, Michael (eds.). *The Victorian City: images and realities*. 1973

Elliot, Henry. *Elliot's new and practical guide through London and its environs by railway, steamboat, or omnibus*. 1859

Emerson, Ralph Waldo. *English Traits*. 1856

Engels, Friedrich. *The Condition of the Working Class in England in 1844*. New York, 1887

England. General Board of Health. *Public Health Act... Report to the General Board of Health, on a preliminary enquiry into the... sanitary condition... of the town of Brighton.* 1849

Gatrell, V.A.C. *The Hanging Tree: execution and the English people, 1770–1868.* Oxford, 1994

Godwin, George. *London Shadows: a glance at the 'homes' of the thousands.* 1854

Greenwood, James. *A Night in a Workhouse.* 1866

—*The Seven Curses of London.* 1869

Haffenden, George. *The Middle Street School, Brighton, formerly the Royal Union School, 1805–1905. A record of one hundred years' primary instruction.* Brighton, 1905

Hale, Edward Everett, the Elder. *Ninety Days' Worth of Europe.* Boston, 1861

Hall, Catherine. *Civilising Subjects: metropole and colony in the English imagination, 1830–1867.* Oxford, 2002

Hall, Fanny W. *Rambles in Europe: or, a tour through France, Italy, Switzerland, Great Britain and Ireland in 1836.* New York, 1839

Halliday, Stephen. *The Great Stink of London: Sir Joseph Bazalgette and the cleansing of the Victorian capital.* Stroud, 1999

Hart-Davis, Adam. *What the Victorians did for us.* 2001

Hartley, L.P. *The Go-Between.* 1953

Hawkins, Henry, Baron Brampton. *The Reminiscences of Sir Henry Hawkins, Baron Brampton.* 1904

Hawthorne, Nathaniel. *Our Old Home* and *English Note-Books.* 1863?

Heald, Henrietta (ed.) *Chronicle of Britain: incorporating a chronicle of Ireland.* Farnborough, 1992

Hibbert, Christopher. *London: the biography of a city.* 1969

Hogben, John. *Hogben's Strangers' Guide to London, etc.* 1856

Hollingshead, John. *My Lifetime.* 1895

—*Ragged London in 1861.* 1861

Holloway, David. *Derby Day.* 1975

Hoppin, James. *Old England.* Boston, 1867

Hotten, John Camden. *A Dictionary of Modern Slang, Cant, and Vulgar Words.* 1859

Howe, Mark Antony deWolfe. *The Life and Letters of George Bancroft.* New York, 1908

Huggett, Frank E. *Carriages at Eight: horse-drawn society in Victorian and Edwardian times.* Guildford, 1978

—*Victorian England as seen by Punch.* 1978

Humpherys, Anne. *Travels into the Poor Man's Country: the work of Henry Mayhew.* Firle, East Sussex, 1982

Irving, Joseph. *The Annals of Our Time: a diurnal of events, social and political, which have happened in, or had relation to, the kingdom of Great Britain, from the accession of Queen Victoria to the opening of the present Parliament. [1837–1868].* 1869

Jackson, Lee and Nathan, Eric. *Victorian London.* 2004

James, Henry. *English Hours.* 1905

Jerrold, William Blanchard. *London: a pilgrimage.* 1872

Kebbell, William. *The Climate of Brighton.* 1859

Kelly, Edward Robert. *Kelly's Post Office Guide to London in 1862, Visitor's handbook to the metropolis and Companion to the Directory.* 1862

Lambert, Miles. *Fashion in Photographs, 1860-80.* 1991

Lampson, Frederick Locker. *My Confidences: an autobiographical sketch addressed to my descendants.* 1896

Litten, Julian. *The English Way of Death: the common funeral since 1450.* 1991

Lockwood, Allison. *Passionate Pilgrims: the American traveler in Great Britain, 1800–1914.* New York, 1981

Macky, John. *A Journey through England. In familiar letters from a gentleman here, to his friend abroad.* 1714

Mankowitz, Wolf. *Dickens of London.* 1976

Marcus, Steven. *The Other Victorians: a study of sexuality and pornography in mid-nineteenth century England.* 1966

May, Trevor. *The Victorian Undertaker.* Princes Risborough, 1996

Mayhew, Henry. *London Labour and the London Poor: a cyclopedia of the conditions and earnings of those that will work, those that cannot work and those that will not work.* 1851

Milton, John. *Tractate of Education, edited with an introduction and notes by Edward E. Morris.* 1895

Bibliography

Morton, Brian N. *Americans in London: an anecdotal street guide to the homes and haunts of Americans from John Adams to Fred Astaire.* 1988

Murray, David Christie. *The Making of a Novelist. An experiment in autobiography.* 1894

—*Recollections.* 1908

Nead, Lynda. *Victorian Babylon: people, streets and images in nineteenth-century London.* 2000

Osbaldeston, George. *Squire Osbaldeston: his autobiography.* 1926

Oxford Dictionary of National Biography. Oxford, 2004

Pardon, George Frederick. *The practical guide to London and its suburbs... with historical, literary, statistical and useful information.* 1862

Pearl, Cyril Altson. *Victorian Patchwork.* 1972

Pearsall, Ronald. *The Worm in the Bud: the world of Victorian sexuality.* 1969

Pepys, Samuel. *The Diary of Samuel Pepys: a new and complete transcription edited by Robert Latham and William Matthews.* 1985

Picard, Liza. *Victorian London: the life of a city, 1840–1870.* 2005

Pike, Edgar Royston. *Human Documents of the Victorian Golden Age, 1850–1875.* 1967

Pool, Daniel. *What Jane Austen Ate and Charles Dickens Knew: from fox hunting to whist, the facts of daily life in nineteenth-century England.* 1993

Priestley, J.B. *The Prince of Pleasure and his Regency 1811–20.* 1969

—*Victoria's Heyday.* 1972

Pritchard, R.E. *Dickens's England: life in Victorian times.* Stroud, 2002

Quennell, Peter (ed.). *Mayhew's Characters.* 1951

Richardson, John. *Camden Town and Primrose Hill Past: a visual history of Camden Town and Primrose Hill.* 1991

Ritchie, James Ewing. *The Night Side of London.* 1857

Robbins, Richard Michael. *The Railway Age.* 1962

Ruskin, John. *The Crown of Wild Olive: three lectures on work, traffic, and war.* 1866

The St Pancras Directory for 1862. 1862

Sala, George Augustus. *Gaslight and Daylight: with some London scenes they shine upon.* 1859

—*Twice Round the Clock: or, hours of the day and night in London.* 1859

Shaw, Donald. *London in the Sixties (with a few digressions). By one of the old brigade.* 1908

Sichel, Marion. *Costume Reference: 6, The Victorians.* 1978

Simpson's Street Directory of St Pancras, with businesses attached, and Court guide. 1862

Smiles, Samuel. *Self-Help.* 1859

Stanford, Edward, Publisher, the Elder. *Stanford's New London Guide.* 1860

Taine, Hippolyte. *Notes on England.* 1872

Thackeray, William Makepeace. *Selected Letters of William Makepeace Thackeray, edited by Edgar F. Harden.* Basingstoke, 1996

Thomson, John. *Victorian London Street Life in Historic Photographs.* 1994 (first published as *Street Life in London.* 1877).

Thormanby (pseudonym of W. Willmott Dixon). *Kings of the Turf: memoirs and anecdotes.* 1898

Thornbury, George Walter. *Old and New London. 1879–1885*

Walton, John K. *Low Life and Moral Improvement in mid-Victorian England: Liverpool through the journalism of Hugh Shimmin.* Leicester, 1991

Weylland, John Matthias. *Round the Tower: or, the story of the London City Mission.* 1875

White, Jerry. *London in the 19th Century: a human awful wonder of God.* 2008

Wilkes, John. *The London Police in the Nineteenth Century.* Cambridge, 1977

Willis, Nathaniel Parker. *Pencillings by the Way.* 1835

Wilson, A.N. *The Victorians.* 2002

Young, G.M. *Victorian England, portrait of an age.* 1936

Nineteenth-Century America

Allen, Walter Ernest. *Transatlantic Crossing: American visitors to Britain and British visitors to America in the nineteenth century.* 1971

American National Biography. New York, 1999

Anbinder, Tyler. *Five Points: the 19th century New York City neighbourhood that invented tap-dance, stole elections and became the world's most notorious slum.* New York, 1981

Asbury, Herbert. *The Gangs of New York: an informal history of the underworld.* New York, 1928

Beals, Carleton. *Brass-Knuckle Crusade. The great know-nothing conspiracy: 1820–1860.* New York, 1960

Bode, Carl. *Midcentury America: life in the 1850s.* Carbondale, Illinois, 1972

Bruegmann, Robert. *Benicia, portrait of an early California town: an architectural history.* San Francisco, 1980

Buntline, Ned. *The Mysteries and Miseries of New York: a story of real life,* New York, 1848

Burne, Jerome. *Chronicle of the World.* Harlow, 1989

Burrows, Edwin G. and Wallace, Mike. *Gotham: a history of New York City to 1898.* New York, 1999

Cobbett, William. *Journal of a Year's Residence in the United States of America.* Gloucester, 1983 (First published London, 1828)

Cofran, John. "The Identity of Adah Isaacs Menken: a theatrical mystery solved". *Theatre Survey,* May 1999.

Coleman, Terry. *The Liners: a history of the North Atlantic crossing.* 1976

Crockett, Davy. *A Narrative of the Life of David Crockett of the State of Tennessee.* Philadelphia, 1834

Daniel, Clifton (ed.) *Chronicle of America.* Liberty, Mississippi? 1989?

Dellenbaugh, Frederick Samuel. *The Romance of the Colorado River. The story of its discovery in 1540, with an account of the later explorations, and with special reference to the voyages of Powell through the line of the great canyons.* New York, 1902

Dickens, Charles. *American Notes.* 1842

—*Martin Chuzzlewit.* 1843–44

Edwards, Samuel (pseudonym of Noel Gerson). *Queen of the Plaza. A biography of Adah Isaacs Menken.* 1965

English, T.J. *Paddy Whacked: the untold story of the Irish–American gangster.* New York, 2005

Falk, Bernard. *The Naked Lady: or, Storm over Adah: a biography of Adah Isaacs Menken.* 1934

Fleischer, Nat. *Reckless Lady: the life story of Adah Isaacs Menken.* New York, 1941

Foster, George G. *New York by Gas-light: with here and there a streak of sunshine.* New York, 1850

Freneau, Philip. *The Poems of Philip Freneau, poet of the American Revolution: edited by F.L. Pattee.* Princeton, New Jersey, 1902

Gale, Robert L. *A Cultural Encyclopedia of the 1850s in America.* Westport, Connecticut, 1993

Galloway, John Debo. *The First Transcontinental Railroad: Central Pacific, Union Pacific.* New York, 1950

Gernsheim, Alison. *Victorian and Edwardian Fashion: a photographic survey.* New York, 1981

Grafton, John. *New York in the Nineteenth Century: 321 engravings from Harper's weekly and other contemporary sources.* New York, 1977

Grattan, Thomas Colley. *Civilized America.* 1859

Hamilton, Thomas. *Men and Manners in America.* Edinburgh, 1833

Harlow, Alvin Fay. *Old Bowery Days: the chronicles of a famous street.* New York, 1931

Irving, Washington. *The Sketch-Book of Geoffrey Crayon, Esq.* 1834

Jackson, Kenneth T. (ed.). *The Encyclopedia of New York City.* New Haven, Connecticut, 1995

Lesser, Allen. *Enchanting Rebel. The secret of Adah Isaacs Menken.* Philadelphia? 1947

Lightfoot, Frederick S. *Nineteenth-Century New York in Rare Photographic Views.* New York, 1981

Lillywhite, Frederick. *The English Cricketers' Trip to Canada and the United States.* 1860

McCabe, James Dabney. *Lights and Shadows of New York Life: or, the sights and sensations of the great city.* Philadelphia, 1872

Mankowitz, Wolf. *Mazeppa: the lives, loves and legends of Adah Isaacs Menken.* 1982

Martin, Edward Winslow. *The Secrets of the Great City: a work descriptive of the virtues and the vices, the mysteries, miseries and crimes of New York City.* Philadelphia, 1868

Moreau de Saint-Méry, Médéric Louis Élie. *Moreau de Saint-Méry's American Journey, 1793–1798, translated and edited by Kenneth Roberts and Anna M. Roberts.* Garden City, New York, 1947

Morris, Lloyd R. *Incredible New York: high life and low life of the last hundred years.* New York, 1951

O'Connor, Richard. *Bret Harte: a biography.* Boston, 1966

Sante, Luc. *Low Life: lures and snares of old New York.* New York, 1991

Sentilles, Renée M. *Performing Menken: Adah Isaacs Menken and the birth of American celebrity.* Cambridge, 2003

Slick, Sam (pseudonym of Thomas Chandler Haliburton). *The Letter-Bag of the Great Western.* 1839

Spann, Edward K. *The New Metropolis: New York City, 1840–1857.* New York, 1981

Stover, John F. *Iron Road to the West: American railroads in the 1850s.* New York, 1978

Trollope, Anthony. *North America.* 1862

Trollope, Frances Milton. *Domestic Manners of the Americans.* 1832

Waln, Robert. *The Hermit in America on a visit to Philadelphia: containing some account of the beaux and belles of that famous city.* Philadelphia, 1819–21

Wenborn, Neil. *The Pictorial History of the USA.* 1991

Werner, Morris Robert. *Tammany Hall.* Garden City, New York, 1928

White, John H. *A History of the American Locomotive. Its development: 1830–1880.* New York, 1979

Whitman, Walt. *Specimen Days & Collect.* Philadelphia, 1882--83

Newspapers/Periodicals
Great Britain

All the Year Round, Bell's Life in London, Blackwood's Edinburgh Magazine, Cobbett's Weekly Political Register, The Cornhill Magazine, The Daily Advertiser, Daily News, The Daily Telegraph, Dublin Evening Post, The Field, Fraser's Magazine for Town and Country, The Gentleman's Magazine, The Glasgow Chronicle, Glasgow Herald , The Globe and Traveller, The Hampshire Chronicle, Household Words, The Illustrated London News, The Illustrated Sporting and Theatrical News, The Illustrated Police Budget, Irish

Times, The Liverpool Telegraph and Shipping and Commercial Gazette, Lloyd's Weekly Newspaper, The Manchester Guardian, The Morning Star, The News of the World, New Sporting Magazine, The Northern Whig, The Observer, The Pall Mall Gazette, The Penny Illustrated Paper, Punch, Reynolds's Newspaper, The Saturday Review, The Spectator, The Sporting Life, The Sporting Magazine, Sporting Telegraph and Daily Record of Music and the Drama, The Sportsman, The Sportsman's Magazine of Life in London and the Country etc., The Times, The True Protestant Mercury.

United States
Albany Evening Journal, Boston Evening Transcript, The Boston Gazette, The Boston Post, The Charleston Mercury, Columbian Centinel, Daily Evening Bulletin (San Francisco), *The Daily Picayune* (New Orleans), *Frank Leslie's Illustrated Newspaper, Harper's New Monthly Magazine, Harper's Weekly, New York Clipper, New-York Daily Tribune, New-York Evening Post, The New York Herald, New York Illustrated News, New-York Spectator, The New York Times, Porter's Spirit of the Times,* later *Wilkes' Spirit of the Times, The Press and Tribune* (Chicago), *Register* (Philadelphia), *Spirit of the Times, States–Item* (New Orleans)

Websites
Websites, ephemeral by nature, do not normally rate inclusion in a bibliography, but there is one martial arts site so comprehensive and with such a look of permanence that it would be wrong to exclude it. EJMAS (http://ejmas.com) is the Electronic Journals of Martial Arts and Sciences. Most useful to those with an interest in the bare-knuckle prize ring is the Kronos section, subtitled 'A chronological history of the martial arts and combative sports'.

INDEX OF FIGHERS, THEIR FRIENDS
AND ENEMIES

291

Index